C000178926

THE **31** PRACTICES

ADVANCE PRAISES FOR THE 31 PRACTICES

"Great to see a practical book about how to live your values at work – and a book that gives useful methods and live examples of the hard work of firstly clarifying your values and then the hard work of living them in the heat of action." **Peter Hawkins, author of Leadership Team Coaching and Professor of Leadership, Henley Business School.**

"An inspiring, powerful and practical tool kit. How to harness fundamental human emotions and align behaviour/practices with core values. A guidebook for greater meaning and success in our lives and in our work." **Sheila McCann, General Manager, Chiva-Som International Health Resort, Thailand.**

"The 31 Practices is a great book for understanding values in a changing organizational environment – due to advances in technology and the way we communicate (social media). The ideas explained by Alan and Alison depict the importance of bringing to life the values of organizations through the behaviour of the people representing them. I enjoyed reading this great work and hope that companies in India and all over the world will consider this book as a compulsory read for their employees." **KK Verma, Harvard Business Review Advisory Board and author of Unlearn Before U Learn, India.**

"The 31 Practices is a comprehensive and insightful overview of behavioural and psychological research and its relevance to the modern workplace. By translating complex ideas into practical actionable steps, this book can help managers make a genuine positive difference in their organizations." **Nic Marks, Founding Director, Happiness Works.**

"Values-based leadership has never been more relevant. The 31Practices framework that is described in the book is a practical framework for developing a values-based culture, one that inspires our colleagues to deliver products and services with meaning and purpose. What we do can be replicated. The values-based approach of 31Practices means that we engage our customers not just by what we do but how we do it, the experience that they have of our organization. That is the real difference that makes the difference." **John Frost, Managing Director, Values Based Leadership.**

"The 31 Practices has the potential to transform organizations. The emphasis on being, knowing and doing will help leaders practice the art of 'whole leadership', integrating mind, heart and body in the way they lead." **Kiran Chitta, Managing Director, Caxton & Co, Singapore.**

"...one of the most thought provoking books of the year. 31Practices combines a methodology for developing organizational (and personal) practices creating organizations (and people) which are truer to their values and thus able to live more rewarding, fuller and more choiceful lives." **Professor Jonathan Passmore, University of Evora, Portugal.**

"This excellent book is great for busy people who only have time to dip in and gain insight into a wide range of organizational issues. Useful for personal development too." **Professor Stephen Palmer, Coaching Psychology Unit, City University, London.**

"This book is an excellent resource for managers, leaders and front-line workers. Its strength lies in the way it is written in an accessible style, combining contemporary theoretical perspectives, beautiful words and imagery with real-world case studies and examples. There is minimal jargon and management speak, but plenty of practical applications of sound evidence from a range of areas including coaching, neuroscience and positive psychology. It brings fresh thinking and offers an innovative approach to the challenges and creative potential of working in uncertain, complex times." **Dr Kathryn Waddington, Head of Department of Psychology, University of Westminster, London.**

"What really excites me about 31Practices is the effectiveness in involving and empowering everyone from top to bottom…if the values are owned and exercised by everybody in the organization, the effect will be truly powerful. 31Practices appears to me to be a wonderfully simple and flexible way of bringing values to life, and harnessing the inspirational power of shared values to achieve the common purpose." **Charles Fowler, Chair, Human Values Foundation.**

"The book will be particularly beneficial to senior management who are facilitating culture change. It will furthermore, help organizations to deliver authentic customer experiences through behaviour being aligned with the organization's values." **Professor John A Murphy, Telefonica O2 Professor Of Customer Management, Manchester Business School.**

"The 31 Practices approach offers you the opportunity to reflect and act to make a sustainable impact professionally and personally. Refreshing, inspiring." **Francois Huet, Managing Director, Big Waves of Inspiration.**

"This book offers an engaging menu of topics for those who have interest in organizational life and individual thriving. It is succinctly and usefully referenced, for those who want more depth or detail, and has very approachable practical exercises. Easy to navigate, it can be dipped into, so the reader can start with what catches their interest and then travel onwards." **Julie Allan, Chartered Psychologist, coaching supervisor and author.**

"The 31 Practices is the book to provoke thinking, clarify awareness, guide to action…Alan Williams and Dr. Alison Whybrow walk together with the reader along the journey of thinking and improving, providing perspectives and structures. This is the best solution for readers to build awareness and translate understanding into action. This book is the best reference for Chinese business leaders and career individuals to have in order to practice 'doing the right thing'." **Ricky QIN Wei, Consulting Partner China, Strengths Partnership.**

"This book brings the concept of 31Practices to life beautifully with inspiring quotes and numerous examples and tales from the coal-face. One quote in particular stands out as a perfect description for both this book and the approach it describes – 'simplicity is the ultimate sophistication' (Davinci). 31Practices is in many ways very simple, and that is what makes it so widely applicable. Yet it has a richness and depth drawing on years of research and diversity of underpinnings including mindfulness, which the authors describe clearly here, which renders it supremely sophisticated." **Liz Hall, Editor, Coaching at Work and author of Mindful Coaching.**

"The focus on 31 themes is a wonderful way to simplify a complex field of philosophy, science and practice." **Ross Peat, CEO, KlickEx, Auckland, New Zealand.**

"In our complex and fast-changing world, it's more important than ever to identify and hold fast to what really matters. This is especially important for organizations that want to embody authenticity and act with integrity, serving and meeting the needs of their diverse stakeholders. In this excellent book, Alan Williams and Alison Whybrow combine scientific insight with simple practical steps to show how we can do this, simply and every day." **Dr. Alex Linley, Director, Centre for Applied Positive Psychology (CAPP), Coventry, UK.**

"The 31 Practices is an absolutely vital handbook for any leader, manager, or business person looking to accelerate their results and build a happier, more fulfilled work environment." **Scott Marcacio, Sales and Marketing Director, Toronics Inc.**

Published by
LID Publishing Ltd.
The Loft, 19a Floral Street
London WC2E 9DS (United Kingdom)
info@lidpublishing.com
LIDpublishing.com

A member of:

www.businesspublishersroundtable.com

31Practices®
31Practices® is a registered trademark owned by SERVICEBRAND GLOBAL Ltd.
31Practices® projects may be delivered exclusively by SERVICEBRAND GLOBAL
Ltd and our growing network of licenced Practitioners. We are currently seeking
Practitioners in various locations and industry sectors.

We reproduce the photographs of Matthieu Ricard with his kind permission.
The photographs remain Matthieu's copyrighted property and may not be
reproduced without his permission.

Unless specifically referenced to an individual person or organization, all stories
within this book are created from composites of the authors' experiences and do
not refer directly to any one individual or organization, past or present.

Printed by CPI Group (UK) Ltd.

ISBN 978-1-907794-35-3

Page design: e-Digital Design Ltd

THE **31** PRACTICES

Release the power of your organization's VALUES every day

Alan Williams & Dr. Alison Whybrow

LONDON   MADRID
NEW YORK   MEXICO CITY
BOGOTA   BUENOS AIRES
BARCELONA   MONTERREY

We dedicate this book
to the alchemy of relationships,
curiosity and serendipity.

Practice makes
more perfect...
Keep practising
Alan

Enjoy every step
of your journey
Best Wishes
Alison

CONTENTS

ACKNOWLEDGEMENTS

Our thanks and appreciation extend to all the wonderful collaborators we have met as we have written this book. The accessibility of resources open to everyone today, facilitated by worldwide increased connectivity, has enabled us to work with some incredible individuals. We have discovered a wealth of experts, masters in their own craft, all willing to share and extend their contribution. We have had overwhelming supportive and positive input.

Serendipity has played its part from the very beginning of the project when we were connected by a mutual colleague, Peter Swead. Then another colleague, Iain Ellwood, recommended that we contact Martin Liu at LID Publishing. And finally, we had the idea of a beautiful photograph to introduce each of the 31 chapters but had no idea that we would find the right kind of photographs for our book AND a happiness guru at the other end of the lens. Our thanks to Matthieu Ricard, his being and his amazing photography. More is shared about Matthieu and his work in Chapter 31, **Photography**. Our intent is that we continue to support his work in Tibet and Bhutan now that we have made that connection.

We have received invaluable feedback and positive appreciation on the draft manuscript from a number of colleagues across the globe, some of whom we have met simply through sharing our project with them. These people hold a rich variety of roles and interests ranging from senior executives in the private and public sector to leading academics and experts in marketing, customer service, complexity, psychology, organisational development and leadership. They are based in an equally diverse range of locations: Australia, Canada, China, France, Hong Kong, India, Japan, New Zealand, Singapore, Thailand, UK and USA. We are proud to be associated with these people and thank them for their interest, time and giving spirit. We would like to extend our thanks to:

- Julie Allan, Chartered Psychologist, Coaching Supervisor and Author, London, UK
- Richard Barrett, Chairman and Founder, Barrett Values Centre, London, UK
- Kiran Chitta, Managing Director, Caxton & Co, Singapore
- John Frost, MD, Vales Based Leadership, Herefordshire, UK
- Steve Flaim, Americas President & Group COO, PTS Consulting, New York, USA

- Charles Fowler, Chair, Human Values Foundation, London, UK
- Liz Hall, Editor of Coaching at Work, Coach and Author, London, UK / Alicante, Spain
- Peter Hawkins, Author of Leadership Team Coaching and Professor of Leadership Henley Business School, UK
- Francois Huet, MD, Big Waves of Inspiration, Carcès, France
- Dr Lesley Kuhn, Senior Lecturer, School of Business, University of Western Sydney, Australia
- Dr Alex Linley, Director, Centre for Applied Positive Psychology (CAPP), Coventry, UK
- Scott Marcacio, Sales and Marketing Director, Toronics Inc., Toronto, Canada
- Nic Marks, Founder, Happy Planet Index, London, UK
- Sheila McCann, General Manager, Chiva-Som International Health Resort, Thailand
- Jacqueline Moyse, Head of Organisational Development, Mandarin Oriental Hotel Group, Hong Kong
- John Murphy, Telefonica O2 Professor of Customer Management, Manchester Business School, Manchester, UK
- Marc Newey, Chief Executive, Roehampton Club, London, UK
- Andy Palmer, Executive Vice President Nissan Motor Company Ltd. & Chairman, Infiniti Motor Company Ltd, Yokohama, Japan
- Prof Stephen Palmer, Coaching Psychology Unit, City University London, UK
- Prof Jonathan Passmore, University of Evora, Portugal
- Ross Peat, CEO, KlickEx, Auckland, New Zealand
- Ricky QIN Wei, Consulting Partner China, Strengths Partnership, Hong Kong
- Dr Ram Raghavan, Founder, Riddlebox, Leamington Spa, UK
- Horst Schulz, Chairman/CEO, Capella Hotel Group and ex-President / COO, Ritz-Carlton, Atlanta, USA
- Matthew Taylor, Chief Executive, RSA, London, UK
- KK Verma, Harvard Business Review Advisory Board, Author of the book *Unlearn Before U Learn*, Delhi, India
- Dr Kathryn Waddington, Head of Department of Psychology, University of Westminster, London, UK
- Rob Webster, Chief Executive, NHS Trust, Leeds, UK
- Trevor Wigmore, Real Estate Executive, New York, USA

FOREWORD

When I am asked to write the foreword to a new book, I usually read the book thoroughly, and then, after reflecting for a few days, search for something to say that adds value: something supportive that provides a fresh and different perspective. Rarely do I come across a book which is as complete as this one. Alan and Alison have left me nothing to say. They have put together an encyclopaedia of understanding about what it takes to build the neural pathways of an organization.

Neuroscience is telling us that when things are not working as well as they could in your life, focusing on what is not working just makes it worse. You have to create a new series of synapses in your brain about what it is you want to happen. This is what 31Practices does: but at an organizational level. The framework that Alan and Alison have put together provides a way of creating a new series of synapses in the collective consciousness of the members of an organization so they embrace a new way of being and behaving. 31Practices provides a way of bonding people together to achieve a common purpose by aligning their values. In so doing, 31Practices creates internal cohesion. In turn, internal cohesion builds trust: trust increases efficiency and reduces costs, thereby increasing performance.

In the "olden" days, when neural pathways were just a glitter in a neuroscientist's eye, I remember reconfiguring my neural pathways by using something we used to call an affirmation. An affirmation was a statement about something you wanted to manifest in your life. It had to be believable, but it also had to stretch you. My first really effective affirmation was, "I design my life the way I want it", which later became, "I design my life the way my soul wants it". Subconsciously, we always design our lives the way we want them, but I wanted to do it consciously. Not only that, I wanted to be sure to design my life in such a way that the gifts and talents that my soul has given me could be made manifest to their fullest extent.

Reading my affirmation every morning before I started work enabled me to make conscious choices about what to do, with whom, and when. I stopped drifting like the flotsam you find in the open ocean and started sailing in the direction that my soul was leading me. By harnessing the winds – making conscious choices – I became more effective in my life.

My second significant affirmation was, "I have no needs". This was a real stretcher. Of course, we all have needs: I just didn't want satisfying my needs to be the sole focus of my life. This affirmation taught me many things. It taught me not to be attached to the outcomes I thought I needed. By believing I had needs, I was constraining the universe to operate in a particular way, when very often what wanted to emerge was something quite different. And, to my enduring wonderment, what emerged under its own volition gave me something that satisfied my needs and the needs I didn't even know I had in a larger and more comprehensive way than I could ever have imagined. I began to realize that as long as I stayed true to my soul, there were forces at work in my life, which, if I hitched my wagon to them, would lead me on a journey that was beyond my ability to ever have conceived. If I could learn to trust my soul, by affirming that I had no needs, then this journey would lead me to a deep sense of fulfilment.

This is the power that reconfiguring the neural pathways of your organization brings you. By collectively focusing on what it is you want to be and how you want to live, you unleash the corporate soul. Your organization becomes all it can become because everyone is heading in the same direction and living with the same vision and values. 31Practices is a brilliant tool for helping your organization or team to achieve its highest performance.

Richard Barrett
Chairman and Founder, Barrett Values Centre, London and author
of *The Values-driven Organisation: Unleashing Human Potential for Performance and Profit*

1

CHAPTER 1 INTRODUCTION

"Simplicity is the ultimate sophistication"

Leonardo da Vinci[1]

In our super-connected world, organizations' brands and reputations are shaped to a far greater extent by the personal experience of their employees and customers. We already know that 70% of customers' brand perception is determined by their experience with the organization's employees[2] and 41% of customers are loyal due to employee attitude[3]. Authenticity from the tip to the root is the new Holy Grail for organizations. This book shows how an organization's values and brand can be translated into the daily practices and behaviour of their employees, drawing a golden thread from the boardroom to the front-line customer experience. The 31Practices method weaves together principles and practices from psychology, philosophy, neuroscience, leadership and business to significantly enhance customer and employee satisfaction and loyalty. This book shares insights into how and why the methodology works. 31Practices has been successfully adopted by large and small companies, across sectors from around the world.

The purpose of this book is threefold:

- First, to share the importance of values-based working for individuals and organizations, and the story of how the 31Practices methodology was created and has been developed over time to support organizations to do just that (Parts 1 & 5);

- Second, to explain the underpinning framework of the approach with a light touch on how this might work for your own organization (Part 2); and,
- Third, to provide an insight into some of the core principles and topics that are central to understanding why the 31Practices methodology works and its relevance in today's context (Parts 3 & 4). These topics have been chosen with careful consideration so that you can explore in more depth the areas that we believe are most relevant to the way 31Practices works.

The book is presented in a simply structured format of 31 "bite size" chapters that you can explore in the way that appeals to you most. We have made a conscious effort to keep the style light and accessible. There is a more academic feel in places as we discuss some meaty topics such as complexity, wisdom, emotion, and a lighter, practical feel in others as we consider the application of the approach in a range of organizational case studies. We could not hope to cover each topic in this book in a way that satisfies each reader's needs or does full justice to the breadth of each field. We have included references and resources for those of you that wish to explore particular topics further.

This book has been created as a practical reference guide to understand why the 31Practices approach works. It goes much further than that alone, offering insight into some core topics that are of use to understanding yourself and your organization more fully, and raising awareness of how 31Practices might energize, enable, and strengthen your organization, you and those you work with. We offer some ideas about the complexities of people, the world we work in and some thoughts on strengthening our collective wisdom and leadership.

We have been delighted to receive feedback that the book occupies a really important middle ground somewhere in the triangle between 'theory heavy' academic texts, theory light 'airport bookshop' management/ leadership texts and theory free but pretty and glossy "concept" materials[4].

Whether this is the first time you've explored the subject of values or are revisiting a familiar topic, we hope that you find The 31 Practices an interesting and useful read, deepening your knowledge and awareness of how and why you would wantan explicitly values-aligned organization.

What this book does not do is tell you how to create and implement 31Practices or what they should be for your organization. Each set of 31Practices is unique to the organization that creates them and we have spent many years developing the way in which we work with organizations to make this as effective as it is. This book doesn't hold your answers, but will help you ask and explore some of the questions that may be helpful, and give you ideas for the direction you may wish to take. Naturally, we would be delighted to assist you in this journey!

The 31 Practices is written for people in organizations all over the world who consider organizational values an important asset and wish to optimise performance through harnessing the hearts and minds of employees and brand value in its broadest sense. The book will be as valuable to senior executives and team leaders in small or medium-sized enterprises as it will be for those in large multinational organizations in any sector, including the public and third sector. It is likely to be of interest to you if you are interested in the functional areas of Marketing, Human Resources, Customer Experience and Organisational Development as well as if you have a more academic interest in these areas and others such as psychology, culture, workplace, leadership and behavioural science.

31PRACTICES[5]

At one level, the 31Practices methodology could not be simpler: create a set of 31 practical behaviours directly related to the organization's values and then, each day, make one practical behaviour the focus for everybody in the organization. Over time, behaviour becomes habitual and consistent at an individual and group level, bringing organizational values to life, and, as a result, releasing untapped potential and raising the performance bar.

The importance of a focus on just one Practice each day should not be underestimated because it allows us to perform in a very conscious way to the best of our ability. Neither should we underestimate what we can achieve. Sometimes people feel that 31 Practices will be too many to deal with but because they are easy to implement behaviours, this concern is quickly overcome. Also, just consider how many small actions you take in making a cup of tea or coffee…but we do not consider this to be beyond our capability.

As an example of one part of the methodology, Figure 1 shows the values and Practices on the credit card size carry card that is issued to each employee in an organization. The values are translated into daily Practices according to the date of the month. For example, in Figure 1 on the 4th of every month, the Practice for all employees is: "We take **pride** in our immaculate **appearance** (personal and facilities) and professional behaviour". While we may assume that immaculate appearance is part of business as usual, on the 4th of each month, every employee is reminded of its importance, and chooses how they personally are going to live that particular Practice – taking their personal level of grooming and the presentation of their work area one step further. This can be something as simple as polishing shoes, taking extra care with ironing a shirt, tidying the furniture in a meeting room or picking up some litter in the car park.

Figure 1: Example carry card content

Values

Customer Service
Showing potential and existing clients that customer service is at the heart of our organisation and governs our every action is key to our success.

Respect
It is important that we show respect for the individual and treat others as we would like to be treated.

Integrity
This is central to the way we do business and crucial to our external credibility and continued respect in the market place.

Excellence
Maintaining competitive advantage and giving the best possible quality and value for money for every project or service we deliver.

Innovation
This is essential to grow our business and continue to be recognised as the market leader.

31Practices

Customer Service
1. We find out our customer **needs** and thrive on **delivery** to build and maintain long lasting **relationships**.
2. We deliver our best to both **internal and external** customers, in a **personalised** way, remembering personal preferences.
3. We are **polite and approachable**, use names and have a genuine smile.
4. We take pride in our immaculate **appearance** (personal and facilities) and professional **behaviour**.
5. We have **detailed standards and procedures** so we know what we need to do.
6. We value **face to face** communication above email and telephone.

Respect
7. We focus on two-way communication – **listening** and giving **clear and constructive** information.
8. We **value the contributions** of everybody and respect differences.
9. We offer and accept **help** and give and receive **feedback**.
10. We are eager to **learn** from others so we can be even better at what we do.
11. We **respond** quickly and positively to requests and maintain a **professional** approach under pressure.
12. We show our **flexibility** because we understand that sometimes things change.

Integrity
13. We follow ethical business practice and are **trustworthy**.
14. We are **honest** (even with not such good news) and **straight talking**.
15. We **deliver our promises** and have a fair minded approach.
16. We are **consistent** in our **positive** attitude, language and behaviour.
17. We enjoy our role as **ambassadors** for our organization, taking opportunities to share our story.
18. We are willing to stand up for our **beliefs** because we **care**.
19. We take **responsibility** to get things done (individually and collectively) and never have to be asked twice.

Excellence
20. We show our **commitment** to be the best at what we do and deliver better than our competitors.
21. We **demand the best** quality people,standards, materials and equipment.
22. We invest in **training** to continually update our knowledge and job skills so we set, meet and exceed standards
23. We plan, **prepare**, have the tools to do the job, and are resourceful.
24. We pay attention to **detail** because we understand that the small things make a difference.
25. We are determined, **never give up** and overcome challenges.
26. We **measure** our performance so we know how much we improve.

Innovation
27. We **continually improve**, by embracing change.
28. We suggest and successfully implement **new ideas**, including small changes.
29. We enjoy finding ways to **make things easier** for our customers and colleagues.
30. We **celebrate** success and learn when things are not quite right.
31. We work together, **sharing** knowledge, information and resources to create new ideas.

31Practices consists of a robust, methodical framework supported by a host of interwoven underpinnings, theories and thinking. This combination reveals a rich and complex approach about bringing to life an organization's values through the behaviour of the people who form and represent that organization. Our experience of working with 31Practices in different cultures has been fascinating. Initially, some felt that it was too "American", but then it was well received by UK organizations. Then it was suggested that it would not be accepted by employees in European countries like France, Germany, Italy and Spain… but it was. Then it was suggested that in the Far East, the culture was far too different for employees to feel comfortable to take part but we have enjoyed some fantastic sessions with organizations in countries such as Japan, Singapore and China. The key has been respect – to take the time to explain what 31Practices is, why it is important and how it works, then to respect cultural differences and allow ownership of making 31Practices work in a locally relevant way.

Importantly, 31Practices is not an alternative approach to goal setting. Goal setting in an organizational context often focuses on "what" is achieved, whereas the 31Practices framework focuses on "how" you behave or the way you are.

One of the strengths of 31Practices lies in the blend between practice and theory – on the one hand, we can say "what works" and "what the benefits are" and, on the other, we can answer in some depth "why" the methodology works. You will gain an understanding of how 31Practices draws on a number of different areas working together in a layered way to create a powerful approach.

Throughout the book, we bring together thinking and practice from great academic minds and well-known achievers in business, but we also introduce the ordinary "day-to-day" stories from our personal experience of working with leaders or being leaders ourselves. While we have included many perspectives, we are sure that there are others that could add further insight. Unashamedly, we will be taking our own personal slant on the theoretical landscape, with a view to bringing to life current theories around leadership, business, and the world we live in.

31PRACTICES – WHY NOW?

Transparency and connectedness: Social media and general media exposure is more intensive and extensive than ever before. Organizations have nowhere to hide and the world is super-connected. This means that employee and customer perception is shared very openly and quickly and the repercussions can be terminal. It is more important than ever for every single touch point to be authentic and positive. In addition, digital natives who have known nothing different to our increasingly technology-based world are starting to powerfully shape contemporary organizations and this audience will strongly influence the way in which values are represented in organizations in the future[6].

The speed of change: The business world is shifting at unprecedented speed. This requires more flexible and decentralized working practices that empower employees to solve problems there and then. Employees require a holistic understanding of what the organization stands for so they can behave in a way that is in line with the organization values without having to refer upwards to make day-to-day decisions.

Business model innovation: A number of organizations are now part of complex organization structures that comprise a web of outsourced functions. Call centres, facilities management, logistics and security provide relevant examples. This development requires organizations to think very carefully about how their values can be delivered consistently when they may sometimes be represented by third parties as part of a virtual organization.

The changing focus of "control": Organizations are no more than the people that represent them. This means it is the organization's stakeholders that control the perception and not the organization itself. For customers, the least senior people have the greatest influence: the cashier, the car park attendant, the bell boy and not the CEO have the greatest influence on how an organization is perceived. For employees, the visible behaviour of leaders, from board members to local team leaders, is key in shaping perception. Other stakeholders such as outsourced service partners and local communities also have an influence on the perception of an organization.

Humans are emotional: There is an increasing body of neuroscientific knowledge which outlines the importance of emotion in the human decision-making process. The basis for a lot of emotional connections is a common sense of values. Increasingly, customers and employees identify with organizations as a statement about themselves as an individual and the "tribe" they belong to. Organization authenticity and being "real" is more important and this places a sharper focus on values – regardless of what your organization does.

Sustainable competitive advantage: Organizations can no longer compete so easily through the products and services they offer when these can be copied (sometimes very quickly). The one remaining point of differentiation is an organization's "personality" displayed through values. And this is more enduring than any new product or service, which have increasingly short life cycles.

Measurable difference: Achieving values alignment can result in measurable beneficial outcomes across a variety of balanced scorecard measures ranging from increased customer satisfaction, to more inspired employees, to increased employee retention, to increased sales and profit.

In summary, there are many aspects of the way organizations work, within a dynamic local and global environment, together with our increasing insights into how people think, feel and behave, that all combine to make 31Practices of particular relevance at this point in time.

HOW TO USE THIS BOOK

The book is written in "bite-size" pieces, intended to be easy to access in whatever way suits you. Dip into the book intermittently or read in a chronological or ad hoc manner. How you make use of the book is entirely up to you.

Each chapter provides an insight into either what the 31Practices method is, why it works, or how it works in practice. In Parts 2, 3 and 4 we end each chapter with a number of exercises you can put into practice yourself or with your teams. We also offer a number of resources for you to explore particular areas in more depth if you wish to do so. We hope that you enjoy the gifts each chapter holds and the further discoveries you may make.

Part 1 – Laying the groundwork
The first part of this book is snappy and tells the story of why and how 31Practices came into being and the journey of evolution over the last 10 years. Chapter 2, *Values* shares some of the thinking, research and philosophy that make values the cornerstone of the approach, with

Chapter 3, *Journey* sharing the story of evolution. This background provides a practical and theoretical context for the methodology that follows in Part 2.

Part 2 – The underpinning framework

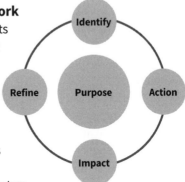

This second part shares the core elements of the underpinning framework, starting off with Chapter 4, *Framework*, which provides an overview of how the elements knit together. This part of the book will enable you to understand what is involved in kick-starting the virtuous circle that the 31Practices framework supports.

Each of the subsequent chapters 5-9(*Purpose, Identify, Action, Impact* and *Refine*) presents the central part of the framework for that core element and brings it to life with stories from our own and others' experiences.

Part 3 – Exploring the principles

The third part of this book starts to explain why it all works. These chapters outline the underpinning psychological and philosophical principles that 31Practices draws on. We have separated those principles that are focused on how we work as human beings and articulate how providing a purposeful, values-based framework in an organizational setting connects with, engages and enables people to operate at their best. The purpose of this part of the book is to enable you to develop your insight into how and why the 31Practices method works from a human perspective.

We hope you enjoy it and remember, you don't have to know any or all of this for 31Practices to work as a practical intervention.

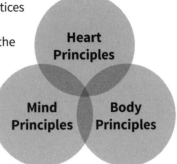

We have organized this section into the *Heart Principles*, focused on being; the *Mind Principles*, focused on knowing; and the *Body Principles*, focused on doing. Despite this attempt at classification, the principles flow into one another, mirroring reality. We can't actually separate with hard lines what is heart, mind and body. All are part of each other, just like a hologram. And, just like a hologram, it doesn't matter which way you look at it, so the best advice is to start with a subject in this section that is most appealing to you and follow your interests from there.

In Section 1, *The Heart Principles*, we work with *Emotion*, *Inspiration* and *Happiness* (Chapters 10–12). In Section 2, *The Mind Principles*, we work with *Mindfulness*, *Resilience* and *Storytelling* (Chapters 13–15). In Section 3, *The Body Principles*, we work with *Practice*, *Strengths* and *Discipline* (Chapters 16–18).

Part 3 offers an understanding of how heart, body and mind principles can come together to resource us (rather than deplete us), and to provide some practical ways for you to harness your own and others energy and resources. In each chapter, some of the central themes from research and practice are presented and brought to life with stories.

Part 4 – The broader context

The fourth part of this book highlights why 31Practices makes sense as a methodology at this point in time. The principles we explore in this part come from the broader system and context that leaders and organizations find themselves in. We cover *Complexity*, *Change*, *Wisdom*, *Neuroscience*, *Choice* and *Leadership* (Chapters 19-24)

These are common "headlines" in business thinking. We have endeavoured to make sense of some of these topics within the daily reality of organizations. While we don't purport to have all the answers, our intention is that in sharing these subjects through our 31Practices lens, we are both provocative and pragmatic, supporting you to develop your insight into how and why the 31Practices method works from an informed but practical perspective.

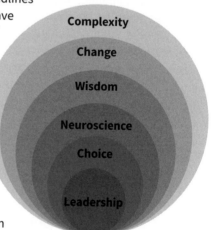

Part 5 – Evolution
This final part of the book shares case study work and examples of where and how 31Practices has developed and been implemented. We share real experiences of 31Practices, the benefits realised and some of the challenges faced. This practical, operational perspective brings to life the thinking we have shared through the book. The principles and methodology remain the same whether you're using 31Practices in a single business unit or for a global organization but, needless to say, the context is clearly different and we explore the implications. We also provide a glimpse of the future of 31Practices with an overview of a personal application, a mobile web application tool called my31Practices.

Site

Case Study

National   Global

For the ultra-busy, we offer a distillation of everything in our book in Chapter 30, *Summary*.

And finally...
This leaves us with Chapter 31, *Photography*, where we share some information about the work of Matthieu Ricard, the photographer who kindly allowed us to use his photographs in the book – we also give details about the fabulous photographs accompanying each of the chapters. In 2000, Matthieu Ricard founded Karuna-Shechen, a global non-profit humanitarian organization. Based on the ideal of "compassion in action", Karuna-Shechen develops education, medical, and social projects for the most destitute populations of the Himalayan region. Our hope is that through this book, we can continue to raise awareness of his work and develop our relationship with Karuna-Shechen.

TO CONCLUDE

We know you don't need reminding that despite the best attempts of researchers and scientists, philosophers and thinkers, there is no agreed, fixed formula that if universally applied would make an organization and all its members successful, fulfilled, healthy and resilient. Each individual, group and organization's evolution is a process of constant interaction with and adaptation to the environment and context they find themselves in – which is why this won't be the last book on the subject.

31Practices is not a "fix all" approach. But it does provide a framework which helps organizations to translate organizational values into a set of very practical day-to-day behaviours and then bring these behaviours to life in a sustained way. We hope you find much within the approach that resonates with your thinking and look forward to hearing your stories of how 31Practices thinking and practice has enabled you to create an even more effective organization.

If nothing else, we trust you will enjoy *The 31 Practices*, that it will give you cause to think about your organization and "the way things work around here", and that it will give you ideas as to how you can release the power of your organization's values every day.

PART 1

LAYING THE GROUNDWORK

The first part of this book tells the story of why and how 31Practices came into being and the story behind the approach. In Chapter 2, *Values*, we share perspectives on core values as this is the basis on which the 31Practices approach is built. We look at what values are, why they are important and their relevance for organizations. Then Chapter 3, *Journey*, is an overview of the 31Practices story over the last decade to provide background and a sense of the evolution.

"It is good to have an end to journey toward;
but it is the journey that matters, in the end."

Ursula K. Le Guin[1]

2

CHAPTER 2 VALUES

"It Ain't What You Do (It's the Way That You Do It)"
The Fun Boy Three and Bananarama 1982[1]

Core values are traits or qualities that represent deeply held beliefs. They reflect what is important to us, and what motivates us. In an organization, values define what it stands for and how it is seen and experienced by all stakeholders (customers, employees, service partners, suppliers and communities).

Values act as guiding principles – as a behavioural and decision-making compass.[2] In an organization, values (explicit or implicit) guide everyone on a daily basis. They are the foundation for the way things work, providing the basis of the corporate culture.

For individuals, as well as organizations, values sit at the gateway between our inner and outer worlds. They describe what is fundamentally important and meaningful to us and directly relate to sense of purpose and to our needs as individuals to survive and thrive.

Richard Barrett and colleagues differentiate between positive values and potentially limiting values.[3] Honesty, trust and accountability are positive values, whereas blame, revenge and manipulation are potentially limiting. Positive values are described as virtues and are strengths that we can draw on to build resources and resourcefulness. Potentially limiting values are fear-based, evoked when our concerns for ourselves get in the way. In this chapter, we focus on positive values.

"Values are the ideals that give meaning to our lives that are reflected through the priorities we choose and that we act on consistently and repeatedly".

Brian Hall[4]

In 2010, Reed Hastings, CEO of Netflix,[5] made public a 126-slide presentation on how Netflix maintains a culture of innovation. Their core values are prominent on their website[6] with clearly defined behaviours and skills. They are serious about their values as core to the company's culture of innovation. Netflix enables employees to embody the values explicitly at work. The presentation went viral.

Following financial scandal in 2012, Antony Jenkins took over as CEO at Barclays in August of that year. In January 2013 he announced that bonuses and performance would be assessed against a new "Purpose and Values" blueprint. In a company-wide letter to staff, Jenkins unveiled his plan to implement five core values in a cross-business code, named "Purpose for Barclays". The five values were respect, integrity, service, excellence and stewardship.

Jenkins wrote: *"I have no doubt that the overwhelming majority of you, no matter in which area of the business or country you work, will enthusiastically support this move. But there might be some who do not feel they can fully buy in to an approach which so squarely links performance to the upholding of our values."*

"My message to those people is simple: Barclays is not the place for you. The rules have changed. You will not feel comfortable at Barclays and, to be frank, we will not feel comfortable with you as colleagues." [7]

Values are moving from a PR exercise to become the guiding compass. We invite you to take the whole business of values, and the values of your organization, a lot more seriously. A public commitment is a commendable start but it then requires rigorous follow through and, for Barclays, time will be the judge of what has been started.

Values are fundamental; some might call them ethics, others might see values as "how we do things around here"; both are right.

In reality, values often exist implicitly, outside formal organization processes and, mostly, under the radar of awareness. The commonly adopted behaviour of people in an organization is a representation of the values and creates the culture, the "felt experience" that stakeholders have. Values impact how the very best thought-out rational processes actually operate in practice. This organization culture is powerful, as Ivan Misner, quoting Peter

Drucker reminds us, *"Culture will always eat strategy for breakfast".*[8]

Awareness of values at an individual level is a starting point to self-insight and understanding.

Awareness of values at an organizational level helps employees and organizations to more easily navigate the complex ambiguous nature of today's business environment.

Articulating core beliefs, traditions and "the way we do things around here" through an explicit set of core values opens things up, empowers employees to make decisions without reference to their line manager for tiny details, enables ideas to flow freely and creativity and innovation to take place.[9] Shared and explicit values offer a level of consistency of experience and engagement that is aligned on a site-by-site, national and global level.

There are simple ways to help people and organizations start to understand their values[10] (see Chapter 6, *Identify* for more).

In summary, people are shaped by what they care about, and where given a choice, will engage in activities that enable them to survive and thrive in any situation.[11] We can live core values to good effect. We can use them to provide:

- a reference for decision making
- clarity and increased awareness about individual behaviours (self and others)
- an unambiguous environment for new employees to start off on the right track
- stories to build the heritage and folklore of the organization
- consistency – viewed from within or from the outside

"Without exception, the dominance and coherence of culture proved to be an essential quality of the excellent companies [we identified] … the stronger the culture and the more it was directed toward the marketplace, the less need was there for policy manuals, organization charts, or detailed procedure and rules."
Tom Peters and Robert Waterman[12]

HARNESSING THE VALUE OF CORE VALUES

Ken Blanchard and Phil Hodges[13] estimate that fewer than 10% of organizations have clear, written values and many take the work on values no further than words. To impact, core values need to extend into the day-to-day fabric of the organization and be a reference for decisions and behaviours at all levels, influencing people daily... And, yes – that means you!

Those in different places in an organization see evidence of culture and values differently. For example, those at the top rate tangible KPIs (key performance indicators) as demonstrative of organizational culture (e.g. financial performance, competitive compensation); those lower down rate their personal experience as important evidence of "values" (e.g. open communication, employee recognition, access to leaders).[14] Both are forms of evidence.

How do you make sure that your stakeholders' experience of your organizational values is explicit and aligned from the boardroom to the front line?

The tone is set by every employee, not just those at the top of the pile. Those at the top model what is important, and are particularly visible in everything that they do – people take notice of how they behave. Yet, wherever you are, you have influence on those around you.

An organization is a system of loosely connected individuals, and, as Antony Jenkins so eloquently highlighted, if you can't personally sign up and "live" the values of the company you are working for, then what are you doing there? The organization is only as good as each of the component parts.

As individuals, we need to turn the lens inwardly if the organization is going to behave in line with core values. What are you doing? If you don't behave as if the core values matter, then others won't either. For values to be really cemented in the organization's culture, everyone must be held accountable for living and demonstrating the values in their day-to-day actions. Embedding values is a challenge.[15] 31Practices offers a methodology to enable this.

For organizations, identifying values is just the first step. It is not enough. Well-written values without good execution will not prevent Enron-sized disasters.[16] Enron's explicit value statements of respect, integrity, communication and excellence masked the real and self-defeating culture at work.

In our own work, we often notice very limited attention paid to values when we first visit organizations. At a recent visit to a pharmaceuticals organization, the values that adorned the lobby were discussed as part of the proposed learning and development strategy. The HR Director responded that sadly, the values were enshrined on the walls of the lobby and in marketing materials, but were not explicitly built into the way things were done. Had we stopped to ask employees about the company's values, they would have in all likelihood struggled to remember them. They would have been even more pushed to explain what the values meant to them as part of their daily life at work.

Enron would be in good company today. Many leadership surveys see corporate values as rhetoric rather than reality,[17] with most employees unaware of their organization's values.[18] And yet, most employees see the potential benefits of having a set of values in the first place,[19] especially if the consequences of living and failing to live the core values are explicitly aligned.

"In the wake of the banking crisis and other corporate scandals, now more than ever, organizational values should be at the forefront of business leaders' minds".

Peter Cheese[20]

Two stories here share the impact of core values – when they are harnessed and when their value is ignored.

The story of Zappos

Founded in 1999, Zappos demonstrates strong values-based leadership. Starting as an online footwear business focusing on customer service, Zappos grew from $1.6 million in sales in 2000 to over $1 billion by 2009. Zappos was sold to Amazon for a reported $1.2 billion in 2009. At the point of sale, Zappos' range included: handbags, eyewear, clothing, watches, and children's merchandise.

CEO Tony Hsieh, commenting on this shift, noted: *"Back in 2003, we thought of ourselves as a shoe company that offered great service. Today, we really think of the Zappos brand as about great service, and we just happen to sell shoes."*[21]

Resisting the idea of values for as long as possible, believing they were *"very corporate"*, Tony Hsieh admits he's *"just glad that an employee finally convinced me that it was necessary to come up with core values – essentially, a formalized definition of our culture – in order for us to continue to scale and grow. I only wish we had done it sooner."*[22]

Hiring / firing decisions were the crux around which Zappos' core values were crafted, enabling a clear articulation of what was REALLY important when it came down to it. If employees were not prepared to hire and fire on the basis of the values, then they were not considered as core.

Core values inform fundamental decisions and behaviours. New hires are asked to sign an official commitment to Zappos' core values right from the recruitment and induction phases of employment.

The story of *News of the World*

News of the World was a national newspaper published in the United Kingdom from 1843 to 2011; at one time the biggest-selling English-language newspaper in the world, selling nearly 3 million copies a week in October 2010.

Its reputation was for exposing the wrongdoings of national or local celebrities, by setting up insiders and journalists in disguise to provide either video or photographic evidence. The newspaper took on the mantle of a trusted people's champion – the nation's newspaper fighting "little people's" battles against the large, rich and powerful.

From 2006, allegations of phone hacking were rumoured. The company is believed to have hacked the phones of citizens, celebrities, and even the British Royal Family to gain inside information. The scandal started to unwind during the case of a murdered child and deepened when the paper was alleged to have hacked into the phones of families of British service personnel killed in action.

Rather than the people's champion, the newspaper was seen to have turned against the ordinary people – soldiers' widows, bereaved parents – and looked much more like the cynical corrupt elite they claimed to expose. There was a deep sense of betrayal that such a significant and trusted "people's newspaper" could allow this to happen. Major advertisers withdrew advertising.

A "whatever it takes" culture had grown and spread at the paper, resulting in the extreme measures taken by employees to deliver results. Carl Bernstein[23] asserts, *"Reporters and editors do not routinely break the law, bribe policemen, wiretap, and generally conduct themselves like thugs unless it is a matter of recognized and understood policy."*

The public backlash and loss of revenue led to News International announcing the closure of the newspaper in July 2011. A 170-year-old business and one of the most successful newspapers in the world ended with the associated financial and personal costs, with senior executives facing trial for breaches of privacy, bribery of officials in public office and obstruction of justice.

The lived values of an organization have a huge impact on reputation and business outcomes. It's also possible to delude yourself and your organization that you're fine, all is well. The way powerful and intelligent people deliberately set aside crucial facts and turn a blind eye to fatal errors and frauds is explored in the book *Wilful Blindness* by Margaret Heffernan.[24] But where actions cut across the beliefs and traditions expected by core communities of stakeholders, standards expected in the profession and the ethical standards and practice embedded in different legal systems, disaster can be a very real outcome for all involved.

SO WHAT?

"I am able to control only that which I am aware of. That which I am unaware of controls me."

Sir John Whitmore[25]

Looking from the best case to the worst case, you can see for yourself the way you can harness core values for good, or ignore core values at your peril. The key factor common to companies that have delivered sustained high performance – at the top of their market for 100 years or more – is a base of values that was strong enough to provide the employees of the company with a common bond – a purpose beyond profit.[26]

In 2001, Eric Flamholtz[27] discovered a strong positive correlation between cultural agreement (a proxy for values or cultural alignment) and the company's EBIT (Earnings Before Interest and Taxes). He concludes: *"Organizational culture does have an impact on financial performance. It provides additional evidence of the significant role of corporate culture not only in overall organizational effectiveness, but also in the so-called "bottom line."*

The power of living values is described by David MacLeod, Chair of the UK Government-sponsored Employee Engagement Task Force and non-executive director of the Ministry of Justice in the UK. He comments: *"All organizations have some values on the wall. What we found was that when those values were different from what colleagues and bosses do, that brings distrust. When they align, then it creates trust."*[28]

The changing landscape for business and organizations will arguably bring the importance of values into even sharper focus.

The internet and social media have brought greater transparency than ever before. As a direct result, authenticity is and will continue to be increasingly important. Some years ago, it was perhaps possible for organizations to invest in marketing and PR to tell the story they wanted others to hear, but now it is becoming increasingly difficult to tell a story that is far from the reality. Organizations are no longer what they say they are but what others say they are.

Ultimately, aligned organizational values are a key to an organization achieving its purpose.

VALUES AND 31PRACTICES?

The purpose of 31Practices is to enable organizations (and people representing these organizations) to reconnect with what is at the core, and live these core values on a daily basis. The approach facilitates authenticity and improves people's sense of well-being with the resulting positive impact on performance that you would expect.

The importance of the people who represent an organization has increased significantly. The general shift from a product-based reputation to an experience-based reputation has resulted in people's perception of an organization being based on their personal experience of those representing the organization. Similarly, employee perception of their own organization is based on their personal experience of how they are treated and how they see colleagues behaving.

For organisations to state their core values is a waste of time unless employees understand what values mean in their day-to-day activities and understand how values can change their daily decisions.[29]

31Practices provides a framework to enable employees to practise behaviours directly linked to the core values every day.

EXERCISE: EXPLORING YOUR ORGANIZATIONAL VALUES

Here we share two simple exercises that can give you some insight into your organizational values.

Exercise 1

This is one style of light-hearted exercise we like to use with some of our clients. If your organization were a group of musicians, what group would you like to be? What would your music be like, your lyrics? What kind of experience would your fans have?

What kind of values would you be portraying as this band? How do these translate into your organizational values?

Exercise 2

Organizational values show up over time – through organizational processes, structures and approaches – the way the organization is – and the way the employees behave in the wider world when representing the organization. It's difficult to "see" your values when they are so much a part of your working context – but you see them at specific, more extreme moments.

- Think about peak moments for the organization – what was going on – what values were being "honoured" at that time?
- Explore low moments – those moments when emotions were running high, frustration was boiling over, people were upset, indignant – what values were being "dishonoured" at that time?
- What are the "must haves"? What is it that the organization "must have" in order to be fulfilled, thrive, survive?

What circumstances led to the peak moments, the low moments or to the must haves? What does this say to you about what the organization values?

Want to know more?

To explore this area further, you may enjoy the following books:
- Patrick M. Lencioni (2012) *The Advantage: Why Organizational Health Trumps Everything Else In Business.* San Francisco: Jossey Bass.
- David Gebler (2012) *The 3 Power Values: How Commitment, Integrity, and Transparency Clear the Roadblocks to Performance.* San Francisco: Jossey Bass.
- Richard Barrett (2013) *The Values-Driven Organization – Unleashing Human Potential for Performance and Profit.* New York, Routledge.

3

CHAPTER 3   JOURNEY

"Culture is the most difficult organizational attribute to change, outlasting organizational products, services, founders and leadership and all other physical attributes of the organization."

Professor Edgar Schein[1]

The journey of 31Practices started more than ten years ago, and has emerged through an evolutionary process to be what it is today.

THE BEGINNING...

Hanbury Manor, a five-star Marriott hotel in UK, provided the first inspiration and the initial principles upon which 31Practices is based.

The Ritz Carlton luxury hotel chain developed their credo: *"Ladies and gentlemen serving ladies and gentlemen"*, offering a sense of purpose that all those serving the Ritz Carlton brand were asked to demonstrate by living a collection of service behaviours called "Basics".

Ritz Carlton was a subsidiary of Marriott and the parent company adopted the "Daily Basics" routine, where everybody focused on one of 22 hospitality behaviours (or Basics) each day. At the time, Marriott had 3,000 hotels. One of the stories from that time was that Bill Marriott (CEO) would telephone a hotel, ask for a department at random, and would expect whoever answered the phone to know the Basic for that day.

A number of performance milestones were achieved at Hanbury Manor between 1997 and 2002: the most improved Associate (employee) opinion survey across Marriott hotels, globally; the most improved guest satisfaction survey in UK; uniquely, "all green" balanced scorecard business measures for three consecutive years; and AA Hotel of the Year. The Basics approach was a key tool enabling this success.

"We are what we repeatedly do. Excellence, then, is not an act, but a habit."

Will Durant[2]

The next evolution of 31Practices was during the creation and implementation of an innovative service delivery model for the corporate offices for one of the Big Four banks. The front-of-house services (catering, reception, meeting rooms, housekeeping, security, audio visual services, telephony) were provided in a number of new and existing properties in the UK for the bank. A key challenge was finding a way to resolve the fragmented approach to service resulting from a number of supplier organizations providing different services.

The bank was not alone with this challenge, it is one faced by numerous large businesses.

It seemed worth adopting something like the Basics methodology as it offered an opportunity to create a unifying culture and approach across the supply chain of different service providers. The Basics methodology had been so effective elsewhere, it seemed to be a good fit for the challenges faced, with some specific improvements.

First, because at Marriott there were 22 Basics, there was no synchronization with the day of the month and the number of the Basic behaviour being applied. Although this sounds crazy, it did have a negative impact on employee perception. One frustrated employee summed it up *"I get confused when it is Basic 15 and it's only the 2nd of the month"*. A simple answer to this was to have 31 behaviours as there are never more than 31 days in a month.

Second, and possibly more profoundly, there was a significant opportunity to integrate organizational values into the methodology.

One of the things that we had noticed and discussed (so it's unlikely to have escaped your attention) was how often the core values of an organization were in beautiful frames in the lobby or the boardroom, sometimes even making it to a cube on an employee's desk – but not explicitly lived through employee behaviours. What if employees received service in their place of work in a style that was aligned to the core values of the organization? Surely those values would be more credible and would be reinforced – and would start to become business as usual. In this way, service style may vary across organizations, but the customer / employee experience will be aligned with the values of the organization. For example, the style of service in the workplace of a progressive, media organization would be expected to be very different from that of a traditional law firm.

With these two considerations in mind, the leadership team in the banking organization created a set of 31 behaviours, all linked back to the core values and service promise called "Our World Class Way". A credit card-sized card was issued to all employees and, importantly, an operating platform was created connecting day-to-day operating processes with the 31 behaviours. The operating platform considered processes and activities such as selection interviews, the induction processes, standard operating procedures, daily buzz meetings, performance and recognition programmes, etc.

In this way, the first version of 31Practices was born. The results at the bank were dramatic, resulting in significant improvements in customer satisfaction (+10%) and cost reduction (a 10-15% reduction). A global property industry innovation award was received for the initiative together with an award from the bank for outstanding customer service. This core methodology forms the underpinning of 31Practices today.

THE MIDDLE...

The company, SERVICEBRAND GLOBAL, was started in 2005 to assist organizations with improving the quality and effectiveness of face-to-face service delivery in built environments. One of the first clients was a global investment bank who wanted to create a consistent culture and service standards in key locations globally.

At this time, the 31Practices name was created and it seemed to be appropriate because of the focus on "practising" the value-linked behaviours on a daily basis. It was during this first project that the power of co-creation was also recognized. A series of workshops enabled cross-functional/organizational contributions as to what the 31Practices should be to represent the organization's values. These high-energy, participative and experiential learning-based events enabled individuals from across the organizational hierarchy to feel ownership for the 31Practices subsequently designed. No surprises then that the level of engagement with the approach was high.

One particular example involved an employee from the post-room in the New York office of the investment bank. Sometime after the launch of 31Practices, he said with pride "Look! Number 16! I suggested that Practice in our workshop!"

Once designed, the organization's unique 31Practices approach is implemented through a series of employee workshops delivered cross-functionally and cross-hierarchically by a team of trained supervisory-level employees. It is important that those who are involved in the roll-out are involved in the day-to-day operation of the organization. Where new facilities are being opened, or new hires engaged, it's important that 31Practices is part of the induction process. Supervisory-level people are the ones that are there day in, day out, side by side with their front-line colleagues. They are the ones that have the biggest influence on 31Practices being "lived".

Once live, employees are able to nominate colleagues who they see displaying the 31Practices excellently (they can even nominate themselves). This works best when a cross-functional group (non-management) is responsible for selecting the best examples on a monthly basis. Nominated employees are recognized and their actions and stories are publicized through the organization and become part of the culture, the "way things work around here" that is central to an organization's impact and brand. This can be a standalone process but is even better when integrated into an existing recognition programme. The organization's heritage is created through the communication of stories.

Notably, employees play a co-creation role and take ownership for development of the way the tool is used, and latitude is given to employees to apply each daily Practice as they wish in their place of work. For example, if the core value is Excellence and today's Practice is "We display meticulous attention to cleanliness", the hotel receptionist may tidy a cupboard, the engineer may sweep the boiler room, the chef may book the de-greasing of the filters, etc.

Finally, while the overall framework and principles of the 31Practices methodology are consistent, the specific details of the 31Practices are unique to each client.

WHAT CAME NEXT...

The next stage of development has been to consolidate the business proposition: develop the commercial model and the brand. 31Practices is a registered trademark with a distinctive logo. It is provided to client organizations on a licensed basis with the premise that clients get the most from this approach when every employee applies each daily practice. The cost of a licence equates to the annual spend on uniform. The eye-catching appeal of a uniformed employee is a good start, but employee behaviour being aligned with the values of the organization is much more fundamental and meaningful. As a client recently shared, *"I spend that much each year on making sure my people look the part, so if this helps them behave right, it is great value"*.

A leadership team event has been specifically included in the implementation phase to design and support the operating platform for 31Practices. How will the methodology be embedded into everyday processes such as interviews, induction, standard operating procedures, daily buzz meetings, recognition programmes and more? Every organization is different and it is critical that 31Practices "fits", is owned, and that leaders feel accountable for the effective use of the framework. This powerful set-up process, together with planned reviews, keeps 31Practices fit for purpose, lived, and impactful.

In 2011, Alison joined the team and lent her considerable knowledge, experience and expertise to help identify the supporting theoretical underpinnings that makes 31Practices such a powerful tool. Little did she imagine that two years later we would have co-authored this book.

Ten years may seem a long time to develop what is, on the surface, a very simple tool, but perhaps this is its strength. The development has been grounded in practical application rather than management theory and books. 31Practices brings an organization's core values to life through the behaviour of every employee, every day. The approach helps instil a common culture across departments, supply chain delivery partners and remote workers. Over time, consistency of behaviour is built through repetition. 31Practices has been used in a variety of local, national and international business environments and has played a major part in the measurable balanced scorecard success achieved in these businesses. It is now available on a license basis for 31Practices Practitioners to promote and deliver to their clients.

"Life is really simple, but we insist on making it complicated."

Confucius[3]

THE CURRENT FRONTIER...

One of the initial reasons for Alison joining the project was to support the development of a personal application of 31Practices, my31Practices. In the "perfect storm" that is globalization, economic uncertainty, family fragmentation, enhanced pace of business, instant communications, unlimited connectedness – we find that we are endlessly busy, both at work and in our social lives. Against this context, it is very easy to "do" without mindful awareness of what we are doing all of this for. The result? We end up "doing" without much thought about how we are behaving – caught in habits of thinking and action that are at best unsustainable, and, at worst, are destructive. Under this pressure, we can very easily feel out of control and lose touch with our personal core values, our core purpose and what creates meaning for us.

But there is another way. People can often see the benefit in joining a gym or creating a fitness regime to be the best they can be from a physical perspective. Might it then be possible that people would benefit from developing mental and behavioural fitness in a more holistic way? To do this starts with discovering and reconnecting with our personal core values: what's really important to us. The next step is to align the way we think, feel and behave and this is where my31Practices can help by bringing these values to life through a set of very practical behaviours every day. In this way, people can be the best they can be. The development of the technology platform to become part of our day-to-day lives will be launched in 2013 and is outlined in more detail in Chapter 29, *my31Practices*.

It has been quite a journey over the last ten years. We started with a couple of core ideas and then built the 31Practices methodology in live, operational business environments, finding out what works well and developing the approach during this time. What has been consistent is the business impact. Some client organizations have been more focused on measurement than others. However, there has always been an improvement in areas such as employee retention and engagement, customer satisfaction and finance (where targeted).

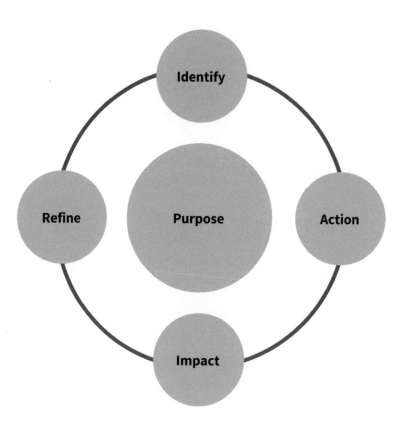

PART **2**

THE UNDERPINNING FRAMEWORK

This part of the book shares the core elements of the 31Practices framework and how it works in an organizational context to enable an organization's purpose and values to be made explicit and lived by everybody representing the organization. Chapter 4, *Framework* provides an overview of how the elements knit together. This part of the book will enable you to understand what is involved in kick-starting the virtuous circle that the 31Practices framework enables.

Each of the subsequent chapters *Purpose*, *Identify*, *Action*, *Impact* and *Refine* (Chapters 5 – 9) presents a central principle of the framework, bringing it to life with stories from our own and others' experiences.

4

CHAPTER 4 FRAMEWORK

"To be nobody but yourself in a world which is doing its best, day and night, to make you everybody but yourself—means to fight the hardest battle which any human being can fight—and never stop fighting."

E.E. Cummings[1]

Without going over much trodden ground, the world is increasingly connected (and disconnected), possibilities and possible selves are endless, work is intense (or boring), money is not an issue (or it is the issue), families are dispersed (or on top of one another) - to step up, to keep up and to deliver to ever-increasing demands, we find ourselves overwhelmed, stressed, anxious, fearful, excited, bombarded. Wherever you are, whatever your circumstances - how do you survive? How do you thrive? How do you flourish?

How do you be at your best whatever the context or circumstances you find yourself in?

How on earth did you get here?

You are sitting on a bench on the south side of the River Thames, London, amid the glass tower blocks behind the warship HMS Belfast. A list of points to cover in your next meeting run through your mind. You stop, taking a few moments to "notice" where you are, notice the sounds, the smells, notice the people scurrying about, others engaged in meetings at the many coffee bars spilling onto the walkway. What's the purpose of all this activity – all this "doing"? What are you really doing here? What was the reason for this meeting? Why were you going? How does this work fit into what is important to you – into what you really want to be doing?

A high-performing team?

A global technology company attracted significant funding through its reputation for a unique product and great service. Great individuals were brought together to deliver the business plan. One year on, the business is seriously off-track from the intended deliverables. The investors are getting edgy and the great individuals are at each other's throats – blaming, defending and disengaging. Scratch below the surface, and you find little to bind the top team together. The connections between the great individuals are disabling rather than enabling, there is no shared purpose, and no agreement as to how they need to work together.

Imagine – what would it be like to have a clear purpose, to be able to make meaning of what it is that you are doing here, to have a shared purpose with those that you work with, where you are clear about how you want to be together and how you want to move forward to deliver that purpose?

The answers, personally and organizationally, are both simple and complex. The simple answer is get to know yourself, your organization, identify what's important and live according to that purpose and those principles every day.

The complex part is the journey that identifying and living core values every day will take you and your organization on – even choosing that journey is not necessarily easy. Even more complex is why on earth such an approach works anyway.

AT THE CORE: BEING VS. DOING

We are often caught in a cycle of doing things, driven by external imperatives and demands. Doing more to achieve – achieve what? Doing more to buy the things to flag our success to others – do we really need it? Doing more to prove our worth – to whom?

How do we break the cycle – more to the point, why bother?

Doing mode

Our brains operate primarily in "Doing mode"[2] using our minds to solve problems, make plans to act, anticipate events, make choices and decisions. Clearly this mode fundamentally enables us to live and achieve our goals. Doing mode doesn't help us thrive emotionally – or be in touch with ourselves, others or the world we live in. Jon Kabat-Zinn[3] notes that staying in "doing" mode, we are in danger of *"Dying without actually fully living"*. It's a significant risk for all given the relentless pace of our lives and the rapidly changing context we live in.

To illustrate the point, in the last two millennia there has been an accelerating pace of change. Our lives and the systems we live by have become increasingly complex and our ability to manipulate our environment extreme. Some people have become immeasurably wealthier in material terms and many others considerably poorer.

Bringing the scale of recent change into perspective, humans have walked on the earth for about 195,000 years, and only 300 of those years have been after the industrial revolution. The rapid technological, social and economic changes in the last 300 years just may not be ones to which we are biologically or socially optimally adapted. Given where we are as a species at the moment and the way we are depleting our personal, interpersonal and planetary resources, it is difficult to see Homo sapiens surviving for another 1,000 years, never mind another 300,000.

In this complex and chaotic world, our lives have evolved such that we are bombarded. We experience information overload and an increased perception of threat such as job and financial insecurity, fears for personal safety, and even the threat of extinction as a species. Our traditional social bonds are more easily fragmented, with people and groups across the social hierarchy left on their own to deal with what seem like overwhelming pressures.

In this context, there is so much that we could be doing, so many possibilities, so much demand: staying in Doing mode perhaps feeds our need to have a sense of control within this chaos.

And yet, we cannot hope to gain control.

Scratching the surface, we find increasing stress, fragmentation, obesity, malnourishment, addiction, pollution. In our hardwired drive to avoid pain, mistakes and threats by thrusting forward and demanding control; we are only ever one step away from the pain we are desperate to avoid.

As our material wealth increases, we see ourselves as "time poor", as our time is totally consumed with "doing" what we need to do, with the purpose of reaching an ever-elusive goal. This, in Prof. Richard Layard's view, is the hedonic treadmill. Despite our increase in material wealth, and our busyness "doing", we are no happier now than we were 50 years ago (see Chapter 12, *Happiness*).

Take the time now to reflect on what you are doing. Step back and consider how you are choosing to live.

If we don't know who we are, and are not aware of the way that we are being, then what we do is mindless rather than mindful. In these circumstances, our doing is only by chance, aligned to our purpose and our values. How can we learn to align ourselves? How can you become the person you keep dreaming you are?

Being mode

In order to have a different outcome to the place that the "doing" mode is taking us, we need to switch tracks.

Not stopping doing (how would we get anything done, make any decisions, live?), but stepping into a different zone. Building the capacity to be present and aware in the here and now to what is happening around us.

Switching modes

There are different starting points to enable you to switch modes, and achieve a different level of awareness of yourself, and a different, more resourceful centre from which to act. Cast your mind back and remember the last time that you recalled questioning what you are doing, beyond the immediate, tangible *"it's part of my job"*; *"I've been asked to attend the meeting"* reasons that come readily to mind.

Have you gone further, perhaps asking: What is this all for?

When have you have taken the time to step back and really consider this question, and perhaps even done something to live in a way that is more aligned with who you aspire to be?

In describing our version of "being", we are perhaps offering a different perspective to that of mindfulness practitioners such as Jon Kabbat-Zin and Daniel Siegel. We are placing the concept of "being" within a consciously shaped awareness of what it is that is core to you – designing a unique personal compass that will guide you towards your chosen purpose.

Imagine how it might be if, in your "doing mode", your actions and behaviours were expressions of your core purpose and values?

Now, consider this in the context of an organization. When did your organization last reflect and question what its core purpose was? The mission and vision, do we really believe in that? Is it truly what we are about? Or was that a tick box activity that met the governance requirements at the time?

What is the purpose of your organization? What is it uniquely able to do that people need in the world right now? What are the core values of your organization (the personality and the way of doing things)? How does the behaviour of those in the organization, from the leadership down to the front line, express your organization's purpose and values? Are those actions and behaviours truly expressions of the organization you want to be? This is the subject of Chapter 5, *Purpose*.

Imagine the energy and resources that might be released if individuals' behaviours and actions were aligned and connected directly with the organization's core purpose and values. This idea has been at the forefront of much work on employee engagement and organizational design over years of research.

This is also where the 31Practices framework and underpinning methodology comes in.

31PRACTICES: THE FRAMEWORK

31Practices has been designed with the explicit purpose of enabling people to live the core values of their organization, being the personality, identity and culture of their organization that is designed to deliver the organization's purpose. In addition, 31Practices offers a way for individuals to live their lives according to their personal core values, their actions expressing their core identity and purpose.

We believe that 31Practices offers one methodology that can provide greater fulfilment and strengthened resilience individually, and greater impact and resilience organizationally. In this book, we focus on the organizational context as we articulate the underpinnings of 31Practices. Our sister text, my31Practices (our second book), focuses on how to apply the 31Practices framework and methodology to your individual situation and is introduced in Chapter 29, *my31Practices*. If you read both, you would notice, and not be surprised, that the underpinning framework and thinking is the same, while the context, stories and impact of the application of 31Practices and my31Practices differ.

31Practices simply helps to translate an organization's core values into practical daily behaviours and to enable employees to live these on a day-to-day basis. It is an approach that is so simple, it is almost common sense.

31Practices is an approach based on doing a little every day with mindfulness, internalization, imprinting and positive reinforcement. It provides a discipline in much the same way as an exercise programme for fitness or a diet. An important difference is that the discipline is deeply integrated into the fabric of the organization.

31Practices offers flexibility so that each organization's set of values and daily Practices are designed and driven by the people who work in the organization. Despite the simplicity, the approach is underpinned by a vast array of theories, principles and ideas that have been developed over decades and, in some cases, centuries.

Purpose
The starting point of the framework is purpose. What is it that the organization is there for? Expressed simply, in a way that engages hearts and minds, the core purpose becomes something that people can get behind.

Having identified your purpose, this is supported by the 31Practices four pillars:
- Identify
- Action
- Impact
- Refine

Identify
The first pillar requires the organization to identify a core set of principles, values, traditions that can act as a guide in this ever-changing, complex, and busy landscape. Building from Purpose, the values are the principles, the "how" that links the here and now to that purpose. The values clarify what is fundamentally important in the way the organization is seen and experienced by stakeholders (customers, employees, investors, communities, suppliers) and the way its people behave.

Action
The second pillar is simply about putting core values into action. Many organizations have taken considerable time and trouble to create a vision and values. For many, this is where the work flounders or stops. The values may be in a frame on the boardroom wall or referred to as "fundamentally important" in the annual report. But if you ask employees about these values, often they do not even know the words; and even when they do know the words, they are unable to explain what these mean to them as part

of their daily life at work. Through daily action, new habits develop and the values are brought to life in the stories and very fabric of the organization.

Impact

The third pillar is to notice what happens as a result of the behaviours that are now being practised consistently across the organization. What is the impact on different stakeholder groups? What is the impact on the employees? On customers? What's the impact on your bottom line? What are the stories that are circulating from customers, from suppliers, from employees? How are employees feeling? What is their level of engagement? As an individual employee, you directly experience the impact. The stories you tell yourself about your role in the organization are likely to change, perhaps you start to embed some different skills, have a different awareness, or feel more engaged with the "bigger purpose" of the organization you work for.

Refine

The fourth and final pillar is to refine and adjust the way in which you are applying the Practices, and, in time, perhaps refining the Practices themselves. The values or what is core and important to the organization is not going to change or shift radically from one moment to the next, but as your awareness and insight grows, you are likely to get a different understanding of how these values are constructed and the best way to bring these values to life. You might refine, reconstruct, re-prioritize, add to or take away from the way you implement your Practices based on greater awareness and experience. A series of reviews are built into the 31Practices approach to assist this process of refining.

Based on a form of the scientific method (and building from models such as Plan-Do-Check/Study-Act), this enquiry-based cycle (identify, action, impact and refine) will extend understanding and bring organizations closer to their goal.[45] Made explicit, this approach can enhance the level of critical thinking, enabling employees to be more purposeful and have greater choice about how they act – rather than mindlessly acting to fulfil a demand.

WHAT MAKES 31PRACTICES WORK?

Why is 31Practices likely to be effective? For this part we turn to a wide range of sources that shed light on what it is to be human: the interplay between Heart, Body and Mind. We often talk about and see these as different "parts" of ourselves. In fact, they are all strongly interconnected and if all three are working together in the same direction, positive things start to happen.

Working in the manufacturing industry in the 1990s, there were many times when a lathe operator, grinder, or driver would share the "fact" that *"you're expected to leave your brains at the gate when you work here"*. Another favourite in a particular manufacturing organization was that *"we are treated like mushrooms… kept in the dark"*. The message here was very clear: you're not meant to think – just do – we don't want to harness the power of your minds.

The energy and resource provided by inspired and engaged employees is a known factor that organizations are keen to tap into, often spending a significant budget on measuring engagement with the aim of creating the right context and environment to enable people to put their hearts into their jobs.

The 31Practices framework is not something that is rigid or fixed, but provides a framework that enables organizations to create the habits of their own success. We believe 31Practices enables organizations to have the yin and yang that Jim Collins and Jim Poras refer to in their book Built to Last. Namely, the 31Practices framework is designed to enable organizations to preserve their core and stimulate progress through:[6]

- continuity and change
- core values and big goals
- stability and discontinuity
- strong cultures and idiosyncratic people
- consistency and innovation
- discipline and creativity
- systematic methods and experimental approaches
- meaning and achievement

The next five chapters give more depth to the steps and stages of the 31Practices methodology.

CHAPTER 5 PURPOSE

"If you want to build a ship, don't drum up the people to gather wood, divide the work and give orders. Instead, teach them to yearn for the vast and endless sea"

Antoine De Saint Exupery[1]

Purpose refers to the very reason that something is done or for which something exists. The broader the aim, the bigger the goal. Purpose is not a given for organizations or individuals; it is something that needs to be crafted and defined, something that has to be believable if it is to be believed in.

Clarifying purpose is the starting point for the 31Practices framework and in this chapter, we explore what makes it so fundamental to our approach.

"Purpose expresses the company's fundamental value – the raison d'etre or over-riding reason for existing. It is the end to which the strategy is directed"

Richard Ellsworth[2]

As human beings, we are keen to make meaning of our existence. Creating stories and reasons for events is something that we do almost without thinking. This search for meaning on a grand scale centres around questions such as "Why am I here?" Creating a meaning and purpose to life – the sense of making a contribution in some way – is one of the factors that leads to happiness and contentment. A meaningful purpose enables people to tap deep wells of energy and resource.[3] In contrast, a life without purpose can leave people with an internal emptiness and an inescapable yearning that many try to fill by tangible and transitory possessions and experiences (for more, see Chapter 12, *Happiness*).

Understanding your individual purpose can be a challenge. Some coaching clients that we work with comment that this is something they have been thinking about for a long time, while others have great clarity about what their purpose is. To speed up the process of finding your purpose, it's often useful to start at the other end of the time line. When you look back on life:

- What do you want to be remembered for?
- What legacy do you want to leave?
- What do you want people to say about you?

Looking at purpose this way can really help you focus.

Roberto Assagioli, a 20th-century Italian psychiatrist, emphasized the personal will required to fully live your purpose. He noted that to live your purpose every moment requires mastery through determination and persistence; however, the reward is intense energy, dynamism and focus as you synthesize and integrate all that you are into each present moment.[4]

From the perspective of organizations, connecting people with a broader purpose in the work that they do taps into the energy and resources that people have at their disposal. The traditional transactional contract between employer and employee, a trade of time for pay, doesn't engage hearts and minds, and can disengage some as people look for fulfilment from their work. It's perhaps no surprise then that many organizational leaders recognize the value of connecting at an emotional level with employees.

Take some of the success stories of modern business: IBM's nimbleness and longevity is attributed to its view of itself *"as an organization loyal to the idea of packaging technology for use by business."*[5] Others that are animated by ideas rather than products include Apple, who package the latest technology in simple, elegant form and sell it at a premium – their purpose is about inspiring and amazing people; Samsung, who are dedicated to making a better world; Amazon, making it easy for people to buy stuff and Facebook, helping people share things with friends easily. You may think Starbucks would be focused on selling coffee but they have a far deeper sense of purpose *"Our mission: to inspire and nurture the human spirit – one person, one cup and one neighborhood at a time".*

Looking at Asia and the very real war for talent in growing economies; community, meaning and a sense of purpose in organizations are even more important because of the sense of pride in the nation, and in increasing self-expression.[6] Ian Mintram,[7] GlaxoSmithKline, Senior Vice President, HR leadership of Emerging Markets, Asia Pacific and Japanese, believes that GSK fares reasonably well in terms of this war because the organizational strategy of contributing more to the wider society taps into a deeper sense of purpose among current and future employees.

In our own business, we ask potential partners what their purpose is. The answer is revealing, and not always something that our partners have thought about to a significant degree. Whatever the response, it enables us to understand whether a partnership with the company or individual is likely to be successful.

WHAT DOES PURPOSE DO FOR YOU?

Mission, vision and values statements are fundamental to strategic planning and good management. At best, they offer a powerful governance tool, bringing clarity, consistency and purpose. To be effective, such statements need to be "lived" and "compel" people to action – connecting people to the broader intent of the organization.

An organization with a clear and compelling purpose is potentially able to evolve without experiencing a level of chaos that is disabling because its overall direction, principles and intent are clear and consistent. This exact point was noticed by a client implementing 31Practices who stated *"it* [31Practices] *provided a sense of purpose for employees at a time of significant change".* In this case, the change referred to was significant headcount reduction.

The board, employees and wider stakeholders gain a sense of pride in working for an organization that stands for something they can believe in, "get behind" and are united by. A meaningful purpose lives beyond your organization's annual report and web page, bringing guidance and inspiration to all your initiatives. This principle of purpose was noted and captured by Jim Porras:[8] a guiding philosophy or spirit takes an organization beyond the mediocre.

Charlotte Rainer describes the shared sense of purpose as the golden thread that becomes a fantastic rope that people can hang on to. In the current context where change is business as usual, this golden thread can be of particular value.[9]

ELEMENTS OF A DEFINING PURPOSE

An effective purpose will:
- **make you feel energized.** It needs to engage you at an emotional level.
- **enable you to act.** It needs to motivate you, to support you to bring your creative, innovative "best self" to work.
- **be lived by those at the top.** To be seen as believable and worthwhile, it has to be something that leaders prioritize and act by.

How does your organization's purpose make you feel?

A defining purpose needs to be something that you can line up behind. Purpose engages the heart. Imagine for a moment meeting someone who told you that their purpose in life was to "enable others to be free". How does that purpose make you feel? This is a really transcending purpose, i.e. it doesn't matter through what means the freedom is enabled. The person enabling others to be free may be a lawyer, a coach, a school teacher, a scientist, a personal trainer, a receptionist, a road-sweeper. What is your defining purpose?

Imagine for a moment that a global conglomerate had the defining purpose of "Changing the world". Immediately, there is something that grabs your attention. Steve Jobs, luring John Sculley, then CEO of PepsiCo, to Apple, famously and ultimately successfully evoked Sculley's sense of purpose by asking *"Do you want to spend the rest of your life selling sugared water or do you want a chance to change the world?"*[10]

Any kind of work has the possibility to provide purpose. Take this story from an unknown source:

A man is walking along a construction site where there are people building a wall. He says to the first person, "What are you doing?" "Earning enough money to live" was the reply. He walked on and asked the next person the same question. This time the answer was "I am building a wall, I have been a bricklayer all my life and I am the best there is". Walking on, the man asked the question of a third person and the answer was "I am building a cathedral in the glory of God".

Bringing this story into a recent context, just remember how engaged the volunteers were at the recent Olympic games held in London, in the

UK in 2012. Similarly, in Vancouver in the 2010 winter Olympic games, volunteers worked extremely hard for no significant tangible rewards; instead, they worked for the opportunity to *"be a part of something"*, *"one of the biggest events in the world"*.[11] Compare this to how employees feel when there is economic uncertainty and the possibility of redundancy. The attitude of volunteers such as those at the Olympics is a function of their choice to be there and the sense of purpose to contribute to a global showcase event.

How does your organization's purpose enable you to act?

Take the NASA employee who was sweeping the floor. When asked what his job was, he replied, *"to put a man on the moon"*. Perhaps this story is an urban myth, but it illustrates the power of purpose. Whatever the skills and resources the man brought to his work (the means at his disposal), he was putting them towards a meaningful purpose. How proud and motivated must he have felt when his alarm clock rang in the morning?

A purpose that goes to the very heart of why the organization exists and enables employees to bring more of their full selves – because they care about the bigger idea – will inspire motivation and engage people. Even if that purpose is about profit maximization, "to make as much money as possible", as long as the purpose is clear, people can buy into it and get behind it, or choose not to, but the choice about what you are engaging in is evident rather than hidden.

Organizations can and do successfully exist without an engaging purpose. But what used to define competitive advantage has shifted from efficiency to effectiveness. Efficiency can be repeated, copied and adapted and is based on structures, processes and hard systems. Effectiveness comes from people committing to an organization enough to use their knowledge, innovation and creativity.

There is certainly no one way to define your organization's purpose as these vignettes show:

- **HCL Technologies** have a purpose that is about engaging the passions of their employees. They look at each employee's top five passions, and the line manager is then required to facilitate and enable employees to realize those passions in their work. This idea works from the philosophy of employee first; customer second. If you ensure a focus on employee engagement, employee empowerment and employee enablement (the three E's), those employees then focus on customer delight, customer loyalty and customer satisfaction.[12]

- **Richard Branson's Virgin group** has "making a difference" as a core purpose. Each year, the group celebrates some of those people who have gone the extra mile around the Virgin world at the Virgin Stars of the Year Awards. With so many different companies, nationalities and personalities represented under one roof, they all have in common the pride they take in their work, and in the company they represent. Virgin recognize that staff are the biggest brand advocates, and focusing on helping them take pride will shine through in how they treat customers.
- **Apple** is about inspiring and amazing people by challenging the boundary of what is thought to be possible. The purpose "enriching people's lives" instils a purpose far greater than just selling or fixing products. Apple has been an immense success story, resting on a fan base that ensures a steady supply of eager job applicants and an employee culture that tries to turn every job into an exalted mission. *"When you're working for Apple you feel like you're working for this greater good"* says a former salesman. One manager said it was common for people offered jobs to burst into tears. Newly hired devotees then become disciples. If there is a secret to Apple's success, this is it: the company ennobles employees.[13]
- **Southwest Airlines** is dedicated to the highest quality of customer service delivered with a sense of warmth, friendliness, individual pride, and company spirit. Co-founder Herb Kelleher has been called perhaps the best CEO in America by Fortune magazine. Under his leadership, Southwest became the most consistently profitable, productive, and cost-efficient carrier in the industry: earning the "Triple Crown" award for best on-time performance, baggage handling, and customer satisfaction for four years running. Kelleher's belief: *"If you create an environment where the people truly participate, you don't need control. They know what needs to be done, and they do it. And the more that people will devote themselves to your cause on a voluntary basis, a willing basis, the fewer hierarchies and control mechanisms you need."*[14]

Imagine if you were able to engender this passion in your own organization.

How do the leaders in your organization live that purpose?

A purpose has to be lived at the top – otherwise it is just a marketing gimmick. If a motivated, energized workforce is essential to accomplishing organizational goals, and if motivated workers will overcome all obstacles, defying the odds, then they must be purposeful, brimming with passion and committed energy. This is where leadership comes in. Leaders have to first be sure of their own purpose – not just in knowing how to get what they want but also in being focused in driving and inspiring purpose throughout the organization. Leaders instil purpose by communicating it through even the smallest behaviours.

The best CEOs are driven by their own purpose and passion and connect other people to that purpose.

Most leaders, directors and business owners feel a sense of fulfilment because they believe they are doing work that matters to them and their company. The challenge is inspiring those that work for them. Leaders can get so absorbed in the noise of the day-to-day business that they fail to pay attention to careful messaging, and can fall short in communicating that inspiring belief to others.

Leaders often say they "don't have time" – but in reality, many leaders we work with spend the time to create a philosophy and plan how they want to lead. If you make time, and inspire those that work for you, the rewards are significant as it unlocks employees' discretionary energy.

Have you got time?

Realigning "doing" with core purpose enables you to build reinforcing habits that have greater impact – not having time is an empty excuse.

At the same time, without the opportunity to share their goals and the things which are important to them, employees that work for you simply lack motivation and creativity and perhaps connection to how they can integrate what they care about into the job that they do. Effective leaders help their people to achieve a common goal by simultaneously helping them realize their own potential.

"As a leader, you must believe in your heart that the people who work with you are truly in it for something bigger than themselves. Then you must be able to communicate in a way that respects their desire to make a difference."

Simon Sinek[15]

Perhaps one defining character of organizations with sustainable performance will be the meaning and clarity of the shared purpose.[16]

....

Discovering your purpose

This exercise is adapted for an organizational context from a post by Steve Pavlina[17] and from the work of Peter Hawkins.[18]

1. Work with a blank sheet of paper or laptop for each person in the group.
2. Write at the top:
   What is our true purpose? What is this organization uniquely able to do that the world needs right now?
3. Write an answer (any answer) that pops into your head. It doesn't have to be a complete sentence. A short phrase is fine.
   DO NOT CENSURE OR JUDGE ANY RESPONSES
4. Repeat step 3 until you write the answer that moves you to tears. This is possibly your collective purpose.

....

Want to know more?

One fabulous book in this arena which is definitely worth a further read:

- Jim Collins and Jerry L. Porras (2005) *Built to Last: Successful Habits of Visionary Companies*. London: Random House.
- A second title written by Nikos Mourkogiannis (2006) *Purpose: The starting point of great companies*. New York: Palgrave Macmillan. makes the point that a choice between values and success is no choice at all – and it is ideas that cause companies to move from good to great.

CHAPTER 6 IDENTIFY

"Achievements on the golf course are not what matters, decency and honesty are what matter."

Tiger Woods[1]

How do you go about identifying your core values as an organization? How do you do it as an individual leader? The starting point is to start noticing what you do value. The clues are evident, especially during the highs and lows of organizational life, but also at significant decision points. What is it that finally pushes you one way or another when a difficult decision has to be made? In this chapter, we share some of the ways to identify your organizational core values and how you might bring those to life through practical behaviours.

Identifying core values is the first pillar of 31Practices. Core values are the principles which, when followed, lead you towards fulfilling your purpose. Operating in a way that is aligned around core values reduces the experience of stress, whether at an individual level or across an organization. It also enhances the resources and capability that individuals have access to. In this chapter we highlight the impact of identifying and aligning around core values and provide some insight into identifying your own values and practical behaviours.

Have you ever walked out of a job interview with a feeling that, despite the job ticking all the boxes, something doesn't quite feel right? You might even take the job and enjoy the role when left to your own devices – if only it wasn't for the organization! This is almost exactly the experience of this hospitality manager when interviewed for a senior management role at a prestigious venue and restaurants location in London, UK.

Sam views punctuality as a basic courtesy. He arrived in good time for the interview, but immediately, there were small signals of the potential values clash: the receptionist was not expecting him, and he waited an hour after the scheduled time before the interview started.

Despite this initial experience, the role which Sam was offered was very attractive – he accepted. Sam remembers arriving for his first day where the pattern of behaviour was evident once again: as before, the receptionist was not expecting him; in fact, nobody was expecting him! He had no office and there had been no communication about his arrival. Business performance success was achieved in the following two years, ranging from gaining a Michelin star for the restaurant to improving annual operating profit by £1 million, but the values mismatch continued. Perhaps the final straw was when Sam's boss would not honour a verbal gentleman's agreement regarding a bonus for improved financial performance. At this point, Sam was pleased to move to another role.

In this story, the almost intangible mismatch between Sam and the way things are done in the organization shows up as a sense of discomfort. The experience, in hindsight, shows the organization is not demonstrating a value that is important to Sam.

"Whenever you experience stress of any kind, look into yourself and ask, "In what way am I compromising my innermost values in this situation?"

Brian Tracy[2]

INDIVIDUAL CORE VALUES

Consider a different experience, one where you may have been lucky enough to find yourself working for an organization that really fits and works for you – whatever the specific job role you have to fulfil – you feel appreciated, capable, connected. What is happening here?

To start identifying what's important to you, what your values are, start paying attention to your gut feeling; what are you picking up that you can't yet consciously articulate?

If we are constantly in situations with groups, individuals and communities where we are required to behave in a way that is out of synch with our personal core values, we will experience stress, dissatisfaction, discomfort, perhaps anxiety and, if left unchecked, ill health.

As human beings, whether we are aware of it or not, we have endless opportunities to adopt a more conscious role in deciding how we want to engage with and respond to our environment. By consciously choosing to live a life that is more aligned with the values that are important to us, and to practise habits of thinking, feeling and behaving that enable us to live those values on a daily basis, there is evidence to suggest that we may well be happier, more satisfied, have access to more resources and have greater resilience.[3] Martin Seligman suggests we will find greater happiness through living life according to core values. Such a life can offer greater fulfilment, a feeling of greater personal comfort and a sense of control (Chapter 12, *Happiness* covers this field in more depth).

For leaders, acting in line with your personal core values is essential to authenticity. Joseph Badaracco,[4] Professor of Business Ethics at Harvard Business School, writes about the defining moments for executives being those times when they dug below the busy surface of their lives and refocused on their core values and principles – raising the question "who am I?" in order to become leaders in the truest sense. This was the root cause of Tiger Woods' well publicised difficulties: whilst he had identified his core values quoted at the beginning of this chapter, he later admitted that "I had gotten away from my core values".[5] This highlights that whilst Identify is a critical stage, on its own it is not enough. The other steps: Action, Impact and Refine are necessary for values to be lived.

ORGANIZATIONAL CORE VALUES

As an organization, if employees are unable to accommodate an organization's values or if values are misaligned, there will be strain within the system. Decisions made will not be aligned, communication will be more difficult and there will be tension day to day. Identifying and making use of core values can lead to greater performance success while ignoring the real core values of our organization may lead to a fast demise (see Chapter 2, *Values*).

Connor O'Shea, the Head Coach at Harlequins Rugby Club in the UK, noted in 2012 that the turnaround in the club's strategy started with a session at a well-known business school, where they worked to identify their core values as a team and how to "live" those values through the way that they interacted and played. O'Shea points to this shift as making a difference in the team game. At that time, Harlequins had risen to the top of the Rugby Football Union league in the UK.

Many private, public and not-for-profit organizations use a code of ethics, a credo or other long-form description of what they believe in. These kinds of values statements help people to make decisions, and to respect the intent and spirit of their organization's purpose and plan – particularly when the context is ambiguous and unclear.

Values operate as "simple rules" assisting people to know how to function when there are no specific rules for a given situation. Policies and procedures guide behaviour in organized work. Simple rules guide behaviours in self-organized work.

As a matter of curiosity, what simple rules can you see around you in your organization? For example, if the values in an organization are about intolerance of risk, together with a push for individual achievement, this mix could easily give rise to observable patterns such as:

- stretching individual performance targets
- competitive organisational processes
- people working in isolation (little or no collaboration)

You might also notice:

- a lack of creativity,
- little or no individual / group learning

This would be a demanding environment to work in.

It is only by identifying and articulating these values and behaviours that people in complex organizational systems can be expected to align behaviours and create an observable and distinct brand. Similarly, if the values and behaviours are not identified, then there is a tiny, momentary, and only random chance of behaviour being aligned across any significant part of an organization.

CREATING EFFECTIVE ORGANIZATIONAL VALUES AND PRACTICES

There are a number of principles that we have developed to support organizations to articulate their core values and practices – and one additional principle we have integrated through the research for this book.

These principles include:
- Aligning values and practices to the organizational purpose
- Making value and Practice statements as simple as possible
- Co-creating values and Practices with employees across the organization
- Encompassing the seven levels of organizational consciousness

Aligned to purpose

To be truly powerful and relevant, organizational values need to align to and support the organization's purpose (see Chapter 2, *Values* and Chapter 5, *Purpose*). With a clear set of values (principles, traditions, beliefs) that are lived at the heart of the organization and aligned to a clear purpose, it is much easier for people to know how to contribute to success. The result is growth of trust between the organization and all stakeholder groups (customers, employees, suppliers and communities).

As more traditional rigid organizational structures and hierarchies increasingly become obsolete, organizations need a strong sense of purpose and shared values and principles to guide decision making.[6]

As clear and simple as possible

Values need to be clear and simple to be effective, defining your organization and its unique personality. What you don't want to end up with is a list of qualities associated with any number of organizations. Avoid lists of single words and make sure you clarify the definition and meaning behind each value. After all, we all believe in integrity, don't we? Most organizations (90%) have "ethical behaviour / integrity" as a core value,[7] but each organization will have a different way of defining or living integrity in their context. Is integrity listed as one of your values? What do you mean by integrity? What excellent examples do you have of integrity being displayed by those around you?

Co-created across the organization

It's easy to imagine that identifying and defining organizational values is purely the job of the leadership team. Yet in what business do those on the executive board know all that there is to know about delivery? Values have to relate across the organization, so start from that point – involve people from across the organization.

In any organizational change process, involving a wide cross-section of employees in collaborative co-creation is beneficial and pragmatic. Put simply, if you're involved in designing something:

- you take more responsibility for ensuring a successful outcome
- you're happier that the decisions made are fair, both in terms of what has been agreed, and how agreement has been reached
- you gain personal fulfilment

Co-creation involving a diverse group can (if designed well) also avoid groupthink.[8]

At the same time, the leadership team have a critical role in designing and crafting with other stakeholders. They have to believe in, drive and get behind 31Practices. Now is not the time to delegate the strategic direction of the company!

Employees play a co-creation role in the design and delivery of 31Practices in their business at a number of levels.

First, employees take ownership for developing and articulating the Practices right at the start. We cannot overstate the positive impact this has – remember the examples from Chapter 3, *Journey*, about the post-room employee in New York and his colleagues who still carry their 31Practices card and use the Practices five years later.

Second, the 31Practices created from the values statements act as simple rules, as behavioural guidelines only. Employees themselves decide exactly how they are going to live the specific Practice on any given day. If the core value is creativity and today's practice is *"We enjoy **exploring** and offering **alternative** options"*, the call centre operator is more inclined to go the extra mile to create the right solution for a customer with an issue, or the learning and development manager might investigate beyond what is already on offer in the organization for a solution to a training requirement.

Encompass the seven levels of organizational consciousness

From the work of Richard Barrett[9] and his colleagues at the Barrett Values Centre, your values will deliver more when balanced across these levels:

1. **Survival** – Pursuit of profit and shareholder value: Creating an environment of financial stability, and focusing on the health, safety and welfare of all employees.
2. **Relationship** – Building relationships that support the organization: Building harmonious relationships that create a sense of belonging and loyalty among employees and caring and connection between the organization and its stakeholders.
3. **Self-esteem** – High performance systems and processes: Creating a sense of employee pride by establishing policies, procedures, systems, processes and structures that create order and enhance the

performance of the organization through the use of best practices.

4. **Transformation** – Adaptability and continuous learning: Giving employees a voice in decision making and making them accountable and responsible for their own futures in an environment that supports innovation, continuous improvement, knowledge sharing, and the personal growth and development of all employees.

5. **Internal cohesion** – Strong cohesive culture: Enhancing the organization's capacity for collective action by aligning employee motivations around a singular mission, an inspiring vision and a shared set of values that create commitment and integrity, and unleash enthusiasm, creativity and passion.

6. **Making a difference** – Strategic alliances and partnerships: Building mutually beneficial alliances with other organizations and the local community to protect the environment, while deepening the level of internal connectivity inside the organization by fostering internal cooperation between business units and departments.

7. **Service** – Social responsibility: Working with other organizations and the stakeholders of the organization in pursuit of societal objectives that enhance the sustainability of humanity and the planet, while deepening the level of internal connectivity inside the organization by fostering compassion, humility and forgiveness.

Organizations that purely value aspects at levels 1-3 are too rigid, fear based, internally focused and self-absorbed to be at the top of their game. Too much energy is spent unproductively focused on protecting the self and infighting. Operating with a focus on levels 5-7 means the organization is not grounded in the pragmatic reality of business. When values are balanced across the spectrum, organizations create a climate of trust, can manage complexity, and can respond or adapt to emerging situations.

Supporting you to articulate values and Practices:

- Articulating values: To achieve your organizational purpose, what are your deeply held beliefs and how do you need to behave? Go beyond the short-term strategies and goals – take a longer-term view.

What are the four or five ways of operating that you cannot do without if you are to achieve your purpose? From Tony Hseih and the story of Zappos, a great way of checking whether your values are really core is the "hire and fire" test. Is each one of these principles something that you would expect to inform decisions about hiring and firing? This kind exploration gives you

your value statements.
- Articulating Practices: For each value, what are the five to seven behaviours that demonstrate this value in action, and are specific to the style and character of your particular organization?

We facilitate creative workshops to generate these Practices. For example, for the value "Impact":
- What would be happening if tomorrow everyone started creating impact – what would that look like? What would you notice?
- What do we consider to be best practice examples of impact?

For the value of "Impact", an organization might produce some of the following:
- *We **deliver** what's needed, when it's needed*
- *We **measure** our performance to know how much we have improved*
- *We think "**what else** could I do?", then do it*
- *We **enable others** to deliver excellently*
- *We **recognize** someone else's contribution – then tell them*

It's possible to generate a set of Practices that can be honed and crafted through a process of employee consultation into your unique organizational 31Practices. Organizations that we have worked with have valued the benefit of our experience and external perspective to facilitate this process.

Want to know more?

If you are interested in reading more about values or perhaps want an off-the-shelf approach to identifying your values, there are numerous organisations willing to oblige. Here are two well-founded approaches that we are happy to recommend.
- The Barrett Values Centre has designed a range of products to explore values at an individual and group level, including positive values and potentially limiting values, and their balance across the levels of consciousness. For more information, see: http://www.valuescentre.com/products__services/
- Similarly, Values in Action (VIA) Institute, building from the work of Martin Seligman, offers a range of values measures, including individual and group-level surveys. And you can discover your personal values at no cost. http://www.viacharacter.org/www/

CHAPTER 7 ACTION

"Do not wait to strike till the iron is hot; but make it hot by striking."

William B. Sprague[1]

Action means doing something, a behaviour, changing something.[2] So, having identified core values and crafted 31Practices, what next? What are the actions that need to take place to demonstrate that each core value is lived, alive and part of "business as usual"? How can you bring to life those core values? Action is the second pillar of 31Practices. The 31Practice framework is designed to enable people to take action on a daily basis that is in line with the core values and organizational purpose.

Knowing what your core values are and what they would look like in practice is not the same as living your core values. To really know about something – to achieve something – you have to move it from an idea, from theory into action.[3] Only then do you truly experience that idea – and deliver. *"You can't think your way there. You must act."*[4] Joseph Badaracco explains that to experience growth as leaders and people, core values have to be played out in the messy reality of organizational life.[5]

"Talk doesn't cook rice."

Chinese Proverb

WHY IS ACTION IS SO POWERFUL?

Action is energizing. The physical benefits of exercise are clear, there is an impact on mental functioning too, including reduced fatigue, improved alertness and concentration. Even when our action does not involve physical activity, the very act of doing something and completing it gives us a sense of achievement and makes us feel good.

Action conquers fear according to Peter Nivio Zarlenga.[6] Mel Robbins[7] introduces the five-second rule: when you have an idea that seems a good one, take action to move it forward within five seconds. As we are hardwired to avoid loss and pain and to reduce risk, we'll persuade ourselves to abandon that idea unless we act quickly.

"Don't wait. The time will never be just right."

Napoleon Hill[8]

Taking action builds habits, and building a broader repertoire of habits means we've got more choice about how to act in any given situation. It takes much repetition of actions or sequences of behaviours before we have integrated those actions into unconscious patterns of behaviour.

Individual action is one thing. Taking action as a group is particularly powerful.

When we see others take action, even when we're not involved in the action, certain neurons fire that help prime us to understand and identify with those others. John Cacioppo, Director of the Center for Cognitive and Social Neuroscience at the University of Chicago, notes that when we see others take action, we mimic that action at a physiological level. He calls this "synchrony". As social animals, synchrony is useful to connect us together. It's often so subtle that we don't realize it's happening.

Imagine, across your organization, whether that is a site, multisite, national or global organization, you know that everyone is engaged in the same daily Practice. This level of coherence is engaging. In the words of one employee, "It feels good to know that we are all focused on the same thing".

This social mimicking effect is further enhanced when it involves people we respect or admire, or people who have authority over us in some way. The action of leaders is magnified! This underlines why the behaviour of leaders is so important. We explore this in more detail in Chapter 24, *Leadership*.

"I have always thought the actions of men the best interpreters of their thoughts"

John Locke[9]

Let's use an example of a private healthcare organization where one of the values is Excellence and one of the Practices is "We display meticulous attention to **cleanliness**". If the chief executive is being shown around a hospital and he/she picks up a piece of litter when walking down the corridor, this sends a strong message to everybody who sees the action (or hears about it subsequently).

Conversely, if a member of the cleaning team has just attended a workshop on the importance of values and living the 31Practices but they see the chief executive step over the piece of litter, they could not be blamed for coming to the conclusion that the whole thing is a waste of time – an equally strong, but negative message then takes hold.

Now it may not seem logical to draw such a conclusion from such a small incident and it may not seem very fair, but we know from our experience of large and small organizations that this is how things work. Inaction or silence can be interpreted as tacit approval and in organizations, senior leaders are role models so their actions and inactions are magnified in importance.

"The maxim is 'Qui tacet consentiret': the maxim of the law is 'Silence gives consent.'"

Sir Thomas More[10]

The take-away here is to pay attention to what you don't do as well as what you do in order to demonstrate what is important to you.

TAKING ACTION TO DELIVER THE 31PRACTICES FRAMEWORK

Having identified your 31Practices (Chapter 6, *Identify*), now it's time to put them into operation day to day.

Getting started requires you to follow some simple guidelines:

Let people know what is happening, what's expected and how employees are going to be empowered. You also need to give time and space to listen to concerns, adapt what is still adaptable, and answer questions.

Our way of doing this has been a series of employee workshops delivered functionally and cross-hierarchically by trained facilitators. Ensure that those involved in championing the roll-out are involved in the day-to-day operations.

Each Practice corresponds to a day of the month. Only one Practice needs to be practised each day. The starting point is to ensure that everyone knows what Practice it is on what day.

- Make the Practice of the day visible: emblazoned across the entrance, in the rest room, on a desk cube, on the white board. Visibility comes from what people talk about, not just what is written down. Make the Practice visible at meetings and in conversation.
- Make the best story about the Practice of the day visible: use the intranet and make it fun, especially early on – give some daily recognition for the best story.

We were running a session to design the operating platform with a client organization and discussing the sorts of activity that they would put in place to reinforce 31Practices. Somebody suggested that when people logged on to their PC, the Practice for the day would show as a screen saver. The rest of the group thought this was a good idea and one of the other members said they knew somebody in IT that would help put this in place the following week. The positive energy around this suggestion was far greater than if we had presented the idea as one of a list of things we were recommending.

Let people know what's expected. This requires top teams in the organization to really model what is expected, so be visible and make your Practice of the day visible to others. Notice and appreciate those around the organization who are displaying the Practice of the day – ask people what they have done that day to "live the Practice".

"Setting an example is not the main means of influencing others; it is the only means."
Albert Einstein[11]

Supervisors have a responsibility to model the Practices and endorse those who model them too. Supervisory-level people are the ones that are there day in, day out, side by side with their front-line colleagues.

Together with the top team, operational supervisors have a big influence on the 31Practices being "lived". Which positions in your organization hold the most influence?

Embed the values and Practices into organizational systems. 31Practices needs to be integrated into the reward and recognition system; the learning and development system; and the communication system.[12] These systems are critical because they run from the beginning to the end of an employee's relationship with the organization.

Scrutinize, alter and integrate as many opportunities as there are to get the message of 31Practices embedded.

Make 31Practices visible in the fabric of the organization.

For example: include 31Practices in interview schedules; the induction process; design of learning and development interventions; the procurement process; standard operating procedures; regular communications; daily buzz meetings; recognition programmes; and the newsletter.

Even in the case of sport, it's action that leads to embedding.

"I've missed more than 9000 shots in my career. I've lost almost 300 games. 26 times, I've been trusted to take the game winning shot and missed. I've failed over and over and over again in my life. And that is why I succeed."

Michael Jordan[13]

If the Practices and values are not built into the fabric of the organization, then as much as people are engaged by the ideas and by the possible impact, people forget. They will revert to older, stronger habits. It takes time for habits to develop, for a new way of operating to make sense. Making the values and Practices part of the organizational fabric keeps them at the front of people's minds while habits become strong enough to develop and be sustained.

A leadership team event is part of the process to design and support the operating platform for 31Practices. Every organization is different and it is critical that 31Practices "fits", is owned, and that leaders feel accountable for the effective use of the 31Practices framework they are creating. This powerful set-up process, together with planned reviews, keeps 31Practices fit for purpose, lived, and impactful.

BUILDING A FUTURE TODAY

"A dream doesn't happen in a day, but it does happen daily, and what you do daily will determine what you are permanently"

Pat Mesiti[14]

31Practices, through daily actions, helps you develop habits of thinking, behaviour and emotion that support you to live your organization's core values – how you behave, the patterns that emerge in the complex organizational system that you work in. The 31Practices framework puts the focus on "how" people act.

31Practices is designed to make individual and organizational success practical and achievable. Each individual employee decides how they will "live" the Practice of the day and what specific action they will take personally.

When actions produce results and we see ourselves performing, this experience of success is reinforced, creating a virtuous circle, and we are encouraged to do more. And even when our actions are not so successful, with the right support, the experience helps us adjust our actions going forward.

"Small deeds done are better than great deeds planned."

Peter Marshall[15]

Want to know more?
One of Brian Tracy's books is a must in this section – try:
- Brian Tracy (2004) *Eat that Frog!: Get more of the important things done – today!* San Francisco: Berrett-Koehler.

8

CHAPTER 8 IMPACT

"You must get involved to have an impact. No one is impressed with the won-lost record of the referee."

Napoleon Hill[1]

To impact means to have a marked influence, a strong effect on someone or something.[2] Assessing the impact of action is the third pillar of the 31Practices framework.

WHAT IS IMPACT?

Impact is often associated with measurement and reward in organizations, and the phrase *"What gets measured gets done"* has been attributed to Peter Drucker, Tom Peters, Edwards Deming, Lord Kelvin and others – it is true. Impact is only seen historically, after the fact.

And measuring something does not always lead to the intended impact. There have been some disastrous examples. Here are two of our favourites:

Case 1
A call centre was focused on the speed with which calls were answered. A standard was set that calls must be answered within three rings and this

was measured and reported on. The call centre operatives were bonused on their performance. Then somebody pointed out that while the targets were met and bonuses paid, there were a large number of customer complaints about the poor quality of service.

Further investigation revealed call centre operatives had a single-minded focus on meeting the three rings standard... and yes, you've guessed it, in order to answer incoming calls, they were cutting off existing calls mid-conversation!

Case 2

A bus company chose to actively manage the timeliness of its service by putting in place a performance indicator stating that drivers would not be late for more than 10% of bus stops. To meet this targeted measure, bus drivers missed out stops completely to catch up time rather than miss the target.

Cutting the deficit by gutting our investments in innovation and education is like lightening an overloaded airplane by removing its engine. It may make you feel like you're flying high at first, but it won't take long before you feel the impact.

Barack Obama[3]

It's easy, very easy, to reward the wrong things, and have actions and behaviours emerge that run counter to what you are aiming to achieve.[4] It's also possible to get it very right. Consider the case of Zappos: in their call centres they will measure time per call, but reward satisfaction and loyalty measures.

What kind of impact will the actions arising from your 31Practices have?

MEASURING AND SUSTAINING BEHAVIOUR

The two examples above demonstrate the risk of over-reliance on simplistic measurement by numbers. Impact also needs to be assessed at a less quantitative, more qualitative level. A combination of carefully considered metrics or quantitative measures (to provide direction) and a collection of qualitative data (narrative, story, open comments) clarifying the impact on individuals and groups of stakeholders provides a much richer picture of impact and the context within which this happens.

While stories might not seem "measurable" by numbers, Henry Mintzberg, the sanest of management educators, proposed starting *"from the premise that we can't measure what matters".*[5] Mintzberg suggested that this gives leaders the best chance of realistically facing up to their challenge. Stories are a particularly fruitful way of communicating (see Chapter 15, *Storytelling*).

To build your awareness of the impact you and 31Practices have, here are some core principles to follow.

Reflection

To see the impact that you have had so far, look behind you and see what kind of footprint or impression is left: on your profession, people you interact with, teams, departments or organizations you have led. What kinds of impact do the actions and behaviours that you pay attention to have across the organization?

This process of reflecting back is key to learning and to moving forward, to create new meaning and understanding as to how to act in the future.[6]

Ongoing feedback

Organizational processes for exploring impact, resetting goals and agendas at a systemic level generally suffer from a significant time lag between the behaviour and the review process, with six-monthly to annual review processes being the norm. This approach does not build the habits that you want to see at play in the organization in a practical and responsive time frame.

If you have identified your core values and set up a series of daily Practices, six months is too long to wait to explore the impact those changes have had. Instead, gathering immediate feedback and immediate stories keeps the values and Practices real and relevant to daily work life, and more quickly builds them into "business as usual" behaviours.

"What gets measured gets done, what gets measured and fed back gets done well, what gets rewarded gets repeated."

John E. Jones[7]

31Practices is about daily practices, not setting big goals with distant timescales that can be hard to reach. Rather it's about paying attention to the incremental impact of living those daily Practices. It's so simple, taking about five minutes a day to notice and record the impact of your Practice.

*For example, let's say today's organizational Practice is "We **offer help** and assistance". You notice a colleague (that you do not know) struggling with a heavy box in the lift lobby.*

It IS a heavy box, as you discover when you help him carry it through to his desk.

When you reflect on the Practice for that day, you remember how your colleague felt when you helped with his heavy box, what he said, how his appreciation made you feel. In this example, there was an instant "recognition" or "reward" for the Practice because the colleague was very grateful for the help. Reviewing the project team you are about to start managing, you may well notice that this very individual is someone who will be a very useful resource in that project – and you've already struck up a positive connection.

For other Practices, it may be necessary to think more about the value or benefit of the Practice. What came from connecting with five colleagues from other departments? What happened as a result of you saying thank you to everyone? What impact did taking special care about your appearance or spending time with a new employee have? Understanding the impact and benefit reinforces the behaviour and makes it "worth doing" again, eventually becoming a habit.

With 31Practices, the Practice for the day ("We **offer help** and assistance") becomes the **cue** that triggers the **routine** behaviour (behaving in line with the Practice of the day) that is **rewarded** by the attention from colleagues and others in the organizational system. This view of habits as consisting of these three core elements (a cue, a routine and a reward) is described powerfully by Charles Duhigg in his book, the *Power of Habit*.[8]

Rewarding success

This final step to habit formation, reward, has been clearly documented by behaviour specialists over the decades. Perhaps two of the most well-known scientists are Ivan Pavlov[9] with his work on conditioning, and BF Skinner[10] whose experiments around reinforcement are well documented. Behavioural psychology, including theories of conditioning and reinforcement, plays an important role in learning and the core ideas are frequently embedded in organizational systems.

"Reward is the most important part [of a habit] - that's why habits exist".

Charles Duhigg[11]

From this perspective, to build new behaviours, it is important to create a reward system that enables people to gain a quick insight into the impact of 31Practices, through the choices and actions that they and their colleagues take. This positively reinforces the value of using the Practices.

In the 31Practices methodology, the organization's "heritage", folklore and culture is created through communication of stories, data and accounts sharing what people have done to live the core values through the daily Practices.

As we shared in Chapter 3, *Journey*, once 31Practices goes live, employees are able to nominate colleagues who they see displaying the 31Practices excellently (they can even nominate themselves). This works best when a cross-functional group (non-management) is responsible for selecting the best examples on a monthly basis. Nominated employees are recognized and their actions and stories are publicized through the organization and become part of the culture, the "way things are done around here" that is central to an organization's impact and brand.

One thing to note, when we talk about reward: it's not necessarily monetary reward that we are referring to. While financial reward is nearly always welcomed, it is recognition that has the more significant and sustainable impact. It is often the act of a senior person making a presentation, a photograph in the newsletter or intranet posting that has the biggest positive impact rather than the value of a reward. We remember a young man who worked in the post-room at a financial institution: he was nominated for going out of his way to track down the right person to receive a package and when he was presented with the recognition certificate was moved to tears.

Sincere, heartfelt recognition has a major positive impact.

You might be surprised at how quickly a powerful catalogue of examples builds. One 31Practices client, a major shopping centre, captured the nominations on a simple Excel spread sheet and reviewed these on a regular basis with everybody in the business. Appreciating impact and what has been achieved is part of the cycle. We would love to identify and develop an official research project using 31Practices. A collaborative initiative with interested partners (organizations and academic experts) could evaluate the impact of 31Practices in a very practical, business focussed way and also promote the power of practice-based evidence in organizations.

CREATING A UNIQUE AND SUSTAINABLE VIRTUOUS CIRCLE

Some evidence exists to suggest Practices become easier over time. The more we practise, the more tuned in we become to the cues or triggers that indicate an opportunity to practise (would we previously have noticed the new starter looking for a meeting room, the person struggling with the photocopier?). The more we practise, the more comfortable we become with the behaviour. As Shannon Phelan, Assistant Food and Beverage Manager at one of our client organizations, said "Over time it's just become natural"

"The brain can be reprogrammed. You just have to be deliberate about it"

Charles Duhigg[12]

Exercise: An impact Self-Assessment

What impact do you have? Look back over your interactions in:
- the last week
- the last month
- the last year
- the last two jobs

What would people say about you and what you've done?

What behaviours are you reinforcing in others?

What do you want to continue to reinforce?

What Practices/daily habits might you create for yourself?

Want to know more?
You may be interested in this video clip of Harvard Business School Professor Clayton Christensen:
- http://www.measureyourlife.com/inday-speaker-series-how-will-you-measure-your-life/.

9

CHAPTER 9 REFINE

"The whole of science is nothing more than a refinement of everyday thinking."

Albert Einstein[1]

Refine means to improve or clarify by making small changes, removing unwanted elements. There is also something in the word refinement that points to a subtle elegance and sophistication.[2]

To refine thinking and actions is part of the learning cycle captured by David Kolb in his theory of experiential learning.[3] Through the process of reflecting described in Chapter 8, *Impact*, we can gain greater insight and understanding into our core values and the activities or practices that best demonstrate these values in practice.

Refining is about making small changes, based on what you are learning from the evidence you are collecting. This adaptive action builds capacity to see, understand and influence systems and is the fourth pillar of the 31Practices methodology. The adaptive action cycle described in Human System Dynamics is essentially what "refinement" is about within the 31Practices methodology. There are three simple questions:

- **What?** What patterns are you now seeing, what is the data and information that you have?
- **So what?** What does the data mean – what are the options for actions that can be taken on the basis of the data?
- **Now what?** Take action and observe the impact it now has.[4]

The process of refinement is one of becoming clearer about your core proposition, what you stand for and how you want to operate. Something that is ultimately refined offers a sense of flawless quality, polished and artful.[5]

Refinement is core to any process of continuous improvement, or quality. From his work on the P(lan), D(o), C(heck), A(ct) cycle, Deming stressed the importance of constant interaction among design, production, sales, and research and that the four steps should be rotated constantly, with quality of product and service as the aim.[6] Deming described his "Deming Wheel" – which we have altered slightly to fit with 31Practices:

- Design the 31Practices framework and content (with appropriate tests).
- Make it and test it: live as well as in theory.
- Put it out into the organization.
- Keep testing it, gather feedback, gather as much data as you can, find out what stakeholders think and why those who are not persuaded have not "bought it".
- Refine the framework and its application, in the light of stakeholder reactions.

Continue around and around the cycle – growing and moving closer towards your purpose with each turn.

Early on in our work in organizations, when Total Quality Management was the new shade of black and embraced with energy in the manufacturing sector, the beef from employees at different levels would be the rigidity of some of the quality processes introduced, and the difficulty of testing and integrating improvements and innovations into the existing system. This very point has echoes with the experiences of those who have really embedded Continuous Improvement processes into their systems such as Motorola and GM. For example, 3M, a company renowned for innovation, had to loosen its sigma methodology in order to increase the flow of innovation.[7]

As innovation thinker Vijay Govindarajan notes, *"The more you hardwire a company on total quality management, [the more] it is going to hurt breakthrough innovation. The mindset that is needed, the capabilities that are needed, the metrics that are needed, the whole culture that is needed for discontinuous innovation, are fundamentally different."*[8]

Finding the balance between a clear structure and process for people to follow, and flexibility and adaptiveness to what is new and emerging is important to consider.

Rob Ashkenas suggests bearing three principles in mind.

- **What's pragmatic here?** What needs customizing to be fit for purpose? What level of discipline is really needed in the review process? What's required in a manufacturing or food-based environment is likely to be overkill in a design or service environment.
- **What's the purpose of the "rule" here?** Is the rule still fit for purpose, should some things be eliminated rather than improved?
- **What's the impact on the culture?** The way things are done around here.

While Ron Ashkena's focus is about enabling breakthrough innovation within a continuous improvement environment, the points apply to the refinement process in general.[9]

The strength of 31Practices is that there is a consistency of direction provided by the purpose, core values and daily Practices but, importantly, the people in the organization are able to test and adjust their specific actions to add most value. This ongoing refinement on a daily basis needs to be mirrored through keeping the 31Practices framework alive, meaningful and above all useful.

REFINING YOUR 31PRACTICES FRAMEWORK – BUILDING YOUR APPROACH

Designing how you are going to refine your organizational 31Practices is an important part of the process.

You will be pleased to hear, that typically, unless there is a fundamental change in your governance structure (as a result of a merger and acquisition process, for example), or there is a fundamental shift in your stakeholder market due to a brand repositioning exercise, your core values are unlikely to change significantly – assuming you have had the right conversations to identify them in the first place.

There is no fixed way to refine your 31Practices framework. Your core values and Practices, and your purpose, are unique to you. However, there are some principles that you should consider:

New user or business as usual – where are you?
If you have just started using 31Practices, like any systemic change process, keeping a closer eye on the implementation, take-up and impact of the framework is going to be important to ensure timely attention to what is emerging during this period of greater ambiguity and uncertainty.

Employees, from the CEO to the security guard, are going to be feeling slightly unsure about the changes and what is required of them even when they are wholly enthusiastic. Some employees will be openly resistant. What level of focus and reassurance is required to enable people to trust that 31Practices will work to support the organization to deliver its purpose? What trusted individuals, deeply familiar with 31Practices, are going to have access to all areas during this initial phase to provide quick answers to questions, ask the questions that others are afraid of asking, challenge assumptions that might be made and provide guidance to the process? What has worked for you in the past when introducing any systemic change?

In the first 3 months, some evidence-based testing is recommended. Once embedded, a six-monthly or annual "refinement" or review is suggested to ensure the appropriate level of attention to effective operation.

Values-led process – what kind of refinement process fits with the values you are practising?

In the 31Practices framework, the core values are central to decision making and give insight into the "way things are done around here". Embody the core values and Practices in the way that you create and enable the review process. For example, if one of your values is innovation, how do you enable innovation in the refinement process? If one of your values is integrity, what integrity does your review process have?

Evidence-based refinement – what data do you need to have to hand?

What is the data that you are going to draw on to review how effective 31Practices has been? Looking at ideas around evidence-based practice and management,[10] it's important to pay attention to four areas of data:

- What data do you have from external stakeholders, from customers and suppliers, shareholders?
- What data do you have from leaders and managers in the business, from the systems and processes that were included as part of the operating platform for 31Practices?
- What data can you draw on from the broader context, the market niche, market share?
- What data do you have from your other employee groups?

Study the data. What has emerged, and what was expected? Here you are looking at both "how" things are working as well as "what" is working /not working. What needs adjusting to improve how things are implemented or supported? What needs adjusting in terms of the detail of the values/Practices articulated?

Sharing and involvement – warts and all.

Providing feedback into the organization about the review process, what has been "heard", what is working, what is changing, is key to the process of refinement. We have also found that sharing the stories and modelling learning at all levels of the organization is beneficial. In this way, 31Practices becomes owned by everybody in the organization and perhaps surprisingly, even a little vulnerability from the leadership team will support others to change and grow.

"Learning is not compulsory; neither is survival"

W. Edwards Deming[11]

....

Exercise:

We share a really simple exercise here to support you to refine actions and behaviours in order to get a different impact. This exercise, known as "start, stop, continue" is one that can be done by yourself – focusing on your individual behaviours and at a team or system level.

Simply share:

- Three things you feel you (the team, the organization) should start
- Three things you feel you (the team, the organization) should stop
- Three things you feel you (the team, the organization) should continue

....

Want to know more?

- Shewhart, Walter Andrew (1980). Economic Control of Quality of Manufactured Product/50th Anniversary Commemorative Issue. American Society for Quality.
- Gerald J. Langley, Ronald Moen, Kevin M. Nolan, Thomas W. Nolan, Clifford L. Norman, Lloyd P. Provost (2009). *The Improvement Guide: A Practical Approach to Enhancing Organizational Performance*, (2nd Edition). San Francisco: Jossey-Bass.
- Deming, W. Edwards (1986). *Out of the Crisis*. MIT Center for Advanced Engineering Study.

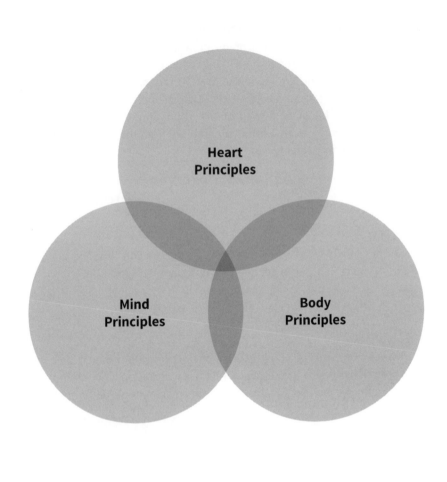

PART 3

EXPLORING THE PRINCIPLES

"If a man is to live, he must be all alive, body, soul, mind, heart, spirit."

Thomas Merton[1]

The third part of this book brings forward, in bite-sized pieces, the underpinning psychological, sociological and philosophical principles that 31Practices draws on. We have organized these into the *Heart Principles*, focused on being; the *Mind Principles*, focused on knowing; and the *Body Principles*, focused on doing.

A greater understanding of the psychology of human beings can help you understand yourself and bring clarity to what at first may seem confusing in those that you lead and work with. Because organizations are a web of interconnecting relationships (that are continually in flux), insight into what might be happening for employees as individuals may enable you to approach the organization as a whole differently. Instead of seeing organizations as rational, linear and mechanical, they tend to be much more unpredictable and more understandable if you have insight into the complexity of the parts.

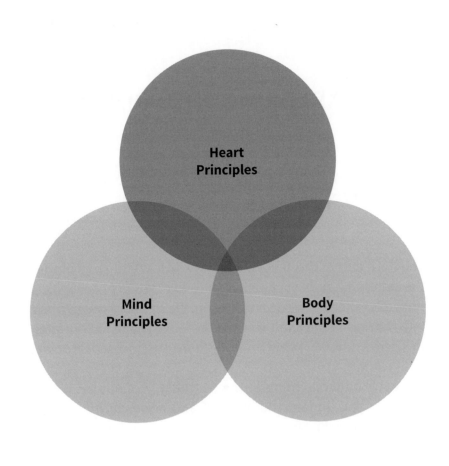

SECTION 1: THE HEART PRINCIPLES

"All the knowledge I possess everyone else can acquire, but my heart is all my own."

Johann Wolfgang von Goethe[2]

The Heart Principles are focused on our emotional and energetic reality, how we experience the world,[3] how we are being. Being is both deeply personal and fundamentally interpersonal, at the heart of how we connect with and respond to others. We start with Chapter 10, *Emotion*, looking at emotion in general as a means of gaining insight into ourselves as emotional beings and what this means. We look at emotion in general as a means of gaining insight into ourselves as emotional beings and what this means. We build from emotions with Chapter 11, *Inspiration* – a sense of being in flow, when we are working at our best with the strong personal and interpersonal benefits that brings. Finally, we move on to Chapter 12, *Happiness* – a state resulting from inspiration. Happiness is now, more broadly recognised as one of the fundamental goals of being human – not the hedonistic, self-focused, consumption-based transitory idea of happiness but rather the mindful, fulfilled, place of contentment that frequently seem elusive.

This build from a brief exploration of emotion through inspiration to happiness reflects a transitional growth that we believe is enabled by living a more explicitly values-based existence. We share how 31Practices links with these three core ideas and why the 31Practices method makes sense from a Heart perspective.

CHAPTER 10   EMOTION

"When dealing with people, remember you are not dealing with creatures of logic, but creatures of emotion."

Dale Carnegie[1]

Emotion is defined as a strong feeling, coming from circumstances, our mood, our thoughts, our history, our experiences, our relationships.[2] Emotion is complex. Emotion directly involves how we interact with others and also impacts how we are affected by experiences either in the present, past or imagined future. Emotions are dynamic.

Emotions are a significant part of our lives. They can fuel us and drain us in equal measure. Unmanaged, emotions can leave us feeling pushed, pulled and out of control, or fuel us with energy, resourcing us. And that is just our own emotional rollercoaster. Working with the emotions of others brings further complexity.

In many organizations, something of a paradox exists around emotions. On the one hand, organizations focus on logic, rationality, process, structure; on the other hand, organizational rhetoric includes the importance placed on employee engagement, on engaging hearts and minds, on creativity and new ways of doing things. Can both exist together?

Yes.

And yet many of us seem to shy away from emotions, worrying about being out of control, unable to handle emotions, incompetence in the face of emotions, being upset. We don't trust ourselves to be able to even go there. We learn that to climb the corporate ladder, emotions have no place in business. Really?

Perhaps we're too ready to think of "emotion" and "emotional" as chaotic, out of our control and in the negative: sadness, crying, anger, anxiety; rather than something we can work with, and the positives: joy, hope, excitement, trust, love, passion, focus.

Take a moment to reflect - if you focus on the negative emotions above, what happens?

If you imagine the positive emotions, what comes to mind?

Of course, we can't just have the positive emotions and cut out the negative. If you try to protect yourself from the negative emotional experiences in your life, you anaesthetise yourself from emotional experiences altogether – dampening the highs and the lows.

"The deeper that sorrow carves into your being, the more joy you can contain."

Kahlil Gibran[3]

SO, WHAT ARE EMOTIONS AND WHAT DO THEY DO FOR US?

Each emotion serves a purpose. A moment of sadness when we reflect, question, critique, reconfigure is an invaluable moment of development and integration. A moment of anger, if it's noticed and brought to light, can offer insight and new perspective into how we might get in our own way or be stopping others grow – what assumptions are we making that are keeping ourselves or others "stuck", what might we need to shift, or how could we support others to shift? A moment of joy and passion can be a helpful guide as to what really engages and resources us.

Our emotional brain is older than the "rational brain" or the frontal cortex.

In the early days of our development as a species, having a hair trigger that could unleash a fast, destructive response towards an attack, or enable a swift escape, would be a survival advantage. We still have that hair trigger, only the circumstances have changed and the attack, real or imagined, is unlikely to necessitate the level of response that an uncontrolled emotional hijack dishes out.

Our emotions are triggered more quickly than our rational mind – *"first feeling, second thoughts"*.[4] It takes the rational mind a moment or two longer to register and respond to an event – we might find we are half way through an "automatic" response when our rational mind kicks in and we wonder why we are shouting at the person who has just said "Boo!" as a joke.

Emotional memories are also stored more vividly and can be particularly strong (but highly inaccurate as the detailed content of memory changes over time). Scraps of current experience reminiscent of an emotionally charged past experience will trigger that earlier emotion.

Emotions play a stronger part in our decision-making than we give them credit for and they are particularly influential when decisions are complex and messy. We are not the efficient and effective rational thinkers that we like to think we are. Emotional biases outside our conscious awareness guide decisions, indicated by gut feel, a racing heart – intuition. And our previous emotional experiences impact significantly on the decisions about choices available to us.[5] Once made, we then rationalize our decision, looking for evidence to back it up.

So if we do find that we are shouting at someone for jumping out and saying "Boo", if we're not careful, we can continue to justify that decision "to shout", thereby creating a scenario that is unreal and unhelpful, simply because we are geared to rationalizing and supporting the decision – reinforcing that it was the right thing to do.

Emotions are triggered by:
- Our thoughts (as well as experiences). If, once we've assessed a situation, we decide that *"Brian is manipulating the figures here"* or *"Leah has really delivered a fabulous report"*, our feelings about each individual, or our emotional response, will correspond with the view we have taken of them. Our emotions line up obediently behind our thought processes, supporting and nurturing the thoughts we are expressing to ourselves and others.
- Our actions and the actions and moods of those around us. We are infected by others' moods. It takes just two minutes on average for us to "pick up" the moods of emotionally expressive people around us.[6] Catching others emotions is a bit like catching a bug – it is infectious. How emotionally expressive or susceptible to others' emotions are you?

Not only are we picking up a significant amount of data from the way things are said, and through others' body language,[7] but there is evidence that we actually feel what others feel in response to events. Neuroscientists, through neural imaging, have identified mirror neurons. Mirror neurons are a type of brain cell that respond equally when we perform an action and when we witness someone else perform the same action.[8] Giacomo Rizzolatti,[9] who was one of the first to discover mirror neurons, sees them providing some explanation of how we develop empathy.

Imagine a situation where you see someone giving a terrible on-stage presentation – you can easily imagine and actually "feel" what it might be like to be there. You see your colleague receiving some great feedback from their manager – you almost feel the impact of that feedback on your colleague – how good that must be.

Emotions are a core element in each of us and help us adapt and deal with basic life tasks such as surviving immediate danger, loss, achieving, reproducing – survival of the species.[10] As social beings, the ability to recognize emotions in others enables us to effectively navigate social interactions. Daniel Siegel sees emotion as central in enabling us to make sense of our world and ourselves in it.[11]

Ignoring and avoiding our own and others' emotions stores up trouble. Emotions don't go away, they get in the way. As Laura Whitworth[12] and her colleagues emphasize, *"it's the hiding, denying, submerging that gets [people] into trouble"* – emotions can keep people stuck, suboptimal, unhappy, and eventually leak out when they *really* don't want them to.

WHAT DO EMOTIONS DO FOR ORGANIZATIONS?

As the binding ingredients in adaptive organizational systems, emotional connection to an organization equates to engagement, whether it's hearts and minds of employees or brand loyalty from customers. Emotional memories are strong and vivid,[13] and at a very basic level, a positive emotional experience leads to a greater likelihood that an action will be repeated. The more frequently and consistently a brand can connect with a customer on a positive emotional level, the stronger and more deeply the customer engages with the brand.[14] Engagement is a winning differentiator.

If your employees can provide your customers with positive emotional experiences, no matter how small, they create meaningful and memorable connections with your brand.[15] In the context of employees, most people (70%) are not deeply connected to their work[16] so there is a lot of untapped resource and potential to draw on. The key to connection is emotional at its core.[17]

The building of an organization that is filled with people who are able to handle their own and others' emotions is a task for individuals and organizations together. Individual leaders of the organization require a degree of personal mastery (including emotional mastery) to be most effective and need to be continually learning and moving forward themselves.

Richard Barrett's[18] work has focused on the developmental mix of organizations who want to really engage their employees. He describes seven levels of organizational consciousness or development. At lower levels of development, where the focus is purely on meeting the basic needs of the business (pursuit of profit or financial stability, and loyalty) there tends to be a predominance of fear-based, rigid, authoritarian hierarchies due to the prevailing anxiety that basic organizational needs will not be met. It's important to meet the basic organizational needs of course, but a focus on these alone leads to greater cultural entropy – greater conflict, friction and frustration. Fear, anger, blame would be a larger part of an organization suffering from greater cultural entropy. And a lot of energy can be spent unproductively, trying to navigate and survive in such an organization.

When an organization is focused on meeting its basic survival needs AND its growth needs, then the organizational context is more open and inclusive. Adaptive systems of governance are in place that empower employees with responsible freedom and support continuous learning, opportunities for growth and greater contribution. In this context, greater passion and motivation exists among employees – greater engagement.

What is the emotional landscape that you are aware of within your organization? Fearful, angry and anxious or engaged, motivated and open to learning?

YOUR PERSONAL EMOTIONAL LANDSCAPE

At a personal level, you can empower yourself to manage emotions better, to build the capacity to pause and assess what is happening and choose how to respond from a variety of possible actions. This will lead to increased performance, connection with a deeper intelligence and intuitive awareness. One of the quickest and most effective ways to achieve this is through emotional self-regulation and generating positive emotions, such as compassion, love, appreciation, and care.[19]

How can you master your emotions rather than allow them to master you?

Emotional intelligence is the ability to monitor your own and others' feelings and emotions, to be able to discriminate among them and to use this information to guide thinking and action.[20] Without this, your negative emotions will continue to control you, get in your way and keep you "stuck" in behaviour patterns that may become unhelpful (even destructive in the ever-changing organizational landscape), and you may not learn how to ignite more positive emotions. Emotional intelligence starts with self-awareness.

Take the story of a passionate general manager. Under tough trading conditions, to underline the need to manage costs, he was known to throw purchase order books and invoices at those employees looking for his signature, yelling at them to get out of his sight. Whilst initially useful to underline an important business message, the outbursts continued, lost the initial impact and started to have a strong negative effect. A strong negative emotional outburst used consistently over time will drive any risk alerts, challenging requests, or innovative developments "underground". The behaviour will disengage employees and create a culture of fear rather than growth.

As the basic currency of relationships (and all that they bring), emotions have a significant impact in the workplace. Daniel Goleman found that the most frequently mentioned factor for derailment among executives was poor relationships,[21] where the executive was too harshly critical, insensitive, and demanding, alienating those that they worked with.

On the other hand, those executives who were successful:
- Stayed composed under pressure, remaining calm, confident and dependable when the heat was on (as opposed to exhibiting moodiness and subject to angry outbursts).
- Took responsibility – admitting mistakes and failures, acting to fix problems (as opposed to denying, covering up, passing on the blame and general defensiveness).
- Had high integrity, were concerned for subordinates and colleagues and prioritizing their needs (as opposed to over-ambitious and ready to get ahead at the expense of others).
- Were empathic, sensitive, tactful and considerate in their dealings with everyone (as opposed to abrasive, arrogant, or intimidating towards others – especially subordinates).
- Appreciated diversity, and were able to get along (as opposed to a failure to build strong, cooperative, mutually beneficial relationships).

Emotions can be used very positively at work. People who are self-aware know their mood, can more easily shift a prevailing negative mood, and move on.

A few years ago, working at a call centre for an international media company, a supervisor, new to the role, shared how he constructively worked with his feelings. *"Every day when I approach the building, I turn around, and tell myself, I can either enjoy the day or hate the day, either way I'm going to be here, so I may as well enjoy it. I put a smile on my face and go to work."*

Imagine being able to withstand the emotional storms and remain connected, at a very human level, to a busy and demanding clientele. Delivering what's required, managing expectations brilliantly and delighting your customers – all without feeling emotionally drained at the end of each shift.

Staying connected with your emotional state at any one time, gaining insight into how your emotions are triggered and developing skills in emotional regulation in what Siegel terms *"response flexibility"*[22] are core to you being the best that you can be at any given moment in any particular circumstance.

Noticing that you have a choice as to how you engage with and respond with your own emotions and those of others will enable you to develop a level of non-reactivity,[23] keep connected to the wider agenda and develop personal resilience (explored in more detail in Chapter 14, *Resilience*). You will have a greater depth of resources and choices available to you during moments of extreme pressure and in the everyday management of a high and intense workload.

In the words of Brian Tracy:[24]

"Just as your car runs more smoothly and requires less energy to go faster and farther when the wheels are in perfect alignment, you perform better when your thoughts, feelings, emotions, goals, and values are in balance."

Exercise using Energy Zones

Self-review

Picking a typical day, how much time do you spend in different energy zones? Looking at the diagram below, there are four energy zones that you might find yourself in at any particular time. The words in each zone give some idea of how you might describe yourself when in any one zone. You will spend time in different zones at different times and in different contexts. In any one day you may find yourself in all four zones, some more than others.

Calm Energy (Optimal): ____%
Tense Energy (Competitive): ____%
Calm Tiredness (Recovery): ____%
Tense Tiredness (Burnout): ____%

Energy zones[25]

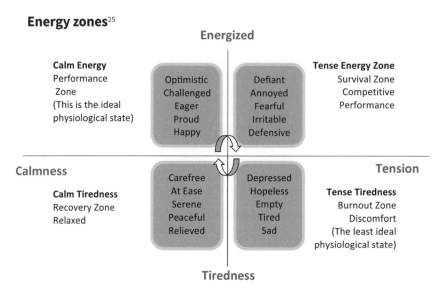

Energized

Calm Energy			Tense Energy Zone
Performance Zone (This is the ideal physiological state)	Optimistic Challenged Eager Proud Happy	Defiant Annoyed Fearful Irritable Defensive	Survival Zone Competitive Performance

Calmness — Tension

Calm Tiredness			Tense Tiredness
Recovery Zone Relaxed	Carefree At Ease Serene Peaceful Relieved	Depressed Hopeless Empty Tired Sad	Burnout Zone Discomfort (The least ideal physiological state)

Tiredness

- What's it like to be in the different zones at work and elsewhere?
- What puts you in each zone? What keeps you there? What moves you on or away from each zone?
- In particular, what do you notice about those times when you are in the Tense Zones (Tense energy or Tense tiredness)?
- What steps can you take to increase the amount of time you spend in the Calm Zones (Calm energy or Calm tiredness)?

MORE ABOUT EACH ZONE

Performance Zone (High Energy Positive Emotions) is where you feel joyful, in flow, happy, energized, stimulated, excited. In this zone, you feel resourced and able to take on challenges and succeed. You are open to experience, perhaps moments of pride fit in here, you feel confident and enthusiastic. In this zone, you feel you can take on life's challenges.

- What are you doing (who are you with) when you are in the performance zone?

- When are you in "flow"?
- How can you intentionally move yourself into this zone and build up a reservoir of positive emotion?
- As a role model, coach, manager, leader, how can you intentionally lead others into this zone?
- Once people are in the performance zone, how can you capitalize on it?

Recovery Zone (Low Energy Positive Emotions). You are in this zone when you are experiencing a calmer, peaceful, energy. A reflective satisfaction and serene happiness where you can recharge. In this zone, you may be relatively carefree.
- How important is recovery in your life?
- In what ways do you give yourself time to recover?
- In what ways do you role model the value of recovery?
- In what ways do you role model the importance of recovery?
- What further recovery strategies can you develop and incorporate habitually into your life?

Survival Zone (High Energy Negative Emotions). In this zone, you experience high energy, but are closed to experience. The energy is directed at blaming or finding fault in others, or defending and maintaining your "self" at all costs. In this zone you may describe yourself as anxious, worried, fearful, annoyed, incensed, perhaps envious. Others may describe you as defensive, angry, impatient, irritable. You are unlikely to be open to new ideas or feedback.
- What triggers you into the survival quadrant?
- Define one of your consistent triggers.
- How does the trigger make you feel (short and long term) and what is your reaction?
- What are the consequences of your reaction?
- Does your reaction make a difference (i.e. does it solve the problem)?
- How can you react differently and move yourself back into the performance zone?

Burnout Zone (Low Energy Negative Emotions). If you are in this energy zone, you are likely to be describing yourself as exhausted, tired, running on empty. On another level, you may be feeling sad, or in the extreme, depressed or hopeless.

EMOTION AND 31PRACTICES

The 31Practices methodology translates the core values of the organization to provide a "living" blueprint as to how employees need to work with each other and so reduces some of the feeling of a tug of war that can happen when people and groups have different ways of doing things.

31Practices enables freedom for each employee in terms of how they choose to "live" the Practice of each day. Through the design of the process, employees know that their collective attention to the Practice of the day is making a contribution to the organization's purpose each day.

This collaboration is underlined day by day, when people witness their colleagues' behaviour and feelings, creating a positive cycle of reinforcement (mirror neurons). Sharing of stories and impact data further demonstrates how each individual can make a difference.

We have seen, first hand, how this process engages employees on an emotional level.

Want to know more?
There are some great resources and projects designed to support you to notice and build your own personal levels of energy;
- The Energy Project. This organisation is about enabling people to sustain great performance by managing their energy more skilfully. Their view is that as human beings we are actually designed to pulse. We're most productive when we move between expending energy and intermittently renewing our four energy needs: sustainability (physical), security (emotional), self-expression (mental) and significance (spiritual). www.theenergyproject.com.
- A short paper on the relationship between thinking and emotions: Luiz Pessoa (2009). Cognition and Emotion. Scholarpedia, 4(1) 4567. http://www.scholarpedia.org/article/Cognition_and_emotion

11

CHAPTER 11   INSPIRATION

"Instead of focusing on how much you can accomplish, focus on how much you can absolutely love what you're doing"

Leo Babauta[1]

Inspiration is the process of being stimulated, mentally, to do or feel something. It's also about stimulating or inspiring others, and there is an element of generating ideas and creativity within the word. It's that internal, intrinsic motivation – internal, intrinsic motivation – the inner "why" that inspires us to action.

Inspiration is that mode of decision-making that really enables us to tap into our intuition and fulfil our destiny.[2] Inspiration propels us from apathy to possibility, transforming the way we perceive our own capabilities. According to Scott Barry Kaufman, *"inspiration can be activated, captured and manipulated, and it has a major effect on important life outcomes."*[3]

We can draw inspiration from ourselves at our very best. As captured by Martine Wright,[4] *"one of my motivations is I truly believe I was meant to do this journey"* after her paralympian debut in the women's sitting volleyball team.

As well as spontaneous and illuminating inspiration that comes from within and from the impact of our actions on ourselves and others, inspiration comes a wide range of other sources too: people, books (a passage or quote, a poem or prose), songs, music and other art forms, and, of course, from the truly spectacular natural world that we live in.

When we ask people we're working with to share who they draw inspiration from, there are some commonalities such as Mahatma Ghandi and Nelson Mandela, some outliers, such as Hitler, and many more varied examples from people's own lives and experience including parents, school teachers, colleagues and public figures of all kinds from authors and artists to celebrities and politicians. What makes one inspiring over another is entirely subjective.

Martine Wright's team members see her as inspirational: Emma Wiggs, her Paralympics GB team mate, says; *"She's incredible, she gels everyone together in the team. Her story, her profile, is what inspires me to get up at 5am in the morning to go to the gym so I can train alongside her."*

Inspiration is spontaneous, focusing people beyond self-serving concerns, moving them towards new ideas.[5] Inspiration enables people to transcend their current horizons, to energize forward towards possibility thinking.

In our organizational work, leaders are often scrutinized as sources of inspiration by those that work for them. Typically leaders fall into three camps:

- non-descript (neither inspirational nor demotivating).
- very demotivating – thus inspiring people to be excellent leaders as they don't want others to have the same devastating experience.
- a source of inspiration, setting a great example for those that work for them.

Sometimes it's the big gestures that are inspirational – for example, a passionate speech at a senior management conference. Often, however, it's the small things that offer inspiration: taking personal care over important correspondence; personally buying presents for birthdays or Christmas rather than giving this job to the executive assistant; even the completely informal incidents like the senior leader simply asking about an employee's personal interests and caring enough to engage with the response.

As people become more senior in organizations, the impact of their behaviour is amplified. Senior leaders have an enormous opportunity to inspire others.

What kind of a leader do you want to be? What legacy do you want to leave? We explore this in more detail in Chapter 24, *Leadership*.

MOTIVATION AND INSPIRATION: WHAT DO THEY DO FOR US?

We are naturally motivated to grow and develop. Inspiration encompasses self-determination, the internal motivation that resonates with Carl Rogers' idea of self-actualization – in the right climate, we will be able to resolve our own difficulties and fulfil our potential.[6]

"Ability is what you're capable of doing. Motivation determines what you do. Attitude determines how well you do it."

Lou Holtz [7]

As part of this growth, we're motivated and inspired to meet our needs for physical safety, control or autonomy, to be connected and have relationships with others, and the need to feel competence or mastery.[8] These needs are fundamental, universal to humans as social beings and keep us socially connected.

Inspiration is purposeful, internally driven, self-determined, and creative. When inspired, you experience knowing exactly who you are and where you're going. You are able to enjoy a state of completeness and wholeness in life, leading to a palpable self-determination. This state is achieved in moments of peak experience, beyond ordinary perception providing a moment of transcendence.[9] The concept of flow, coined by Mihaly Csikszentmihalyi, builds on the idea of peak experience. Flow is a single-minded immersion, harnessing the emotions in service of performing and learning. Emotions are not just contained and channelled, but positive, energized and aligned with the task at hand.[10]

Inspiration has impact, leading to greater resourcefulness, raising people's beliefs in their abilities, self-esteem and optimism.[11] Inspiration is also associated with a greater sense of purpose and gratitude in life.[12]

Within organizations, it's believed that an inspiring work environment leads to greater creativity and motivation for employees and greater performance of the system overall – enhancing productivity, trust and engagement.[13]

Pursuit of work mastery, being open to experience, and fostering a positive mood make you more likely to be open to experiencing inspiration. And, it doesn't have to arrive in a large package, small accomplishments can boost a virtuous inspirational cycle,[14] with achievements building the

121

drive to set inspiring goals, which, in turn, builds achievement.

When we are completely self-driven, where values, behaviour and consequences are totally integrated, where we are doing things because we really want to do them, then we are more likely to get started, sustain our effort and do so with greater intensity. We are more likely to feel and be inspired.

A MODEL OF MOTIVATION AND SELF-DETERMINATION[15]

This model from Deci and Ryan shows how the level of motivation impacts.

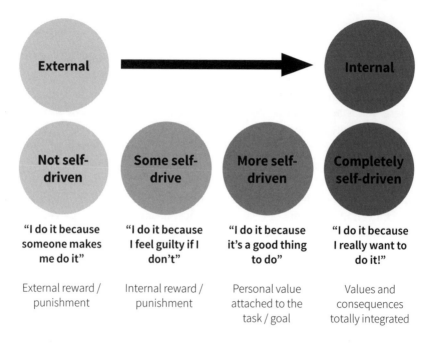

External			Internal
Not self-driven	Some self-drive	More self-driven	Completely self-driven
"I do it because someone makes me do it"	"I do it because I feel guilty if I don't"	"I do it because it's a good thing to do"	"I do it because I really want to do it!"
External reward / punishment	Internal reward / punishment	Personal value attached to the task / goal	Values and consequences totally integrated

To channel our emotional energy into the tasks that we want to achieve, our motivators need to be aligned internally and externally. External motivation on its own does not lead to inspiration. To harness emotions at work, there has to be some level of fit between the values and purpose of the individual and the organization. The closer the fit between individual values and purpose and organizational values, purpose and vision, the greater the likelihood that individuals will be inspired by their work.

Where we are looking to be inspired, to achieve moments of flow in our life and work, paying attention to what drives us is going to help us achieve that sense of well-being and happiness. Where we find ourselves feeling "trapped", doing something that does not give us emotional satisfaction, it will be difficult to sustain any level of performance.

The drivers of inspiring organizational environments and leadership include:[16][17]

- Purpose and vision – Using strategic vision and organizational purpose to motivate and inspire.
- Progress – seeing steps and movement towards the vision, guided by purpose.
- Authenticity – including credibility and transparency and also attention to learning – being prepared to be vulnerable and grow.
- Servant leadership – with a focus on we rather than just "me"; empowering employees at all levels.
- Affirmation – noticing, naming and nurturing the talents of others.
- Story – connecting people to purpose and to each other; accumulating and sharing internal knowledge; gathering and integrating external information.
- Challenging the status quo and enabling creativity.

These drivers impact what gets us started, what keeps us going and what energy and intensity we bring to what we are doing. Together, the drivers lead to greater engagement from customers and employees and greater intent to stay with the brand.[18]

INSPIRATION AND 31PRACTICES

Using the seven drivers of inspiration it is easy to see how 31Practices works:

Purpose and vision – 31Practices is directly related to the organizational purpose and vision and the way in which these are delivered from the CEO to the front line.

Progress – 31Practices are demonstrable behaviours and through recognition programmes and performance review processes, the degree to which they are being "lived" can be monitored. There is also a formal 31Practices review process.

Authenticity – 31Practices are co-created by an organization's employees and are directly connected to the organizational values. As such, they are a set of behaviours that are "real". Leaders at the very top of the organization are models for the success of 31Practices, thereby enabling authenticity from root to tip.

Servant leadership – 31Practices provides leadership with an ideal opportunity to signal behaviour, lead by example and also to recognize the behaviour of employees.

Affirmation – An organization's 31Practices are affirmations in themselves because of the style in which they are written: We use present tense and mark **important** words in bold.

Story – 31Practices is linked to a recognition programme so that the behaviours can be positively reinforced by communication of stories to create the heritage of the organization.

Challenge and creativity – 31Practices provides a statement of the general direction of behaviour and all employees are encouraged to use it to challenge themselves and others. In addition, employees are given latitude as to how they apply the Practice each day.

Want to know more?
- This is a very accessible, fun video clip: Dan Pink – What motivates people – http://www.youtube.com/watch?v=u6XAPnuFjJc
- No chapter on inspiration would be complete without recommending the work of Mihaly Csitszentmihalyi (2002). *Flow: The Psychology of Happiness: The classic work on how to achieve happiness.* London: Random House. This seminal work was first published in 1992.
- *The Little book of Inspiration*, written by Steve Backley, Roger Black and Humphrey Walters is accessible and short (less than 150 pages).
- If you are interested in delving into the subject of motivation in much more depth, there is the significant edited work of Edward L. Deci and Richard M. Ryan (1985). *Intrinsic Motivation and Self-Determination in Human Behaviour.* New York: Plenum Press

CHAPTER 12 HAPPINESS

"There can be no happiness if the things we believe in are different from the things we do".

Freya Stark[1]

Happiness is a state of being.[2]

Studied for decades, the question "What makes us happy?" has been posed all around the world, over time, and in different ways. Happiness is an important emotion, and has a role in the survival of the species.[3]

Feeling good is an overall motivational state that keeps us alive. The avoidance of loss and pain and the search for good feelings is the mechanism that has preserved and multiplied the human race.[4] The impact of happiness has been demonstrated in different studies to improve health, life expectancy,[5] recovery from setbacks and much more.[6]

Dr Ross McDonald describes most as wanting love, acceptance, respect and esteem from others. They want romance, happiness, success and a sense of positive purpose. And given the fundamental nature of these needs, people will give huge attention to anything that suggests it will satisfy them.[7]

Happiness consists of positive emotion (hedonic pleasure), and assessments of flourishing, meaning and purpose (eudaimonic well-being) – both are important in evaluations of life satisfaction.[8]

Happiness is not only an individual quest, but is something

organizations are keen to enhance among employees because there are organizational benefits to a positive, engaged, and energized workforce.

Well-being is part of the measure of human capital, which is finding its way into the annual reports of listed companies. There is little doubt that management of health and well-being in the workplace reduces healthcare expenditure and yields a significant return on investment.[9]

If we look at happiness and unhappiness as two ends of a health dimension – the cost savings alone of reducing unhappiness (both in direct financial terms and down-time resulting from unhealthy employees) should raise the priority of the "happiness" agenda in the workplace. At the other end of the dimension, optimal health is a factor in optimal productivity;[10] engaged employees are associated with innovation, described as moving the organization forward[11] and with putting their discretionary effort into driving growth and performance.[12]

And the quest doesn't stop at organizations. Nations too are keen to enhance the overall "happiness" of their populations. With an ageing population and the growing health challenges across the age spectrum combined with the benefits that happiness can bring, happiness is a vital economic issue.

The 2012 World Happiness report argued: *"if we continue along the current economic trajectory, we risk undermining the Earth's life support system ... necessary for human health and even survival in some places".* There is hope: *"if we act wisely, we can protect the Earth"* and at the same time *"raise quality of life broadly around the world ... by adopting lifestyles and technologies that improve happiness while reducing human damage to the environment."*[13]

THE HAPPINESS DELUSION

"We human beings are terrible at predicting what will make us happy"

Ronald D. Siegel[14]

One of the challenges we face is that we think we know what will make us happy – your instant response to Siegel's statement is likely to be *"of course I know what makes me happy"*. To find out if you're on the right track, we invite you to read on.

What if Ronald Siegel is right? – let's assume he is for now. Why are we so poor at working out what will make us happy?

One part of the answer is simple – we compare ourselves with others to determine whether we have enough to make us happy. If we are in a better material position than our comparison group, then we are more likely to be happy (of sorts), whereas if we're in a worse material position, it reduces our happiness. Lord Layard, a leading economist and researcher into happiness, has coined the term "the hedonic treadmill" – he equates our need for material possessions to the needs of drug addicts: the more we have, the more we need to have to feel the same level of happiness.[15]

In life, there are always those who have more than us and we are exposed to constant messaging across society about what we should aspire to in terms of lifestyle and possessions in order to be happy. The amount we have *in comparison* to others can lead to us us overinvesting, distorting our lives towards working and making money (activities that do not necessarily make us happy and often make us unhappy) and away from other activities that actually increase our happiness in more sustainable ways.[16]

National measures of happiness are distorted along the same lines – feeding the comparison agenda. In general, Governments use a basic economic equation to measure happiness:

Greater income = Greater happiness

This way of looking at happiness feeds the comparison agenda. The media and consumer marketing add to the messaging. Television advertising, for example, is designed to deliver carefully crafted suggestions that happiness, social acceptance, success and respect are all associated with very high levels of material consumption.[17] Income can buy you new circumstances and new experiences, such as having more money to spend, buying a new house, or buying a new car. People soon get used to what they have.[18] Before long, you feel you *need* the new car and the new house. Going back to the old car, the old house, you'd feel much less happy than you did before you had the new experience.[19] As our income level increases, what we believe is our "necessary" income level increases too.

From our work exploring employee engagement across organizations, despite great satisfaction when a much hoped-for change has taken place, the initial euphoria soon reduces to create a new baseline.

Even being "poor" depends on comparison to social norms. Poverty is defined in relation to the average income levels in a country and in terms of what "most people" in a country would consider basic necessities.[20]

Defined in this way, poverty becomes a cultural, subjective idea. By this kind of reckoning, one aspect of poverty in the UK is now defined as not having your own bedroom as a child – for previous generations, it was not having enough food, not having shoes, or having to share your bed with siblings.

The idea behind this comparative approach is that unless the poorest can keep up with growth in average incomes, they will progressively become more excluded from the opportunities that the rest of society enjoys and as a result, be less happy.

What people "should have" in order to be happy in comparison to others is core to the culture of consumer-based economies at every level.

In reality, increased income only increases happiness in limited circumstances – when it lifts you away from hard physical poverty. In western countries, while life may be materially better, happiness has not increased since 1950.[21]

Our own experience of this comparative effect happens approximately once a year and coincides with a visit from the financial advisor. Although we tend to be optimistic, appreciative individuals, content with what we have in material terms, after an hour or more of looking at figures and hearing stories of what we could do if we had more, exploring risk and reward tables and hearing tales of clients with a much greater disposable income, the mood plummets. It takes about 48 hours to rebalance. This temporary upwards change in social reference group can seriously affect our temporary feelings of happiness at that point.

As examples, take the annual visit of the financial advisor, or a child's request for the latest gaming technology or the latest fashion accessory. Although you might see yourself as optimistic and appreciative, content with what you have in material terms, all of these examples create a focus on comparisons with others that can impact on your happiness and it can take some time to rebalance.

Our addiction to consumerism in order to achieve the happiness that we aspire to can, and often does, have a negative impact on overall happiness. The "keep up with the Jones' mentality", the obsession with what others have, means that we are depriving ourselves by continually trying to achieve happiness through focusing our attention away from ourselves.

This hedonic treadmill we find ourselves on creates dysfunction, associated with increased depression and anxiety among other things – and in particular, a general dissatisfaction with life.[22] Our pursuit of happiness is perhaps actually making us miserable.

PERHAPS LESS IS MORE

There are some interesting examples of individuals and countries that take a different approach to happiness. What could you and your organization learn from these?

The story of the Kingdom of Bhutan

Bhutan, one of the most isolated countries in the world, has more monks than soldiers, measures Gross National Happiness, and sees the *"individual's quest for happiness and inner and outer freedom as the most precious endeavour"*.[23] The country has limited exposure to "western" influences: there are neither fast food chains nor even traffic lights.

In 1999, television and the internet were legalized as part of the journey to a modern, democratic nation. The impact was complex as the tiny Buddhist country that was steeped in ancient tradition wrestled with modern, less controllable cyber influences. In April 2002, the remote kingdom suffered its first crime wave, including fraud, violence and murder. While direct cause can't be attributed to television and internet access alone, dramatic changes to Bhutanese society occurred that led to increasing crime, corruption, an uncontrolled desire for western products, and changing attitudes to love and relationships.[24]

We have access to the internet, television and clever marketing – we can't turn back to a time when these things were not integral. But perhaps we can learn to live more wisely and with greater happiness within this technology enabled world.

The story of the poorest president

President Mujica of Uraguay is characterized as the poorest president. Once of many rebels that were part of the crushed Tupamaros guerrilla organization, Mujica was shot six times and spent 14 years behind bars – until democracy returned to Uruguay and he was freed in 1985. Most of his detention was spent in harsh conditions and isolation.

Those years in jail, Mujica says, helped shape his outlook on life. In a recent interview, he notes *"I don't feel poor. Poor people are those who only work to try to keep an expensive lifestyle, and always want more and more"*.

"This is a matter of freedom. If you don't have many possessions then you don't need to work all your life like a slave to sustain them, and therefore you have more time for yourself,"

"I may appear to be an eccentric old man... But this is a free choice" [25]

The story of the laundry worker

There was a newspaper article some years ago about a lady in China who worked in a laundry. She worked seven days a week, from early morning into the evening and did not have holidays. The article explained how hard she worked, how menial the job was and how cramped the conditions were. But it then went on to explain how they had asked the lady how she felt about her work and life. The answer may surprise you but the lady said she loved her work and had a very happy life, saying she never wanted this to change.

If you're wondering how this lady could love her circumstances and gain so much happiness and fulfilment from her life, we bring to your attention that nowhere in the story does a high income, material possessions or comparisons with others feature.

"People are just as happy as they make up their minds to be."

Abraham Lincoln [26]

WHAT DOES MAKE US HAPPY?

The answer is both simple and complex.

"Happiness is when what you think, what you say, and what you do are in harmony"

Mahatma Gandhi[28] **(1869–1948)**

In other words, when you "walk the talk" of your own life, identify your own path and follow it. This is core to the thinking and philosophy behind 31Practices and in tune with Oliver Burkeman's view of happiness as akin to authenticity.

"Happiness is not something ready made. It comes from your own actions."

Dalai Lama XIV[29]

Kennon Sheldon and Sonja Lyubomirsky[30] talk about changing your actions, not your circumstances, to achieve sustainable gains in happiness. The work to explore well-being and what makes us happy is growing and thriving. Leading pioneers in this field (Martin Seligman along with others[31] such as Professor Carol Ryff, Dr Alex Linley and Lord Layard) draw together work across a range of disciplines to identify factors which lead to happiness and well-being. These include:

Having control and choice about aspects of our lives: Of course, control and choice is more likely in certain circumstances; for example, those in leadership roles have greater responsibility and autonomy (and greater well-being).[32] However, we do have choice at all times in our life; it's just that often we're not aware of it. Victor Frankl highlights our choices even in extreme circumstances (see also Chapters 14, *Resilience* and 23, *Choice*).

"The last of the human freedoms is to choose one's attitude in any given set of circumstances, to choose one's own way"

Victor Frankl[33]

Positive relationships with others: signifying love, friendship and trust.[34] Mood and quality of life are more related to the quality of close relationships than to wealth. The quality of relationships between people and the experience they have sharing continuous creativity and learning, is even fundamental to excellent business processes.[35]

What investments are you making in your relationships both inside and out of work? How do you signify your appreciation and positive affirmation of others? Stephen M. R. Covey equates our relationships to our deposit account – the more you invest, the greater the return.[36] How does the balance sheet read for your relationships at work and in your personal life?

Satisfaction with our financial situation: Apart from physical poverty, where we are hungry, homeless and in physical danger, happiness with finances is simply an attitude of mind – who are you choosing to compare yourself to? No matter how much you have, if you're reading this book, you're more likely to belong to a minority with much more than most. So, give some of what you have away, generosity is good for you. Givers can e not only happier but more successful too.[37]

Having a meaning and purpose to life: The sense of making a contribution and doing things for others. From Tony Robbins through to existential philosophers, purpose and a meaningful life are seen as a core element to happiness. Existential angst (or the "mid-life crisis") is rife as people wake up to the hedonic treadmill they are on and start to wonder what their purpose really is.

Feelings of competence and personal growth: Choose goals that stretch you, but are attainable with high probability.[38]

Our health – eat well, exercise regularly: There is a growing literature supporting a link between exercise and mental health, including better mood.[39]

Self-acceptance: the "real" version, "warts and all", rather than the aspirational version. As well as positively appreciating others, appreciate what you bring. We are often our harshest critics. Enabling people to find a sense of worth, independent of social position, income, medals and honours, is significant.

Our personal values, philosophy of life and our inner self: We are happier if we can appreciate what we have, avoid constant comparison with others and are able to control our moods and feelings. Understanding our values and putting these values into practice is a core aspect of living a happier life.[40]

Across a range of disciplines, these factors are viewed as core to well-being, motivation and happiness. To sustain a state of being happy, there seem to be two routes. First, for a measure of success it is essential to focus on more than income and the material experiences. Second, pay attention to how you engage in and appreciate each moment of your life.

"The foolish man seeks happiness in the distance. The wise grows it under his feet."

James Oppenheim[41]

Unhooking ourselves from the hedonic treadmill may do more than enable individual happiness. Present Mujica[42] of Uruguay accuses most world leaders of having a *"blind obsession to achieve growth with consumption, as if the contrary would mean the end of the world"*. Whereas, blind obsession with growth and consumption is a zero sum game – that will lead to the end of the world… for human beings at least.

HAPPINESS AND 31PRACTICES

Fostering well-being and happiness among employees can be rather paradoxical for organizations. People come to work in order to get paid, and it is important for organizations to get comparative rates of pay right. Employees will also focus on how much they are paid in comparison to others, and whether those rates are fair. It's part of being human – it is unavoidable. At the same time, rates of pay alone do not determine happiness and being overly focused on pay at the expense of all other aspects of work is not likely to lead to an engaged workforce.

From the brief overview of what makes us happy, it's easy to see that there are many other ways to enable happiness and well-being in organizations.

The 31Practices approach is closely aligned with many of the factors listed above that promote greater happiness and well-being: employees choose how they interpret the Practice of the day, giving them **control and choice**; we have found that the clear direction provided by the vision, values and Practices establishes a stronger sense of belonging, **purpose** and **positive relationships**; when linked to a recognition programme, stories are captured and publicized, creating a feeling of **competence and personal growth**; finally, 31Practices is a very practical approach and a journey where it is understood that sometimes things will not go as well as they might have done, providing an environment of **self-acceptance**.

"There is no way to happiness, happiness is the way"
Thich Nhat Hanh[43]

....

Exercise: Increasing your personal happiness – some tips

It's easy to view happiness as a right, as an inherently "human" condition. However, there is no reason why we should be happy – biologically. Instead, it's more helpful to see attaining happiness as a skill. In this way, practising "being happy" makes more sense and makes happiness actually more attainable. You can make a substantial difference to how you feel[44] by developing happiness practices in your life.

Appreciate what you have and appreciate others. We all have many choices in life, one of which is whether to focus on all the things we don't have (of which there might be many), or to focus on all the things we do have (of which there are likely to be many). There's no doubt that gratitude and appreciation will significantly increase your chances of experiencing happiness.[45]

Think about five things each day that you are thankful for and let others know.

Perform random acts of kindness. A random act of kindness is a selfless act to help or cheer up others. Others won't expect you to perform these kindness acts, but will definitely appreciate your efforts.

Cultivate optimism. Practise optimistic thinking when faced with a problem. That is, not overly positive thinking, but optimistic thinking.

Weed out and reduce unhelpful thoughts. The Dalai Lama has been quoted saying that *"The central method for achieving a happier life is to train your mind in a daily practice that weakens negative attitudes and strengthens positive ones."*

If you do choose to engage in these practices, and we recommend that you do, notice how they impact your felt sense of happiness and your energy.

....

Want to know more?

There are numerous resources to explore that might support you to develop sustainable happiness, and to fulfil your personal exploration of research in to happiness and positive energy – or simply to make you smile.

- The starting point would be the work of Lord Layard: Richard Layard (2011). *Happiness: Lessons from a new science*, second edition. London: Penguin.
- Lord Layard is one of the founding drivers of a movement for happiness: Action for Happiness. For more information about events, publications and resources see: http://www.actionforhappiness.org/
- Matthieu Ricard's book on happiness is also highly recommended. We often see happiness as a "right" (apparently it's enshrined in the American Declaration of Independence that we should be free to pursue happiness); however, achieving happiness is something that we need to work on as if we are learning a skill. Matthieu views happiness in this way – as a skill. Matthieu Ricard (2006). *Happiness – a guide to developing life's most important skill*. New York: Little, Brown and Company
- Ronald D. Siegel, assistant clinical professor of psychology at Harvard Medical School, is interviewed about positive psychology, the scientific study of happiness. http://www.health.harvard.edu/video/positive-psychology/what-it-takes-to-be-happy.htm

SECTION 2: THE MIND PRINCIPLES

"I know but one freedom and that is the freedom of the mind."

Antoine de Saint-Exupery[1]

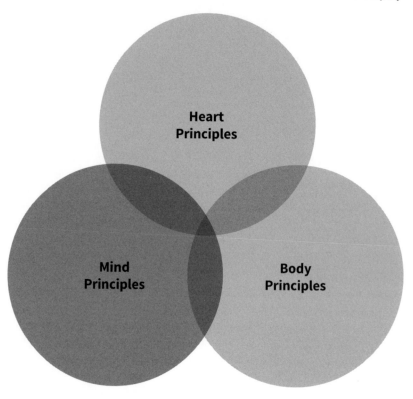

Heart Principles

Mind Principles

Body Principles

The Mind Principles are focused on our inner landscape – knowing ourselves: how we think and what we think about. The Mind, described as the "personalization of the brain",[2] provides us with our identity. The mind is constantly busy: assessing and evaluating past actions, scenarios and conversations, creating hypothetical futures and strategies, and conversations associated with those future possibilities.

Our minds can enable us to focus, recover, perform, connect and experience fulfilment and move forward. Our minds also hold our strongest critical voices. In this section, we discuss the topics of Mindfulness, Resilience and Storytelling, exploring some of the phenomena of our inner world and how we might develop our skills at working with our own inner resources to gain greater self-awareness and awareness of how to engage with others.

Chapter 13, *Mindfulness* provides insight into the power of the mind and an understanding of how to be more aware on a moment by moment basis so that you can step away from unhelpful emotional states and potentially build more resourceful emotional states. Chapter 14, *Resilience* will support you to understand how you can build personal resilience and how this can be undermined by the way you think about the world around you. Catching an unhelpful thought in the act, noticing and unpicking it to create more helpful beliefs is a skill that is likely to serve you well to build greater response flexibility. It provides the opportunity for you to make the most of your personal resources as well as those of others around us. The Mind Principles section is rounded off with Chapter 15, *Story telling*, allowing a different perspective on both our inner worlds (the stories that we tell ourselves constantly) and our outerworlds (the stories that we tell others and are told by others) and gives insight into the power of stories.

Storytelling, together with Mindfulness and Resilience, give insight into the mind as an interactive and responsive aspect of our selves, and provides three ways of enabling our inner world to be a well of resource. In each chapter we explore how the 31Practices method can be enhanced by working explicitly with the Mind principles.

CHAPTER 13 MINDFULNESS

"Whatever the present moment contains, accept it as if you had chosen it."

Eckhart Tolle[1]

Mindfulness essentially means moment-to-moment awareness of heart, mind and body. It's about purposefully and non-judgementally paying attention to the unfolding experience of each moment.[2] This awareness enables you to make choices about how and what your mind attends to, how you act and how you react to events. The idea of noticing "with friendly curiosity" makes mindfulness a compassionate activity. This developed awareness is available to everybody through mindfulness practices.[3]

MINDFULNESS – WHAT DOES IT DO FOR US?

Mindfulness practices are not new; they have emerged from traditions in middle and eastern collectivist cultures for whom meditation and other techniques promoting enlightenment and self-mastery are more central. From our own observations, we believe these practices are of growing interest in western cultures where ideas of individualism and environmental mastery have typically dominated.

Mindfulness is about creating distance from our immediate experience so we can take a moment to reflect, review, and consider how to move forward. This ability to be more of an impartial spectator on the noisy emotions and thoughts that are constantly produced internally develops to the extent that we can more easily choose what to attend to and how to respond.

Being "mindful" of the state that we are in (happy, angry, sad, bored) and the thoughts that drive that state enables us to choose to be in a different state at any one moment. Mindfulness is not about denying anger, or bottling up frustration. It's about skilfully choosing not to get frustrated or angry in the first place – choosing that a different response will achieve the purpose that we want to achieve.

Without attention to our inner world, we can find ourselves tossed along on wave after wave of thought and emotion without any insight about how to manage this onslaught; reacting on "auto-pilot" to whatever emerges.

In the workplace, you may notice when people around you spend more time worrying to themselves and to others about just how much work they have to do, how unfair it is, or how difficult it is. You may have witnessed how this creates distress and keeps them "stuck", unable to move into a more resourceful state. In this situation, people often find it difficult to step back and see themselves, what they are doing and the impact of their approach on themselves and others. They've lost the necessary distance to appreciate the bigger reality.

Mindfulness is like getting back into the cockpit of your own mind and giving yourself more control.

As well as internal awareness, mindfulness raises awareness of the context you're in – observing things as they *are* rather than believing they *should* somehow be different. When you see things as they are and don't label or judge the events taking place around you, you are freed from your normal habits in how you choose to react to them.

Images of mindfulness practice tend to invoke the need for years of retreat, Buddhism and hours of daily meditation. Actually, in a recent study of students at Dalian University, Yi-Yuan Tang[4] and his colleagues demonstrated that a programme integrating body–mind aspects of meditation can, when practised for 20 minutes a day for five days, enhance self-regulation, attention, ability to be present in the moment and reduce the baseline stress level (measured by the level of the stress hormone – cortisol).

An interesting convergence between traditional mindfulness practices and developments in neuroscience now enables us to understand the physical basis for the impact and value of mindfulness practices.[5]

"One man that has a mind and knows it can always beat ten men who haven't and don't"

George Bernard Shaw[6]

MINDFULNESS AND ORGANIZATIONS

So what sense does this all make in the context of organizations? The work of Daniel Siegel (and others) indicates a number of aspects of physical and mental functioning are enhanced through mindfulness practice including:

- improved emotional regulation
- improved ability to heal and sense of well-being
- enhanced interpersonal relationships (through attuned communication, greater empathy, intuition and response flexibility)
- a greater ability to focus and attend to the present moment[7]

Reviewing the potential benefits, the question is not "What sense does mindfulness make in the context of organizations?", but rather, "In what context would mindfulness *not* make sense in organizations?"

There is evidence globally about the negative impact of stress on health and well-being; on toxic emotion in the workplace (impacting both the individual concerned, colleagues, and the organizational system); on poor working relationships (making it harder to get things done); and the impact of stress on society manifesting in mental and physical ill health. If mindfulness really is a practice which enables individuals to increase their health and effectiveness (in and outside of work), there is little to argue against embracing it.

A number of respected businesses have implemented mindfulness programmes,[8] including Apple, McKinsey & Company, Deutsche Bank, Procter & Gamble, Astra Zeneca and Google.

Mindfulness at Google

Google has a fast-paced, hard-driving culture.[9] Co-founder and CEO, Larry Page, promotes a *"healthy disregard for the impossible"*. In this pressurized culture, mindfulness training has a standing and reputation you might find surprising. Chade-Meng Tan, who introduced the programme, is both a lifelong Buddhist and rich (due to being only the 107th person Google hired) – but that isn't enough to sustain the reputation of the mindfulness programme.

An engineer at Google sees *"business as a machine made out of people"* with the mindfulness training as *"a sort of organizational WD-40, a necessary lubricant between driven ambitious employees and Google's demanding corporate culture. Helping employees handle stress and defuse emotion – helps everyone work more effectively"*[10] *"in a high IQ environment, IQ is not the differentiating factor, but emotional intelligence, EQ, is".*[11] There are many personal experiences shared at Google that evidence the value gained from the mindfulness training, enabling people to get a handle on their experience of stress and strong emotion.

Mindfulness at General Mills

General Mills is a large global food provider, with offices and manufacturing facilities in over 30 countries. Global brands include: Haagen-Dazs, Old El Paso, Green Giant and others. General Mills has offered mindfulness training for seven years and it has become part of business as usual. The founder of the programme, Janice Maturano, states mindfulness is *"about training our minds to be more focused, to see with clarity, to have spaciousness for creativity and to feel connected – to be compassionate to ourselves and to others."*[12]

The mindfulness programme at General Mills has demonstrably increased effectiveness. Nearly four times as many employees focus daily on their personal productivity after participating in the mindfulness programme (up from 23% before to 83% after). Most senior executives who attend the programme also report a positive change in their ability to make better decisions, with nearly all reporting becoming better listeners.[13]

Mindfulness, it seems, impacts on employee performance, well-being, and will inevitably impact on the organizational system. It doesn't have to be introduced as something separate to other development initiatives. On leadership development programmes, mindfulness practices may be introduced as simple breathing exercises or the practice of "presencing": bringing attention and focus to the present moment.

MINDFULNESS – SOME CORE PRINCIPLES

"Every human has four endowments – self-awareness, conscience, independent will and creative imagination. These give us the ultimate human freedom... The power to choose, to respond, to change."

Stephen R. Covey[14]

Awareness leads to choice

The core purpose of mindfulness practice is enlightenment, or the awareness of the reality of things. Clear understanding of what is taking place right now prevents us being deluded.

It sounds simple.

Yet, so often, we are wrapped up in the noise of our minds, drawing our attention to the future to an imagined event, or to some past event. We associate emotions with these events and become hooked into what might be possible (future), or perhaps some restless replaying of a past frustrating conversation. Living in the past or future prevents us being aware of what is happening to us in this moment.

Right here, right now, we are on auto-pilot, letting our assumptions and habits guide our immediate responses. Greater mindfulness enables us to bring ourselves back to now, and make more skilful choices about how we want to respond in the moment – choosing how we want to feel, what we want to think and how we behave.

The compassion within mindfulness practices allows us to accept ourselves (warts and all) without judgement, enabling us to examine more closely those things about ourselves that we might struggle with or want to deny about ourselves.

For example, take the senior manager who gets emotional when frustrated with colleagues in the work place. He is so upset by his loss of control and appalling behaviour that he cannot accept that this is him. He refuses to accept the evidence (feedback) and locks it away.

Imagine being able to look at those emotional outbursts without judging himself (with a compassionate mind). He may then, through careful exploration, understand the triggers, and with a little more discovery, understand some of the different choices he had about how he might respond. He might learn to stop, breathe, notice what is happening to him, reflect, and respond based on choice rather than based on a knee-jerk habit.

With skilled mindfulness habits, rather than avoiding uncomfortable experiences, we are much more likely to simply notice them, be curious about them, choose what response we want to give and move on.

"Feelings come and go like clouds in a windy sky. Conscious breathing is my anchor."

Thich Nhat Hanh[15]

Focusing

One of the myths of business is the "skill" of multitasking. Multitasking is shifting attention back and forth between activities very quickly. Mindfulness practice helps you focus your attention more effectively, being fully present to the activity you are engaged in – getting it done and moving on.

Multitasking does not make you effective.[16] A study at Kings College London found workers distracted by email and phone calls suffer a fall in IQ more than twice that found in marijuana smokers. In this super-connected world, we are constantly scanning for opportunities and staying on top of contacts, events, and activities in an effort to miss nothing.[17] According to one study, it can take up to 25 minutes to fully re-engage with the task you have distracted yourself from by answering an email, or responding to an interruption.

The art of paying attention is something that great minds attribute to their success, and equate to greater wisdom. Integrated learning requires focused attention rather than the scattered crumbs of attention we might be tempted to give when "multitasking".

Mindfulness is one route to being able to carefully attend and be present to the current moment, learning to focus on what is now the priority, while putting distractions out of our minds.

"There is time enough for everything in the course of the day, if you do but one thing at once, but there is not time enough in the year, if you will do two things at a time."

Lord Chesterfield[18]

Presence

Mindfulness practices enable us to be more present. When we are more present, happy to accept rather than struggle for control, we release energy, relax, let go of judgements and regrets. We look fully and open-mindedly at where we are, giving greater choice. We enjoy greater health, well-being, and clarity.[19]

Peter Senge and his colleagues describe Presence[20] as full consciousness, being fully aware in the present moment and open to what might emerge (beyond assumptions normally held). Presence is also about letting go of old identities and the need for control. All these aspects together allow things to emerge – "letting come".

Some see presence and the capacity for reflection as the true attribute of wisdom.[21] Mindful presence can enable us to see that information is contextual rather than truthful or "fact".

Overfamiliarity, routines, habits all prevent us from paying attention to what is really happening now because we see what we expect to see – we make reality fit our assumptions. In this state, we don't let things emerge or new ideas come forward. Building our ability to be present helps us to slow down and see what is happening rather than seeing what we expect to happen. Greater awareness, where we are performing tasks in situations that are highly familiar to us, means we can cultivate conscious awareness and greater competence.

MINDFULNESS AND 31PRACTICES

31Practices is a methodology designed to bring greater attention to how you are "being" rather than a focus on "doing" alone. Core to 31Practices is enabling individuals and organizations to be mindful of their core values and purpose, and how they might practise those values and achieve their purpose, by focusing on just one at a time, each day. Over time, focusing on one Practice at a time builds strong habits that support individuals and organizations to be the best that they can be.

A key part of 31Practices is for people and organizations to notice what they are doing, make choices about how they are being, and to raise awareness about their impact on different groups of stakeholders.

The principle of one Practice a day not only builds strong habits, but also allows us to bring that one Practice to mind and be present with how we are "being" and what we are doing about that particular Practice. Perhaps all employees know that they should display "meticulous attention to cleanliness, tidiness and presentation". However, to have this front of mind and taking responsibility for what you do about it today makes a difference. Suddenly, you see things that you would not have seen and you are ready and prepared to act... so you do.

This idea of one Practice at a time as part of awakening or enlightenment is, as we discovered, not new. In writing this book, we came across the 37 Practices of the Bodhisattva.[22] A Bodhisattva is "one who seeks awakening"[23] and enlightenment. We like to believe that 31Practices is in good company.

....

Exercise – The mindfulness continuum

The alternative to mindfulness is living a life where you are on auto-pilot (mindless): living without thinking "how", responding without thought, continually at the mercy of ever-changing conditions that you give yourself absolutely no control over – the world around you, and your unchecked responses to that world, has you hooked. You have little or no awareness that you are "hooked" and no skills to unhook yourself. There are many points along the continuum between the two extremes. You might like to try this exercise yourself or with your colleagues/team.

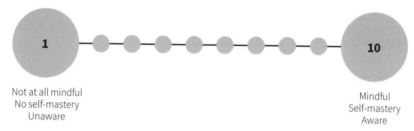

Not at all mindful
No self-mastery
Unaware

Mindful
Self-mastery
Aware

1. Where are you on this continuum now?
2. Do you believe that it is helpful to have control over your emotions and behaviours?
   If your answer to question 2 is sometimes, or yes, please answer questions three to six below:
3. To what extent do you feel you have a choice about how you feel when you are experiencing a particularly strong emotion (e.g. anger, fear, happiness, sadness)?
   Where would you put yourself on the continuum between 1 and 10 when experiencing strong emotion? Put down different ratings for different emotions if they give you a different sense of choice.
4. During what % of your day do you feel you have a choice?
   Looking back at your answers to questions 3 and 4 – what do you notice? What patterns do you see?
5. Are there times when you really DO feel that you have a choice about your emotional response and / or physical response?
   Great…you've left the starting blocks on the road towards greater mindfulness.
6. Are there times when you really DON'T feel you have a choice about your emotional and even behavioural response?
   Welcome – join the majority of people on the planet – you've got some way to go before reaching the "self-mastery" end of the continuum.

....

Would you like to have a sense of greater choice, mastery and mindfulness? If so, read on to explore some simple techniques.

Mindfulness: some simple techniques

"Mindfulness isn't difficult, we just need to remember to do it."

Sharon Salzberg[24]

Noticing: At Google, one of the practices taught on their Search Inside Yourself programme is simply: Stop, Breathe, Notice, Reflect and Respond.

- **Stop** what you are doing
- **Breathe** (three in and out breaths from your gut not your chest)
- **Notice** yourself – your emotions, your five sensations
- **Reflect** – what do you need to do here? What is your intention? What is your purpose here?
- **Respond**
  Building this collection of practices enables you to catch yourself even in the most potentially emotional of situations and choose how you want to respond.

Mindfulness exercises for the super busy:

- Spend at least 5 minutes each day doing nothing
- Get in touch with your senses by noticing the temperature of your skin and background sounds around you
- Pay attention to your walking by slowing your pace and feeling the ground against your feet
- Anchor your day with a contemplative morning practice (e.g. breathing meditation or any other)
- Before entering the workplace, remind yourself of your organization's purpose and recommit to your purpose
- Throughout the day, pause to be fully present in the moment before undertaking the next critical task

"By letting it go it all gets done. The world is won by those who let it go. But when you try and try, the world is beyond winning."

Lao Tzu[25]

Want to know more?

These alternatives on further reading around the mindfulness approach the subject from different perspectives. Ultimately, all lead to the same destination.

- Daniel J Siegel (2007). *The Mindful Brain: Reflection and attunement in the cultivation of well-being*. New York: Norton.
- Bhante Henepola Gunaratana (2002). *Mindfulness in Plain English: A Practical Guide to Mindfulness of Breathing and Tranquil Wisdom Meditation*. Somerville, MA: Wisdom Publications
- Liz Hall (2013) *Mindful Coaching: How mindfulness can transform coaching practice*. London: Kogan Page.

This seminal book on Presence and Theory U offers a rich story-based journey to the discovery of the power of presence in organizational work.

- Peter Senge, Joseph Jaworski, C. Otto Scharmer and Betty Sue Flowers (2005). *Presence: Exploring profound change in people, organisations and society*. London: Nicholas Brealey.

CHAPTER 14 RESILIENCE

"Our greatest glory is not in never falling, but in rising every time we fall."

Confucius[1]

Resilience is a common ingredient in heroes of myth and legend, a personal quality that is aspired to by many of us and sought after in leaders. The popular view of resilience (and the everyday definition) is about bouncing back, springing back into shape after pressure has been applied, elasticity, recovering quickly from difficulties, toughness.[2] But the real human experience of resilience is defined a bit differently: *"A resilient response to adversity engages the whole person, not just aspects of the person in order to face, endure, overcome and possibly be transformed"*:[3] coming back rather than bouncing back[4] and returning to a different place (transformed), with new insights and new awareness. So not quite the same as you were before.

There are countless modern examples of incredible resilience where individuals have faced adverse, potentially insurmountable challenges, and have come through transformed (often both physically and mentally). One example is Italian ex-Formula 1 driver Alex Zanardi[5], who lost both legs following a crash in 2001 and won gold in the cycling event at the London 2012 Paralympics.

A second example is that of Michael Watson[6], a former champion boxer who suffered considerable brain damage. He was told he would never walk again. He refused to accept this prognosis and taught himself to walk. Michael successfully completed the 2009 London Marathon over a six-day period – his determination and achievement was amazing to witness.

From more of a business perspective, there are some famously well-known resilient figures, and some less well known:

- Walt Disney[7] was turned down over 300 times before he secured financing for his dream of creating *"The Happiest Place on Earth"*. Today, millions of people have shared in "the joy of Disney".
- Legend has it that Colonel Sanders[8] was refused 1009 times across America over a two-year period before he heard a "yes". He was over 65 years old at the time, determined to franchise his chicken recipe. KFC is now one of the largest food franchises in the world.
- Jean-Dominique, the editor of the French fashion magazine, *ELLE*, had a massive stroke that left him completely immobile except for the movement of his left eye, but he devised a means to communicate through blinking and used this method to pen his memoir.[9]
- Richard Cartwright[10], a *Big Issue* seller in Newcastle with a love of reading, used his profits to buy books, sourced from local charity shops and library sales. Now his company has over 140,000 titles, with 27,000 listed online, employing four local residents.

These stories provide a flavour of what might be seen as resilience. Michael Neenan[11], a seasoned therapist, coach and author, describes resilience as a process of self-righting and growth – and a resilient person as someone who is strong and capable *and* able to be vulnerable.

Resilience is something you can develop, individually and across an organization. While developing personal resilience is down to individuals, mobilizing individual inner resources can enable groups and whole communities of individuals to tolerate, learn from and grow through adverse events.

It's easy to see the need for resilience in some roles – those that deal with life, death and "emergency" on a daily basis (medical staff, military service personnel, or emergency response employees).

Other roles, those dealing with emotional situations and circumstances that might be less dramatic, but still highly impactful, also require resilience – front-line employees in demanding customer environments or even call centres where the main purpose is to deal with customers who have complaints.

And less obvious still, personal resilience is a particular necessity where you are more isolated. For example, it may be understandable to think of running a business or corporate profit centre as a privilege, an exciting opportunity to demonstrate performance and success and likely to be well rewarded. But the opportunity is often coupled with the frequent absence of formal support, and a strong link is drawn between the person heading the business and business results. Success and failure are highly visible. Isolation is something felt and experienced by those leading organizations and resilience is a core skill in such roles.

Resilience is rapidly becoming an essential business skill for all. Think of the constantly changing context that we live and work in: an overcrowded, busy, ambiguous environment where there are few ideas that are not questioned; where there are more possibilities than limitations; where success is seen as something everyone can easily attain; where social patterns and extended support networks have disappeared or are diminished. All these factors contribute to greater isolation and chaos so it is hardly surprising that growing your resilience skills is increasingly important.

For organizations, the business and social changes described are set in the context of a challenging global economic environment, leading to pressure to do more with less. Those who have jobs are often stretched significantly, while those made redundant find it increasingly harder to find equivalent employment. People and organizations find themselves facing uncomfortable situations more regularly or even a whole mindset focused on survival rather than performing to their best.

Resilience for organizations points to their capacity to learn, anticipate, respond flexibly to events and to recover. Developing a resilient organization is about making second nature the capability to adapt and find a way through, often using different thinking and approaches.

Just as individual resilience supports the development of organizational resilience, no organization is an island. The resilience of an organization is dependent on the resilience of other organizations within its network (suppliers and customers). The resilience of an organization supports the resilience of a sector, the individuals and communities that depend on the organization, and the geography in which it exists.

WHAT DOES RESILIENCE DO FOR YOU?

"Inner resilience is the secret to outer results in this world"

Tom Morris[12]

For individuals, increasing your ability to face, endure, grow and learn through adverse events enables you to experience a different quality of life regardless of your circumstances or context. Perhaps it is possible to experience enduring personal happiness through greater resilience – resilience is seen as the bedrock of positive mental health.[13] Resilience is a factor in longevity and well-being. It provides you with a rooted flexibility rather than being blown about like a leaf with every shifting breeze.

In terms of the day-to-day impact at an individual level, greater mental resilience generally means you are likely to be:

- more open to people, less defensive and closed
- calmer, experiencing a lower level of stress or anxiety
- able to move forward more easily, allowing things to pass, rather than getting stuck in what has just happened
- more able to make realistic decisions (based on what is happening now, what you are doing, what others are dong) rather than being caught up in limiting ideas about what "should" happen, what others "should" be doing, or what you "ought to", or "have to" do
- better able to openly ask for what you want and need
- more consistent and less emotionally "hijacked"
- seen as approachable and liked by others – you are less likely to upset others as a result of a fiery temper and irritability
- more adult in your approach, less demanding through either childlike sulkiness or an overbearing parental style.

Having little or no resilience, on the other hand, increases the impact of everyday stressors, and increases feelings of anxiety and depression.

The impact of stress at a macroeconomic level is huge, with the World Health Organization forecasting that depression will be the second leading contributor to the global burden of disease by 2020.[14] In the UK, the economic and social costs of mental health problems in 2003/04 were estimated at £98 billion; globally, the cost is estimated at 3-4% of each country's GDP.[15]

In terms of organizations: in the UK, stress, anxiety and depression accounted for 56 million working days lost in the UK in 2004,[16] with each case of stress-related ill health leading to an average of 31 working days lost a year.[17] This picture is replicated in other countries: for example, in the United States, job stress is estimated to cost US industry more than $300 billion a year in absenteeism, turnover, diminished productivity and medical, legal and insurance costs.[18]

Throw into the mix the idea that most organizations face a shortfall in resources from people who are present at work, but not performing at their best due to events (at home or at work) that distract their focus, and you can clearly see the compelling business case for building resilience.

BUILDING RESILIENCE

Getting started – paying attention to your inner world

"What lies behind you and what lies in front of you pales in comparison to what lies inside of you."

Ralph Waldo Emerson[19]

As the Stoic philosopher and Roman slave, Epictetus, pointed out: *"People are not disturbed by events, but by the view they take of them"*. This doesn't mean that bad things don't happen. It does mean that we can view the same event from very different perspectives. And it is how we think about things that ultimately means we either get past events or we get "stuck" in an event.

Take the story of Alex Zanardi, the ex-Formula 1 Driver: he could have chosen to be defeated by the loss of his legs – he could have, understandably, chosen to see himself as an invalid who needed to be looked after for the rest of his life. But he chose a different path and the results speak for themselves.

Srikumar Rao,[20] speaking at Google, brings our attention to our inner stories, our inner stream of consciousness. There is a constant inner voice commenting on the experiences we are having, the people we are near, the people we are thinking about, what we have just said or thought. We ignore this stream of consciousness at our peril as our beliefs, assumptions, judgements and biases all show up in this inner dialogue and the dialogue can be helpful, helping us move forward, onto the next track, or keep us stuck like a scratch on a CD (or vinyl record!), forever repeating phrases that hold us in a particular place – keeping us angry, keeping us fearful, keeping us playing small.

These attitudes and beliefs, these inner stories that you hold, have the **biggest** effect on your resilience.[21] Your thoughts and beliefs are a key driver in how you feel and behave.

Imagine a rather innocuous situation with someone at work; let's call him Joe. Every time you make a suggestion to change something to Joe, you get a lengthy justification of why things are as they are and why something can't be done. If you give Joe feedback on even the smallest thing, there is a strong defence and nothing seems to be taken on board. The impact? Eventually, you might give up trying to collaborate, share your ideas or give feedback.

What might be going on for Joe? Joe may believe any number of things about himself or others. He may hold a view that he's really a phoney and it's only a matter of time before others find him out. He can't easily take on ideas because he believes *"if I was any good, I'd have thought of that idea myself"*. He is closed to feedback because he thinks *"I should be perfect and not being perfect means I'll get found out to be a phoney."* It's these pervasive, unrealistic and irrational beliefs that close Joe down, and lead to the responses you experience as his colleague.

What impact would it have if Joe was able to reframe his beliefs about himself, perhaps believing he was "good enough" although he could learn from his colleagues, perhaps accepting that striving for perfection means things don't get done, so perhaps going for 80% before sharing with others is the target?

The impact of this "reframe" goes further than Joe. It impacts on his day-to-day interactions with colleagues and the whole organizational system around him.

Does Joe sound familiar? Maybe not the specific words, but this hidden inner world holds all sorts of fears that we're worried about being exposed – perhaps you really don't know what you're doing, perhaps you're not intelligent enough…

Actually, the only one who's thinking these thoughts is you and the more you think like this, the more stress you will experience, the fewer resources you will have at your fingertips and the less resilient you will be. The more stress you experience, the greater the volume of the critical voices.

If, instead, you can harness a positive inner world that resources you – if you can shine instead of playing small – imagine what you might achieve.

THE POWER OF YOUR INNER WORLD

Neenan (and others) talk about the A – B – C of understanding what we do and why we do it (see diagram below).

A
Situation, person, event, or even our own memory or images

outer world

B
Beliefs or ideas about the world, how we, others, things should be

inner filter

C
Actions, thoughts, feelings – may be more or less helpful and effective

outer world

Our inner beliefs and ideas about the world are a little bit like a hall of mirrors. The event is distorted as it's reflected through our internal belief filters, and our responses to an event depend on how things have been distorted.

When we get angry, upset or confused, our choices of how to act are limited.

When have helpful beliefs, appreciate our resources and resourcefulness, then we have much more choice about how to behave and more resources to draw from.

Building individual resilience comes through positive emotions and optimism, humour, flexibility of thinking, reframing events, acceptance, altruism, social support, coping style, and exercise, and other factors.[22]

Most of the time, we are unaware of our thinking. Instead we assume we are rational human beings, responding as anyone else would to a particular situation. We're completely oblivious to the distortions we have made to a situation – unaware of the unique hall of mirrors that we have filtered our experiences through. That is why Srikumar Rao is right when he says we ignore our stream of consciousness at our peril.

The good thing is that our beliefs and ideas about the world are learned through experience, and we can change our ideas as we become aware of them and try a different approach. It's not always that easy though, as we've held onto these ideas sometimes all or most of our adult lives. Freeing yourself up from unhelpful and limiting ideas about yourself and others can be life-changing.

"It is not the mountain we conquer but ourselves."
Sir Edmund Hillary[23]

Greater awareness of your inner world leads to the possibility of new thinking, leading to new actions, beliefs and feelings.

In organizations, the pattern is no different; the ABC model can be applied.

Let's imagine a particular organization which wants to consolidate and enhance its existing retail niche. A new, creative approach is required to the way that service is provided. Imagine, at the first thought-generating session, you are brave enough to offer up an idea of your own and it gets immediately dismantled or squashed; you are not going to offer another idea. The situation (A) – request for ideas input has led to you being told you are wrong and a sense of personal discomfort (C). Next time around, you're not going to offer an idea when requested as you believe that you will be told your idea is wrong (B). You may carry this belief forward throughout your career, despite changing contexts. This inner filter gets in the way of your creativity and your ability to bring all your resources to your work.

Imagine instead that your very first idea had been appreciated, had been savoured, built upon, integrated with other ideas and developed as part of the new service model. What a different belief system you might adopt.

This insight into the power of your inner world and the way your thoughts, actions and feelings are all intricately linked is used at the highest levels of performance, and is key to developing and sustaining performance and well-being.

In elite sports, "getting the mind right" is a basic phenomenon – yes, you need to train, to be at the top of your personal physical performance to be a sporting champion – but your mental preparation can make the difference between running a good race and running your best race.

BUILDING RESILIENCE AT A PERSONAL AND ORGANIZATIONAL LEVEL

"Promise me you'll always remember: You're braver than you believe, and stronger than you seem, and smarter than you think."

Christopher Robin to Pooh (by A. A. Milne)[24]

There are numerous ways in which you can build your resilience. The ideas below are a few core offerings that come from a range of sources – and as you will see from other chapters, are not limited to enhancing resilience.

Self-acceptance: So often we are unfairly critical of ourselves. Accepting things is not about complacency, it's about accepting and not judging – not beating yourself up.

For example, accept that you're not perfect (nobody is!) and the feedback that you're receiving becomes really helpful and useful. Make a realistic appraisal and, from this position, make changes. A stronger self-acceptance allows quicker self-righting and growth.

Befriending yourself: This is about imagining what you would say if a colleague or friend was in the same situation. The chances are you would not be so harsh to someone else as you are to yourself. So instead of thinking, *"I was hopeless at the job interview"*, stand back and think about someone you have great respect or care for. What would you say to them? Take the advice you would give to them and give it to yourself. Perhaps your inner voice would then say *"Although I could not answer all the questions, in the circumstances, I gave it my best shot. At least it was good practice for my next interview"*. In other words, you're not ignoring the outcome, but you are able to build and move forward from the adverse experience.

Demagnification or "deawfulising" events: It is very easy to blow a situation out of all proportion and this will only serve to increase your stress levels. Although events may be difficult to deal with or unfortunate, ask yourself: *"Is it really awful?"*; *"Is it the end of the world?"*; *"Is this a hassle or a horror?"*

One story highlights this approach: a catering manager returned home late one night just after 1am but his wife, a paediatric nurse, was still awake in bed. *"How was your day?"* she asked. *"Don't ask. It was a disaster. Things never go wrong but tonight we had a dinner for 500 people and there was a problem in the kitchen. The vegetables for the dinner were not as hot as they should have been and the organizer was furious. He was shouting in my face. It was horrible. It has taken me 20 minutes to find a car park space and I am due back at work for 7am."* Her silence made him take a breath and ask *"How was your day?"* She responded: *"Three babies died on me today"*. Since that conversation, he has been able to deal with any situation he has faced in his career in the service sector.

Look for your strengths: Do more of what you are good at, do more of what works. For example, if you are good at establishing productive working relationships, volunteer for team-based projects.

Look for meaning: Consider what is happening to you, even when you would prefer that it wasn't happening to you. What can you learn? What is good about this bad situation? Another hotel example (demanding service environments can really test resilience) provided an early lesson for a young hotel trainee manager. It was a Boxing Day fancy dress party with lots of (mostly elderly) people dancing around the room in various outfits. Suddenly, a female Robin Hood collapsed, unwell. At first there was panic but then a manager took charge, announcing that there would be a short break and asking people to go to the hotel bar or their rooms and an ambulance was called. The lady was taken to hospital and the party resumed, albeit in a more subdued fashion. The learning here was the importance of meeting the needs of those in the room – the lady who had collapsed needed immediate attention, her family needed care and some privacy and everybody else still wanted to enjoy their Christmas as much as possible. The trainee observed the importance of remaining calm, taking control, making decisions and considering the impact of decisions on all those present.

Be curious: What can you discover? Surprise yourself. Let's take somebody who had been in awe of juggling from a young age and thought people were blessed with some natural gift to be able to do this. Then, after randomly receiving juggling balls as a present, he decided to give it a go. A few days later, after a couple of hours each day practising (and failing many times) he could juggle three balls. Surprised... and thrilled!

And finally, exercise: Yes, there is no getting away from it, exercise is good for physical and mental health. In terms of resilience, it can lift your mood, reduce stress levels and make you more alert. It may also improve your self-image.

"In the middle of difficulty lies opportunity"

Albert Einstein[25]

RESILIENCE AND 31PRACTICES

At the organizational level, the 31Practices approach is linked to building greater organizational resilience. The focus with 31Practices is on setting a very clear understanding of what the organization stands for, the role that the employee plays in representing them, and a unity of purpose.

This clarity helps all employees to perform at their best, mentally and physically, as they can more easily trust the assumptions that they are making. They have a clear view of the shared assumptions in the room and can therefore work with more confidence and trust that others will have (at least some) of the same internal filters.

Recently, an automotive executive commented on the great benefits that would be generated by an employee in a car showroom in New York, knowing that the Practice of the day was to focus on personalizing the customer service, and at the same time knowing that everyone in branches in Paris, or Beijing or Moscow had the same focus that day. He saw how this would create a sense of belonging to the larger organization and an enabling inner belief.

Want to know more?
- Srikumar Rao offers an insightful talk to Google about his book *Are you ready to succeed: Unconventional Strategies to Achieving Personal Mastery in Business and Life*. The talk can be accessed on http://www.youtube.com/watch?v=u20vVbhpM50
- A well known oldie in this area is Tim Gallwey's series of inner game books. The first in the series: *The inner game of Tennis* was first published in 1975. The books are very readable and definitely recommended. Tim Gallwey (1986). *The Inner Game of Tennis*. London: Pan books
- The second resource we point you to is one that we have referenced frequently in this chapter. It's highly readable. Coming from the world of psychotherapy and coaching, rather than the world of sport, the context is different, the underpinning ideas are similar – and there are some really useful practical exercises throughout. Michael Neenan (2009). *Developing Resilience: A cognitive-behavioural approach*. London: Routledge.

CHAPTER 15 STORYTELLING

"Over the years I have become convinced that we learn best – and change – from hearing stories that strike a chord within us…..Those in leadership positions who fail to grasp or use the power of stories risk failure for their companies and for themselves"

John Kotter[1]

A story is an account about events and people (fact and/or fiction) that can be told for different purposes: to garner excitement and entertain, to inform, to share how something developed or might develop.[2] Stories are how we organize our experiences and make sense of what has happened to us.

Stories don't happen in a vacuum. As individuals, we gather stories about ourselves from friends, family, the jobs we have had, people we have worked with. We integrate these into our personal story – and are free to edit – adding and deleting perspectives and insights as fits our dominant ideas about ourselves. Our personal story constantly changes shape, growing as we grow throughout life.

The same goes for business; the story of a business has a starting point and a future point and a narrative that connects the two that makes sense of the business as it has developed, grown, reshaped and changed again and again. An organization's story is heavily influenced by the accounts of different stakeholder groups – to the extent that your organization's story is what others say about you, not necessarily what you say about yourself.

"I realised the importance of having a story today is what separates companies. People don't just wear our shoes, they tell our story."

Blake Mycoskie Founder & CEO, Tom's Shoes[3]

Stories can really work to support and feed a business reputation, or destroy a trusted brand very quickly. In Chapter 2, *Values*, it is easy to see how reputations fall when organizations fail to address cultural failings that run counter to the trusted brand.

WHAT'S IN A STORY?

"After nourishment, shelter and companionship, stories are the thing we need most in the world."

Philip Pullman[4]

Storytelling is at the heart of our existence as human beings. We have used stories to share experience, culture, traditions and learning for most of human history. Stories connect us to others, to our past, our future and to the wider universe. Modern humans have been on the earth for about 195,000 years.[5] Writing was not invented until about 3000BC. It's hard to imagine a world without written information within our current context of information overload and yet we are designed from such a world.

Without the written word, oral skills provide the main form of purposeful communication. It's no surprise that there is a certain amount of receptivity to stories that makes a good story hard to resist. We are sense-making, social creatures, and stories provide a familiar way of making sense of information.

We think in stories.

If this doesn't ring true for you, pay attention to the chatter in your own head. We've discussed the power of this inner world in Chapters 13, *Mindfulness* and 14, *Resilience*. What are the stories that you are telling yourself? Psychologists have come up with many names for the internal stories we hold: schemas, scripts, cognitive maps, mental models, metaphors, or narrative.

Stories fit our need to be able to predict what will happen next so we can prepare for it. At the very least, we are hardwired to avoid loss and harm (emotional and physical) and curious as to the impact of something on someone else so that we can make some assumptions about the impact of the same event on us. We use stories to support us to make decisions, justify our decisions, and persuade others about what they might do.

"Story, as it turns out, was crucial to our evolution— more so than opposable thumbs. Opposable thumbs let us hang on; story told us what to hang on to".

Lisa Cron[6]

Peter Guber describes stories as the *"cornerstones of consciousness"*.[7] Stories provoke our memory and give us the framework for much of our understanding.

As well as our inner stories, stories impact directly on those that we share them with, whether one to one, groups or an entire business.

In the business world, at some point, the idea of telling a good story got lost. In the words of Jason Hensel, *"the vast majority of business communications is deadly dull"*.[8] And yet stories are so powerful. Psychologist Pamela Rutledge sees that stories are the *"pathway to engaging our right brain and triggering our imagination, making us participants in the narrative. We can step out of our own shoes, see differently, and increase our empathy for others. Through imagination, we tap into creativity that is the foundation of innovation, self-discovery and change"*.[9]

The story of Joshie at Ritz Carlton (shared by Chris Hurn) goes like this. Chris's son had left his favourite toy at the Ritz Carlton on Amelia Island. Facing a distraught son, Chris told a little white lie. *"Joshie is fine,"* he said. *"He's just taking an extra long vacation at the resort."* His son seemed to buy it, and was finally able to fall asleep, Joshie-less for the first time in a long while.

That night, the Ritz Carlton called to say that they had Joshie. He had been found, no worse for wear, in the laundry and was handed over to the hotel's Loss Prevention Team. The father mentioned the story he told his son and asked if they would mind taking a picture of Joshie on a lounge chair by the pool to substantiate the story. The Loss Prevention Team said they'd do it.

A few days went by, and a package was received from the hotel. It was Joshie, along with some Ritz Carlton-branded "goodies" and a binder that meticulously documented Joshie's extended stay at the Ritz – showing:

- Joshie wearing shades by the pool (the original request/suggestion)...
- Joshie getting a massage at the spa...
- Joshie making friends with other animals... stuffed and real...
- Joshie driving a golf cart on the beach…
- Joshie was even issued a Ritz Carlton ID badge, made an honorary member of the Loss Prevention Team, and was allowed to help by taking a shift in front of the security monitors.

Needless to say, Chris and his wife were completely wowed and the story will be talked about for many years to come – creating a strong sense of emotional connection with the Ritz Carlton brand.

The blog of this story[10] received plenty of attention – connecting people to the Ritz Carlton brand in a very different way to a traditional corporate advertisement.

A recent study at Princetown University[11] showed how our brains synchronize when we listen to stories. Using brain-scanning techniques, the researchers could see that the areas of the listeners' brains being triggered were the same as those being accessed in the storyteller's brain, in the same sequence, as the story unfolded. The greater the level of understanding of the story, the more the speaker and listener brain images dovetailed. When there was no understanding of the story, where the same speaker spoke in a different language, no synchronization was seen.

"Stories are the most effective form of human communication, more powerful than any other way of packaging information"

Peter Guber[12]

MAKING USE OF STORIES

For individual leaders: Stories are essential as they unify and make sense of our sensory experiences. There is no central command post in the brain, only millions of highly specialized local processors, brought together by an interpreter module in the left brain hemisphere.[13] This built-in storyteller generates explanations about our perceptions, memories and actions and the relationships among them. We create ourselves through narrative. Stories really don't just come from "out there" – we listen to a constant stream of stories every day in our own head. The stories we tell ourselves are telling us where to focus our attention, they give clues about how we see ourselves in the world. Our internal stories are far from fact-based. We create our stories, just as any story is created.

And, just as the cast of characters in a play have their roles, our stories give insights into the role we take in our own life. Are your stories a wealth of support, a resource to draw upon? Or do they keep you focused on your anxieties, and fears – what you can't do, what you need to be scared of?

The greatest freedom comes from knowing that we can recast the role that we play in our lives, changing unhelpful stories to be more helpful, more realistic, and more of a resource. While some stories might have had elements of "truth" decades ago, even perhaps a few years ago, or more recently still, stories go past their "sell-by date" and some well-recited stories can cast us in a role that is no longer true.[14]

Take one very capable professional client; let's call her Jane. In her story, Jane felt her own needs were unimportant, it was her role to enable others to shine, to support others to realize their goals. Jane was admired in her field and received a lot of feedback appreciating her supportive approach. Exploring her story a little more, she felt uncomfortable sharing her own needs with colleagues. Pushing a little further still, Jane felt that her colleagues would no longer "like" her or may even get angry with her for saying what she really needed and sharing what she really thought in a situation. Jane was suffering from stress, at the level of early burnout.

These outcomes that Jane feared; were they really true? Or even likely? The only way to find out is to start doing things differently. This is exactly what Jane did. She identified one or two situations where she felt safe to say what she needed and thought. Not surprisingly, no one got angry. In fact, against Jane's expectations, people responded really positively to her expressing herself more clearly. On reflection, Jane thought she was probably a bit more "human" as a result. Jane rewrote some critical parts of her story; being supportive *and* receiving support from others was a healthy two-way flow and enabled Jane to stay well, thrive and achieve even more.

For organizations: storytelling in communities gives shape to the foundations of a community, the "what" and "how" of past events and future possibilities brought to life through a tale. Organizational values are learned through the stories told in organizations. What is it important to pay attention to here? How do we do things around here?

We learn to navigate an organizational context in exactly the same way we navigate other social contexts. We listen to the stories to understand what it is important to hold on to and what to let go.

When organizations, brands or individuals identify and develop a core story, they create and display authentic meaning and purpose that others can believe and identify with, participate in – emotionally through their own imaginations, and share with the storyteller and others. Peter Guber describes stories as *"state of the heart technology"*, turning the listeners into *"viral advocates of the proposition, whether in life or in business, by playing the story – not just the information – forward."*[15]

The hotel MD, walking around on a Sunday, visited the employee restaurant. There was nobody there and it was a mess: dirty plates left on tables, upturned chairs, discarded newspapers, cups with coffee dregs, debris on the floor. So he started to clear things up. Then a young chef arrived and offered to help: *"I don't have anything else to do in my break"*. In about 20 minutes the place was clean and tidy. The following week, ahead of a holiday weekend, the MD went to see the goods receiving area and asked the clerk if he could make time on the holiday Monday to give the whole area a spring clean. The response? *"If our managing director can clean our restaurant I am sure I can give this a good clean"*. Do you think that an email restating the health and safety reasons for keeping the restaurant clean and tidy would have had anywhere near the same impact as this story being told among the employees?

Stories are rarely pure fact – the "goodies" that show the storyteller in a better light are often positively embellished, the "baddies" sometimes unfairly represented. The critical thing is that these "myths" become the reality.

Of course, social media has changed the dynamic and, now, personal stories can have a much greater impact – in a positive and a negative way.

You might be aware of Dave Carroll's guitar broken by an American airline. He posted a YouTube clip of a song about his experience. Four days after its launch, a million people had watched "United Breaks Guitars"; United stock went down 10% at about this time, shedding $180 million in value (while the cause and effect is hotly disputed, the whole incident did not help United's cause). The clip has now received upwards of 12.9 million hits.[16]

TELLING STORIES WITH SKILL

"You may tell a tale that takes up residence in someone's soul, becomes their blood and self and purpose. That tale will move them and drive them and who knows that they might do because of it, because of your words. That is your role, your gift."

Erin Morgenstern[17]

Storytelling really is a skill. If you're a good storyteller, you transfer experiences directly to the audience's brain – they feel what you feel. They empathize, are horrified and delighted at the same points. Like any skill, practice helps. But where to start? What are some of the basics?

Authentic: The success of a story rests on the resonance, authenticity, and richness created by the storyteller.[18] It's easy to see that when we enjoy a good story, we are not just paying attention to the "content", we are paying attention to the storyteller – the energetic presence of the author, the tone of voice, inflections in speech – and the congruence between the two. On these points alone, a story may thrive or die. Stories provide us with a potentially authentic experience, so the authenticity with which a good story is told triggers whether we believe or disbelieve what we are hearing.

Golden rules: Peter Guber[19] shares some secrets from his considerable directing experience about how to tell a good story.
- *Rule 1:* Give the audience an emotional experience. The heart is always the first target in telling purposeful stories. Stories must give listeners an emotional experience if they are to ignite a call to action.
- *Rule 2:* Use metaphor and analogy as this evokes images and turns on our memories with all their rich sensory and emotional associations. Stories motivate us because we see in them echoes and possibilities for ourselves.
- *Rule 3:* It's wise to prepare your stories in advance. But before you launch into your script, take some time to learn about your audience. What you discover will determine how you tell your story. You want to make sure your audience is with you. You can't get anywhere without them.

Basic structure: Stories follow a structure. Joseph Campbell's[20] work draws out the structure of ancient legends and myths and describes a basic pattern, which is commonly referred to as the Hero's journey. The language of the Hero's journey is engaging and emotive. The basic underpinning structured offered is:[21]

- Who would be the main characters in your story?
- What is the task?
- Who or what is helping?
- What is getting in the way?
- How does the main character get around this?
- What is the outcome or end?

This structure is so familiar to us that our brains are geared to anticipate the next part and the possibilities of what happened next, are already forming in our minds before the speaker has uttered the words. Julie Allan[22] and her colleagues build from this underpinning structure, offering a rich insight into the science and art of storytelling.

Creating a strategic narrative
- Where are you?
- Where have you been?
- Where are you going?
- Ensure employees are part of that narrative
- And repeat the story over and over again
  Most importantly, when telling a story: speak from the heart.

STORYTELLING AND 31PRACTICES

"The destiny of the world is determined less by the battles that are lost and won than by the stories it loves and believes in."

Harold Goddard[23]

Stories are core to the 31Practices methodology. To start with, there is the central story that is woven around organizational purpose and the principles and Practices that are designed to deliver that purpose. This chimes with the "call to adventure" – the departure phase of Campbell's heroic journey.

There is the story around how you create your 31Practices as an organization: the main characters involved, the foundations, expectations and reputation that are you building.

There is the story around what is happening as the journey unfolds. This "bigger story" is created from the many stories that individuals share each day as they put the daily Practices into operation. This part chimes with the "belly of the whale" as the helpers and saboteurs become apparent and people learn how to navigate the 31Practices, its impact and refine it to ensure greater success. The stories about "how to do it well", "the impact on me", "the success I had" that people tell each other here are crucial to amplify. As in the words of Lisa Cron, the stories tell us what to hang onto and what to let go of as the culture shifts to align more explicitly behind organizational purpose. It is for this reason that 31Practices is embedded most effectively when it is aligned to recognition, communications and learning and development, capturing and then communicating these stories, turning myth into reality.

One of the most crucial sets of stories to really work on includes the stories from the organizational leaders. Make sure that those at the top of the organization are sharing what they are personally experiencing and doing this on a daily basis initially in order to send the signal through the organization. THIS IS IMPORTANT. If you don't, interest will wane, confusion will abound and the initiative will fizzle as the old culture and ways of being steadfastly and implicitly remain.

There are stories around integration and mastery where people integrate the 31Practices into their daily routine without question. Stories of recognition from others and impact on stakeholder groups need to be shared.

To paraphrase Harold Clarke Goddard:[24] The destiny of **your organization** is determined less by the battles that are lost and won than by the stories it loves and believes in.

Want to know more?
- Andrew Stanton, writer of *Wall-E* and *Toy Story*, shares the clues to writing a great story in his TED talk of March 2012. http://www.ted.com/talks/andrew_stanton_the_clues_to_a_great_story.html?quote=1388
- Julie Allan and her colleagues wrote an incredibly rich and practical book about narrative in organisations. Ahead of its time when it was published, the book is packed with goodies for anyone wishing to gather insight and improve their technical skills as a storyteller. Julie Allan, Gerard Fairtlough and Barbara Heinzen (2001). *The Power of the Tale: Using Narratives for Organisational Success*. Chichester: John Wiley & Sons Ltd.

SECTION 3: THE BODY PRINCIPLES

"What the mind has forgotten, the body remembers long after."

Lilias Folan[1]

The Body Principles are focused on what we are doing in the world through our behaviour, our actions. Once we have defined the organizational purpose, the values and the Practices, how are we actually living those? How do we actually do what we set out to achieve? What are the ways we need to act, and think about acting in order to foster living those Practices? What are the habits that we are developing and, as a result, what is the impact or legacy of what we have done?

Knowing what we do impacts every time - ourselves, others and the situation we find ourselves in. This brings to our awareness the importance of choosing what we do carefully. In this section, we discuss *Practice*, *Strengths* and *Discipline*.

This whole section is essentially about habits. Just as our minds are an interactive aspect of our selves, constantly in flux, so too are our bodies and the physical habits that we create.

In Chapter 16, *Practice*, we explore three aspects of habits giving insight into the basics of habit formation – moving from an idea to action. This gives awareness of how to shape new habits and eliminate or minimize unwanted ones.

Chapter 17, *Strengths* simply refocuses our attention from improving weaknesses, moving from a problem focus and blame, towards the benefits of working with the flow, looking at what works and doing more, and the power of appreciation. So when we aim at building habits we're building on things that are likely to prevail, be sustainable and enable others to do the same through the environment we create.

Finally, in Chapter 18, *Discipline*, we explore how to really stretch towards the success we dream of and hope for.

Exploring these principles will show how every action we take (or thought we have) creates our daily experience of life. Fundamentally, if you want to change something, you need to change what you do – now, today, in this present moment.

"Knowing is not enough; we must apply. Wishing is not enough; we must do".

Johanne Von Goethe[2]

CHAPTER 16 PRACTICE

"The more I practice, the luckier I get."

Gary Player[1]

Practice is about applying an idea, belief or method rather than the theories related to it. Practice in this chapter is also about repeatedly performing an activity to become skilled in it.[2]

"Practice is a means of inviting the perfection desired."

Martha Graham[3]

The value and benefit of practice is taken for granted for performers at the highest level in fields such as sport, music, and art. Can you imagine teams like the New York Yankees in baseball, Toronto Maple Leafs in ice hockey, Dallas Cowboys in American Football, Manchester United in soccer just turning up on match day? In the arts, would the cast of Cirque du Soleil, the musicians of the Berlin Philharmonic Orchestra or the dancers of the Bolshoi Ballet just turn up on the day of the performance? Even the Rolling Stones practise.

From the sporting world we see that anyone who wants to learn and improve needs to commit time and effort to practise, to notice what works and doesn't, to keep training until a routine is improved, perfected.

How does this translate to organizations? Training exists of course – focused on new recruits or "teaching" new skills and technical knowledge that may be required. Skilled execution is highly valued. But, in most organizations, there is not much focus on practice – and a lack of focus on reflection – on learning from that practice, considering what worked, what didn't work and what to adjust next time. In organizations, practice and reflection are the missing links between the theory – the idea, and skilled execution.

A further common assumption that we make is that skills are purely physical and visible – some are, but many skills are not. Have you ever noticed the routines of top sports people coming out to deliver their personal best at any sporting event? The external habits are easy to see, the touching of a chain, adjusting a cap. These are backed up by a host of internal habits and routines. Skills bloom from a fertile and resourceful set of inner beliefs, ideas and attitudes.

"The mind is what separates a fair player from a true champion"

Kirk Mango[4]

WHAT DOES PRACTICE DO FOR YOU?

Practice enables you to broaden your repertoire, to deepen your knowledge, insight and capability. The brain, once thought to be a "fixed" entity, is malleable. Purposeful practice builds new neural pathways and constant repetition deepens those connections, making that new option a readily available choice.

The result of all this practice? The seemingly super-sharp reaction time of various ball sports is an illusion. In standard reaction time tests, there is no difference between, say, a leading tennis player compared to people in general. BUT, the player is able to detect minute subtle movement in the server's arm and shoulder which from years and years of practice has led them to read the direction of the serve before the ball has even been played. It's this practice that has created unconscious patterns and distinctions that the player responds to equally unconsciously – resulting in the seemingly super-sharp responses in the professional game.

Wayne Gretzky, a Canadian ice hockey player, has been described as the greatest ice hockey player ever by many in his field. His talent captures this attention to the context of a game rather than focusing on distinct actions alone. *"Gretzky's gift…is for seeing…amid the mayhem, Gretzky can discern the game's underlying pattern and flow, and anticipate what's going to happen faster and in more detail than anyone else."[5]*

The same is found in experts in many fields. They instinctively know – based on years of practice. They are able to pick up minute distinctions and patterns that the rest of us are blind to.

The story of a Cleveland firefighter, shared by Malcolm Gladwell.[6] The fire was in a kitchen in the back of a one-story house in a residential neighbourhood. On breaking down the door, the firefighters began dousing the fire with water. It should have abated, but it did not.

The fire lieutenant suddenly thought to himself, *"There's something wrong here"*. He immediately ordered his men out. Moments later, the floor they had been standing on collapsed. The fire had been in the basement, not the kitchen.

When asked how he knew to get out, the fireman could not immediately explain the reasons – the implicit knowledge, built up over years of experience, triggered an almost instinctive reaction – which saved his life and those of his fellow crew members.

The story of a head chef. A catering company introducing software to calculate the cost of producing a dish (data for the recipe and cost of raw ingredients) decided to compare the cost calculated by the package with the calculations from the head chef. The difference between the two costs was minimal. The head chef had practised this calculation thousands of times over a number of years with variations in price and recipe, developing an instinctive subconscious ability to make an accurate calculation.

Purposeful practice is the primary contributing factor (above natural talent) to excellence in sport and life.[7] To be a truly practised at a skill or habit, hours of sustained practice are required – estimated at 10,000 hours (2.7 hours a day for 10 years[8]). This finding has been validated across professions. The focus and attention to the practice and learning from that practice is fundamental.

At this level of competence in a particular skills context, you have developed what is described as reflection-in-action – where you are critically aware of what you are doing while you are doing it – judging each moment for its suitability against an inner set of criteria – at the same time that you are actually doing the activity.[9] It's this attention to practice that enables you to keep performing at your best.

"It's not necessarily the amount of time you spend at practice that counts; it's what you put into the practice."

Eric Lindros[10]

LEARNING THROUGH PRACTICE

How do we learn through practice? As in many things, attitude – how we approach the task and what we expect of ourselves – is of paramount importance. Here are some ideas to bear in mind about the process of learning through practice.

It's uncomfortable – you feel vulnerable, exposed. Through practice you are making the unfamiliar familiar. When you do something for the first time it feels clunky, uncomfortable. You are likely to feel a bit self conscious at best, and downright scared of failure and associated shame at worst – you might feel absolutely sure that everyone else notices that this is the first time you've done this, certain that others can see all your mistakes. Initially, your performance might take a turn in the wrong direction – getting slower rather than faster – as you start to work out how to integrate a new awareness or activity into your repertoire. With repetition, that painful self-awareness subsides and you now can perform the task (whether it's speaking to an audience of 300, operating the photocopier or completing an

UNCONSCIOUS INCOMPETENCE	CONSCIOUS INCOMPETENCE
WHAT YOU DO, SAY & FEEL: Oblivious to the need for change	**WHAT YOU DO, SAY & FEEL:** Acknowledges changes you need to make
Denies change required	
Places responsibility elsewhere	Seeks to understand change required
Creates an overly positive picture	
Avoids action	First tentative steps at practice
Frustrated perhaps angry, fearful	Anxious, worried, vulnerable

PERFORMANCE

DENIAL & RESISTANCE

ACCEPTANCE

TIME

internal approval form) with confidence and elegance. You've integrated the learning into "business as usual" and you're ready for the next challenge.

Practising something new takes you into a four-stage learning and performance cycle.[11]

- Unconscious Incompetence – you don't know that you don't know – and you might react with some defensiveness to feedback or the awareness that you might need to change something. You feel vulnerable when you start to become aware.
- Conscious Incompetence – you know that you don't know and you still can't do it – it's uncomfortable, confidence drops, you might be more worried and you still feel vulnerable.
- Conscious Competence – you know that you know how to perform the new skill – but it requires attention, focus and energy. You start to feel more confident and are practising and stretching your new skill.
- Unconscious Competence – you don't know that you know – it just seems so easy. Your new skill is an integrated habit – you perform the skill without conscious effort.

CONSCIOUS COMPETENCE

UNCONSCIOUS COMPETEICE

WHAT YOU DO, SAY AND & FEEL:

Acknowledges the value of practice and learning

Seeks opportunities to practice further and improve

Prepared to take risks and stretch further

Feeling more comfortable with the discomfort, curious and positive

INTEGRATION

EXPLORATION

WHAT YOU DO, SAY & FEEL:

New skill and insight is integrated into repertoire

Effortless and increased performance

Looking to the next horizon, the next stretch

Feeling energized, confident, focused

Is this model familiar, or if you haven't seen the model before, do the stages of learning sound familiar? And the thing is, you don't get the learning if you don't go through the stages of incompetence (unconscious and conscious). The saying goes "No pain, no gain". To reduce the level of pain, remember that feedback is only data. Be curious about what you might learn rather than be defensive. This gives people around you permission to grow and learn too. Interestingly, people often respond very positively to the humanity displayed when you are open about your learning.

A fifth stage to this model has been described as developing reflection-in-action, or reflective competence – avoiding the onset of complacency leading to mistakes and a degradation of the skills that have been learned. In part this is ongoing critical reflection, and it's also about maintaining a "beginner mind" (see Chapter 18, *Discipline*). Building this reflective competence is something that can support you to build mastery.[12]

"Failure" is part of the territory – Paradoxically, failure is a key part of success. Framing failure as an opportunity to learn is a key to building success. For example, Shizuka Arakawa, one of Japan's greatest ice skaters, reports falling over more than 20,000 times in her progression to become the 2006 Olympic champion.

It is relatively well known that Thomas Edison "failed" many times before he had success. One story is that while Mr. Edison was inventing the light bulb, a young reporter came to interview him. At this point, Mr. Edison had tried over 5,000 different filaments for the light bulb with no success. The young reporter asked *"Mr. Edison, what is it like to have failed over 5,000 times?"* To which Mr. Edison replied, *"Young man, I haven't failed at all. I've succeeded at identifying 5,000 ways that don't work!"* Edison's drive wasn't diminished at all. He continued and made more "mistakes" before he finally "succeeded" in creating the first filament light bulb.

"Practice is the best of all instructors."

Publilius Syrus[13]

Excellence comes from pushing at the boundaries of what is thought to be possible – Practice leads to excellence from constantly stretching to reach a much higher goal (often a goal that only the coach/manager thinks is possible). Thus practising with (and being with) the best is critical to drive up performance and mindset.

"When you are not practicing, remember, someone somewhere is practicing, and when you meet him he will win"

Ed Macauley[14]

One of the reasons Brazil is so successful at soccer is because most of the footballers played futsal. The surface, ball and rules create an emphasis on creativity, technique, precision and more frequent passing.

Linking heart, mind and body – practising any skill (even imagining success at a particular skill – see Chapter 22, *Neuroscience*) is a full mind, heart and body event. As you build new physical skills, you're laying down and deepening neural pathways. As you develop competence and strength in a particular skill, you're building up the positive emotions associated with execution. Practice in something can lead to belief in your ability to do it. This principle is one that informs coaches and practitioners working in the area of somatics and embodiment.

So if you embody confidence, in how you stand, walk, and engage with others, you will believe that you are confident – try it.

"In theory, there is no difference between theory and practice. In practice there is."

Yogi Berra[15]

SO WHAT?

How can organizations create the culture and space for practice in order to grow and learn, improve and deliver excellence? Individual practice at work is a systemic question – it's about the prevailing culture, skills and process – as well as individual focus and motivation.

Specifically, what is the **"feedback culture"** of the organization? To what extent do people receive good quality feedback in a relatively "safe" environment (i.e. not a critical performance environment) so that they can learn and improve – getting it right when it really matters?

An organization with a blame culture will limit people's motivation to practice. And it will suffocate learning and growth. Employees will look to hide and deny mistakes rather than own and learn from them. Such an organization will limit its ability to adapt and change, and within a fast-changing global context, such a limitation may well lead to demise.

It's not just about avoiding a blame culture – how can you establish an environment of striving to achieve the best and an expectation that this will be achieved? Everybody then benefits from the virtuous circle of being with others who are excellent at what they do. This "multiplier" effect impacts across groups and communities:

- The city of Reading, UK produced more outstanding table-tennis players than the rest of the country put together.
- Spartek (a small, impoverished area in Moscow) generated more top 20 women tennis players than the whole of America.
- The high altitude Nandi area in Kenya has produced more marathon runners than anywhere else in the world. The area is so poor that children would regularly run to school (up to 20 km away).[16]

What are the processes in place to support practice?

Take the example of the executive meetings in a media organization. Part of these meetings were dedicated to presentations and input from key senior employees. Securing a slot to present to the executive group was key to developing your profile as a senior employee with the prize being future consideration for promotion to the executive group. Each senior manager presenting was carefully supported to scope, map out and practise their presentation. At each stage, feedback would be given and integrated into the next iteration until an incredibly slick and professional presentation was crafted for delivery to the executive group.

Practice and learning take time and focus – and often the pressure to deliver means the time to implement the theory is missed – and a lot of time and money is wasted in the process.

Every person who has responsibility for leading others, from the supervisor to the CEO, needs skills to support practice and learning. And they themselves need to be supported to learn and grow in these "soft skills".

PRACTICE AND 31PRACTICES

31Practices is about putting values into practice every day. Left on the boardroom wall, or turning up only on the marketing and recruitment literature, means the values are theoretical at best. To become part of the fabric and the way of being, the values have to be practised.

Because there is a Practice each day, everybody in the organization has the opportunity to practise one behaviour directly related to one of the core values. For example, an organization may have the core value "Relationships", and a Practice to bring this value to life, "We **invest time** with stakeholders to build long lasting **relationships**". On the day of this particular Practice, all employees are therefore very mindful and consciously looking for opportunities to build strong relationships with colleagues, customers, suppliers, communities. The impact? Let's consider:

"Today, instead of sending an email update, I took the time to call the project sponsor and ask her what she was noticing, and what did we need to start, stop, continue in her view. I learned that a key team member was in the process of resigning for personal reasons – something that was not widely known – this information enabled me to think through the delivery schedule and prepare a shift in resource to come into play when the news was made public. The call took five minutes – it would have taken me longer to compose the email. I felt great."

Over the course of one month, you live each of the organization's values through a number of different Practices. Initially, like any new activity, you may feel uncertain, perhaps even a little anxious: "Am I doing it right?" Over time, the Practices are repeated, becoming habitual – you don't have to think about them and they become automatic. You will find that you start adopting the Practices more generally, not just the one that day.

This works across small and large groups. Marriott's Daily Basics programme was based on the same principle and operated across 3,000 hotels globally.

A key point for us is that, just as with sport or other activities, hours of purposeful practice of behaviours and attitudes that are hard-wired to the organization's core values will result in a strong values-based culture (if we take the view that culture is the "way things are done around here").

MAKING PRACTICE A REALITY

Try this exercise with a group of colleagues – it's about how you connect with and greet people.

Ask everybody to walk around the room in a random fashion.

Explain that you are going to shout out a number between 1 and 10. When you shout a number, the idea for the participants is to greet the person nearest to them in accordance with the number they have just heard you shout. The number 1 represents a poor effort at greeting and welcoming the other and 10 represents excellence.

When the greeting has happened ask the participants to walk on.

Repeat with different numbers so that they practice greeting at different levels and finish with a high number.

After the exercise, ask people how they felt about receiving greeting 8, 9 or 10. In our experience, people really enjoy receiving a warm, friendly greeting. Then ask them to be honest with themselves and consider what number greeting they give to others each day. Again, we find that people often admit to giving between 5 and 7. You can leave them with the thought that, if a warm greeting feels so good, then why not give this warmth each day. It is their choice and it is easier with practice.

There is another very simple way to experience the benefit of practice: start something that you have never done before and practice regularly and to the right level of quality. This could be something very basic like juggling, memorizing and repeating some phrases in a foreign language or playing a tune on a musical instrument.

Want to know more?

- Matthew Syed (2011). *Bounce: the myth of talent and the power of practice*. New York: Harper Collins
- An example of some of the research studies looking at the details of the impact of practice is provided by the paper by Avi Karni et al. Avi Karni, Gundela Meyer, Christine Rey Hipolito, Peter Jezzard, Michelle M Adams, Robert Turner, and Leslie G. Ungerleider (1998). The Acquisition of skilled motor performance: Fast and slow experience-driven changes in primary motor cortex. Proceedings of the National Academy of Sciences (USA). http://www.pnas.org/content/95/3/861.long

CHAPTER 17   STRENGTHS

"Climbing to the top demands strength, whether it is to the top of Mount Everest or to the top of your career."
Abdul Kalam[1]

A strength is a good or beneficial quality of a person. It implies power and intensity and also refers to the ability to withstand pressure.[2] As people, we have fairly stable strengths – ways of behaving, thinking or feeling that can lead us to be on top of our game and achieve valuable goals, if we make good use of them.[3] Seligman[4] talks about strengths as our values in action. Our strengths may be underplayed or overplayed, but it is very likely that we have much more capacity and resource than we make use of, perhaps than we might even dream we have.

Business culture has an almost obsessive focus on improving areas of weakness, supporting leaders, managers and all employees to address their deficits. This idea of "fixing people" misses a potentially much bigger opportunity – that is, to build people's strengths and allow them to flourish.

The underpinning assumption in the deficit approach is that in order to grow, develop and succeed in business, you have to take a linear route through the leadership and management pipeline, proving yourself at every level in order to step onto the next. This approach can be fundamentally flawed. The very character traits that are trained out of you at one level might be those that will enable you and the organization to thrive at another. Thinking about leaders in less "linear" terms might enable us to work with a more complex and emergent model that frees up the inherent strengths and talents that we have within the existing organizational frame.

Susan Tardanico[5] shares a poignant story around the potentially flawed deficit focus:

"Some years ago there was a brilliant scientist at BBN, the company that built the original Internet, who had an amazing ability to envision the future and invent solutions to problems most people had not yet even anticipated. His list of patents for advanced network technology was so impressive that the company did what companies almost always do. It promoted him to management. Suddenly the scientist floundered, his strengths as a focused and brilliant inventor subsumed by meetings, employee issues and operational reviews. He was given developmental courses to help overcome his introversion, unconventional thinking and lack of business acumen. What had been his strongest assets were now his liabilities. He was notably weak as a manager. As that became obvious, his self-esteem and the respect he had enjoyed at the company melted away, and his value to the organization dissipated. He failed, and he ultimately left."[6]

The deficit approach to leader development – creating the all-rounded perfect leader – plays to the idea that leadership is something that individuals "do", when more and more we see that a leadership team is a more effective focus. In some of the board work we have been involved in, we have seen that having a realistic confidence and understanding of the strengths that the MD/CEO brought and the ability to recognize and engage the strengths and skills of others around them was a significant part of success, engaging others in the team and building a forward momentum.

Consider these two cases observed. In one case, the MD steadfastly defended his unrealistic view of his intellectual brilliance, which led to a drive for control and such political manoeuvring in the top team that his more capable team members were stunted in the contributions they were able to make. The subsequent infighting limited the organization's potential and nearly led to a split in the very early part of a management buy-out process. Contrast this with a second example, where careful feedback to the future CEO about the intellectual capability across the executive team led to a shift in team dynamics that removed previous blocks and enabled much more constructive board-level dialogue – and ensured the continued engagement of a key player in the team, who had until that point been disillusioned and was at risk of leaving. For more on this, see Chapter 24, *Leadership*.

Over the last decade there has been an increasing focus on working with strengths[7] and positivity as a lens through which to facilitate growth and success.

This focus has emerged from a number of underpinnings, including business and leadership theories, strengths research, solutions-focused work, appreciative inquiry, and the blossoming of the positive psychology movement which has been aided by the prolific work of Professor Barbara Fredrickson[8] and Martin Seligman[9] among others.

In this chapter, we are looking at strengths in the round, by exploring what a focus on strengths might give us as individuals and organizations, looking at reframing and refocusing the lens towards what's working and what we're aiming to achieve; exploring what an appreciative environment might offer.

OPPORTUNITY THINKING

"We can't solve problems by using the same kind of thinking we used when we created them."

Albert Einstein[10]

As human beings, we are very comfortable with problem-focused thinking. In fact, our brains are hardwired to avoid loss, rather than to optimize gains.[11] Our dominant thinking pattern perhaps easily draws us a deficit model – indeed, only about a third of people can readily name their strengths.[12] The emergence of psychology has demonstrated this deficit approach beautifully – for the first 100 years of psychological study, the dominant research frame was to work out how to "fix" people who were not well, to understand dysfunction, rather than to focus on what makes people function well, what makes people happy, what enables people to perform at the top of their game, to be excellent. A shift in the frame of psychological research and insight took place when Martin Seligman enabled the profession to see how blinkered it had become.[13] The Positive Psychology movement has since flourished.

Focusing on strengths
These recent developments really encourage us to focus on growing our

strengths. Focusing on what we're good at acknowledges that all people really can't be good at all things.[14] And, instead of focusing on improving our weaknesses so that we are good at everything, we would get more out of focusing on strengths as that is where we have much greater potential for growth.[15]

Problem talk vs Solution talk

Shifting how we frame events and the language we use is key. It may seem to be stating the obvious when we say focus on the solution, not the problem – and by this we mean keep focused on purpose, impact, outcomes, strengths and resources. It's about presenting what is happening, what is currently not working in light of what you're trying to achieve, what would be better, not just focusing on "fixing what isn't working" – because if you don't know what you're trying to achieve, or what is working, you are going to create more problems.

Interestingly, the more people talk about problems, the more they find problems and more entrenched in those problems they become. Focusing on what is done well, and doing more of it, highlighting resources and reframing to encourage possibility thinking frees people up, opens minds and generates creative outcomes.[16]

Appreciative Inquiry (AI) methods focus on increasing what an organization does well rather than eliminating what it does badly. What is it that makes an organization perform at its best, when it is most constructively capable? How do we ask questions that strengthen an organization's positive potential?[17]

"Change is happening all the time….. Our role is to identify the useful change and amplify it."

Gregory Bateson[18]

Positive emotion

Positivity is shown to build personal resources and resilience, improve thinking,[19] enhance creativity and lead to quicker recovery from setbacks.[20] It's even associated with longer life and greater virtue.

Wise leaders are characterized by tolerance and open-mindedness – which is easier to attain when relaxed and in a positive mood.[21]

"In contrast to the constructions of negative emotion, [when we are in a positive mood] our mental set is expansive, tolerant, and creative. We are open to new ideas and new experience."

Martin Seligman[22]

Reframing

Working with strengths, positive emotion and with a focus on the resourcefulness of people and organizations has a positive impact. It's not about ignoring all that isn't positive, ignoring the gaps, ignoring what's not working. It really is about reframing way you look at the everyday challenges and opportunities. It's about language, but not just about language. It's definitely NOT the Pollyanna[23] principle resurrected. Some basic principles to follow:

- Reframe – look at situations with a view to what you are aiming for (what the solution is).
- What do you bring? What do you already have? What do you have, but have forgotten that you have? What past patterns and experiences can you draw insight and ideas from?
- Appreciate what you have already; give praise for what is being done well.
- Notice what works and do more of it.

Working with strengths is a matter of focusing the lens differently, seeing the reality through a resourceful frame (rather than a deficit frame). It's about seeing the problems you are currently facing with a view to the end game that you want (rather than simply fixing the problem). It's also about not trying to fix what is already working – and that requires you to notice what's working (as well as what's not).

"If we did all the things we were capable of doing, we would literally astound ourselves."

Thomas Edison[24]

SO WHAT?

What does a strengths-based approach, a resourceful frame do for us?

We know focusing on strengths is good for individuals and improves many aspects of their performance. What about organizations? Emphasizing

193

strengths in performance conversations increases performance, focusing on weaknesses reduces performance.[25] When encouraged to apply their personal strengths to the job, new employees are helped to become more connected, more engaged and more likely to stay.[26] Employees who are more able to do what they do best every day are likely to be more productive and increase customer loyalty and retention.[27] Teams increase performance and reduce attrition where strengths are highlighted.[28] Leaders who invest in their own and others' strengths increase the engagement levels of those they lead.[29]

In a competitive business context, where any growth is regarded as an achievement, these ideas deserve serious consideration. And this is using a resource that is already in place (your workforce)… it's just not operating optimally.

CAN YOU BE TOO POSITIVE?

Yes – Barbara Frederickson and Marcial Losada[30] have both studied how the ratio of positivity to negativity (the P/N ratio) impacts. High ratios of positive to negative emotion distinguish individuals and teams who flourish (those who grow and thrive) from those who languish (those who weaken and lose energy). However, if you have too much positivity (above 11.6 positives to 1 negative), there is no challenge or stretch. Things are too linear in a positive way and complacency sets in.

The Losada line[31] – the ratio at which the positive feelings and experiences start to build and stretch, leading to learning and growth, flexibility and resilience – is 2.9 positives to 1 negative.

"I love those who can smile in trouble, who can gather strength from distress, and grow brave by reflection. 'Tis the business of little minds to shrink, but they whose heart is firm, and whose conscience approves their conduct, will pursue their principles unto death."

Leonardo da Vinci[32]

Positivity and negativity operate as powerful feedback systems: negativity dampens (or "shrinks") anything that deviates from a particular standard, while positivity amplifies or reinforces, resulting in expanding behaviour.[33]

The tension between the negativity and the positivity creates a complex system that promotes growth and learning.

When we shared this idea with a group of military leaders, the logical question came back: *"Does that mean that we have to precede every piece of negative or constructive feedback with three or more positives?"* And the answer is definitely a firm "no". It's more about seeing a relationship a bit like a bank account. Making sure that on the whole you're putting in many more positives than negatives, but each piece of feedback doesn't need to have a particular structure. So when something is worth appreciating, appreciate it. When something isn't up to scratch, or isn't having the desired impact, share it.

You'll be surprised too. Sometimes you think you're giving someone something negative – giving them feedback that you are finding difficult to share with them – but the receiver on the other hand is hugely grateful because you've really helped them gain insight and understanding about how to be more effective. What you thought was a withdrawal on your relationship bank account turned out to be a significant investment!

As a rule of thumb, remember to genuinely and authentically appreciate those around you.

STRENGTHS AND 31PRACTICES

Martin Seligman describes strengths as values in action.[34] 31Practices is about putting values into action, every day. Supporting organizations to identify their own values provides the consistent building blocks for an organization's practices and processes and language to create a strengths-based culture.[35]

Supporting employees to identify their values-based connection with the organization they work for would enable people to exploit and optimize their prevalent strengths and contribution to the organization in a way that is more purposeful than transactional.

Greater clarity of the values that an organization stands for, and the ways in which "things are done around here", enables greater choice for employees and potential employees. No matter how fantastic a person is on paper, they can only bring their best in an environment and context that enables them to bring their strengths forward. Work on values demonstrates that misalignment of personal and organizational values leads to suboptimal performance.[36] Working within a framework of strengths yields more positive emotion with the benefits that that brings.

STRENGTHS EXERCISES

How do you create an environment where you can flourish? Where you enable others to flourish? Where you are able to bring your resources and resourcefulness? Where you can optimize your collective strengths? Here are two sets of exercises, one focused on you and one focused on your strengths focus with others. Harnessing your strengths first requires you to become aware of your strengths and the resources you hold within yourself.

Increase your experience of positive emotions, appreciation of your resources and use of your strengths

"Be the change that you want to see in the world"
Mahatma Gandhi[37]

Three good things: At the end of each day, just reflect on three good things that you appreciate about the day – note them down.

Hero/heroine moments: Identify a personal "sparkling moment" in your life over the past few months, a moment when you felt in flow, performing to your best, having the impact that you wanted. Note down the details:
- *What was it about the moment that made it sparkle for you?*
- *What do you remember most about yourself at that moment?*
- *What might others have noticed about you in that moment?*
- *What else?*

What are you really pleased about as you reflect on this moment?
Repeat this 2-3 times, until you have a small collection of sparkling moments to review. Keep the sparkling moments safe and accessible. Review and add to them frequently.

Identify and use your character strengths: Martin Seligman identified 24 character strengths. Complete the VIA strengths inventory and identify your signature strengths (the top 5) at www.viastrengths.org.
Once identified, put your strengths (or values) into practice daily.

Expanding to the wider organization

Invest in your relationships: Map out your key relationships (work and/or home). What is the ratio of positive to negative comments that you give to each of those relationships? Note that down on your map.

Which relationships are below the "Losada line" (have less than three positives for every one negative)?

Focus on raising the number of appreciative and positive comments for those relationships in danger – what happens?

When you start a meeting: Start with three good things. If you are chairing, share the three good things that have happened and invite others to do the same.

Performance review – if you are receiving a performance review or conducting one for somebody else, focus on strengths and see what the results are.

If a member of the team is not so strong in an area, think of somebody else who is and see if they can help.

Want to know more?

As you may notice, working with strengths and happiness are not unrelated. As Ronald D. Siegel points out, Positive Psychology is the scientific study of Happiness. Working from a "strengths-based perspective" is a core area of study for positive psychology and happiness.

- A robust book on the subject of strengths is: Martin Seligman (2002). *Authentic Happiness: Using the new positive psychology to realise your potential for deep fulfilment.* London: Nicholas Brealey Publishing.
- Martin Seligman's work exploring signature strengths and how people use their strengths has culminated in some useful global research and a number of "strengths" profiling tools. Some of these are free for individuals to use and can be accessed through: www.viastrengths.org.

CHAPTER 18   DISCIPLINE

"Preparing others to live a life of success and happiness… starts with discipline."

Lou Holtz[1]

The word "discipline" is derived from the Latin root disciplinare (to teach). It is about instilling values and behaviour through positive learning, shaping or correcting behaviour. It's about setting norms and limits and training,[2] perhaps to follow a specific teaching or code. Linked to discipline is disciple – someone who, of their own free will, chooses to follow a master, a guru, a teacher. Who or what are you a disciple of? What systematic instruction, training or code of conduct are you choosing to follow?

Discipline is a mark of love and compassion, not punishment.[3] This story from Lou Holtz of two men and their dogs is a good illustration.

"Let me cite an example of two young men, each of whom owned a new puppy. The first one loved the dog and showered it with love and affection. Anything the dog wanted to do was okay. There were no restrictions on the dog.

"The other young man loved his puppy also, but he put a choke collar on the dog. Anytime the dog did something he wasn't supposed to, the choke collar took effect. It wasn't long before the dog realized there were limitations on his freedom. A year later, the man took the choke collar off the dog and gave it great freedom. The dog ran around the neighbourhood and everyone loved it. The reason the dog was given freedom was because the owner knew it would respond to his commands. It would not bite, destroy or abuse its

freedom because it understood what would and would not be tolerated.[4]

"*The man who showered his dog with love could never allow the dog any freedom because it wouldn't respond to any commands, nor did it understand that there were always limitations on what could and could not be tolerated.*"

Developing discipline facilitates the development of responsibility. Relying on others to tell you what to do and how to do it leaves you helpless, unconcerned about what the right thing to do is and ignoring the consequences of your actions (well, you're not responsible for them, you were just following instructions!).

Developing discipline puts you in the driving seat of your experiences, both physically and emotionally. You are more keenly aware of the impact and consequences of your choices. Choosing your own path, rather than letting others determine it for you, leads to greater confidence, health, resilience and happiness.

"In reading the lives of great men, I found that the first victory they won was over themselves... self-discipline with all of them came first."

Harry S. Truman[5]

Developing discipline does get you past imposed limitations – whether you impose them on yourself or accept the limitations that others have for you.

One of Walt Disney's often quoted statements is: *"If you can dream it, you can do it"*, but only when you have the discipline to turn those dreams into reality. At the Disney Institute, development programmes share Disney's secrets with a vast array of other businesses. At first, senior executives were concerned but they eventually concluded there was no risk because no one else had the same level of discipline. No one else worked as hard as Disney to do what they did.

"I believe everybody is creative and everybody is talented. I just don't think that everybody is disciplined. I think that's a rare commodity."

Al Hirschfield[6]

This idea of getting past limitations is echoed in the world of martial arts – discipline equates to "emptiness" or the absence of fear, hatred, anxiety, arrogance. As focus and attention improve, there is a greater feeling of power, peace of mind, wisdom and love. In martial arts, first you learn to notice yourself. Then you must look at things with non-judgement... only then are you able to understand the mind and finally learn to let go.[7] This is the goal of disciplined practice.

Leaders at every level in an organization have a significant role embodying and teaching organizational disciplines and modelling organizational practices – and those at the very top of the organization set the benchmark. It's not easy to create a disciplined environment, where people can enjoy success and gain confidence – but it can be very effective. A disciplined approach fosters trust, confidence in the organization, team productivity, a desire to achieve and a clear sense of "the way things work around here".

Purposeful discipline, paradoxically, seems to make life easier.

"Most powerful is he who has himself in his own power."
Seneca[8]

DEVELOPING AND SUSTAINING DISCIPLINE

"I am an ordinary man who worked hard to develop the talent I was given."
Muhammad Ali[9]

Self-discipline is a type of selective training, creating new habits of thought and behaviour toward improving yourself and reaching goals. Self-discipline is a positive effort. It's about mental training and working hard.

No sustained success, achievement, or goal can be realized without some level of discipline. It is singularly the most important attribute needed to achieve excellence or outstanding performance. The absence of immediate pay-off is what makes discipline elusive. Consider the Olympic champion training on Christmas Day or the executive studying for exams after finishing a gruelling day. Consciously learning a new discipline in service of a particular outcome is about mental training and working hard.

The starting point: Defining your purpose
Discipline and motivation are the yin and yang of success. You are motivated towards success, yet you create the road to success by the disciplines that you put into place.

What is the purpose of the discipline? What is the goal you are striving to attain? Greater happiness? Spiritual awakening? Reaching an organizational vision? Creating a brand?

Discipline without purpose has a clear danger of running to rigidity, reducing creativity and innovation, stifling growth and ignoring what might be seeking to emerge.

Once you've clarified your purpose – it's then about creating discipline to deliver. More is written in Chapter 5, *Purpose*.

Creating discipline

- Learn how to focus your mind and energy on your goals and to keep going until they are realized. Use visualization techniques to clarify what you're aiming for. These techniques are used by high-achievers and top athletes. By imagining the future in great detail, they can start to "feel" how rewarding it is to achieve that success, get a sense of the benefits and understand more clearly the path that will get them there.

  Muhammad Ali used this "Future History" technique to say that he never climbed into the ring to face somebody he had not already beaten (through visualization).

- Start small – one step at a time. If you're keen to build more effective working relationships, create a space of 15 minutes to speak to one of the key people that you interact with in your role. Connecting with just one person from across your network each day will support you to build stronger and more personalized relationships. People often make the mistake of creating big goals which are unrealistic and never get actioned.

- Cultivate a mindset where deliberate choices determine behaviour rather than simply reacting to emotions, circumstances, or other people. Practice saying "No" to feelings and impulses. Pause, breathe and reflect before taking action. Together these practices help to build a habit of keeping things under control. Try waiting an hour to open an email for no reason other than to exercise your willpower. Endure temporary discomfort with the purpose of greater gain at a later date. See Chapters 13, *Mindfulness* and 14, *Resilience* for more on these topics.

"Self-discipline begins with the mastery of your thoughts. If you don't control what you think, you can't control what you do. Simply, self-discipline enables you to think first and act afterward."

Napoleon Hill[10]

- Create an environment that makes the desired discipline easier and more pleasurable than the procrastination. Remove temptations (like the desk drawer of sweets and treats). Instead, surround yourself with inspiration and encouragement – photos of what you want to achieve or your "gurus" or a phrase that particularly resonates with you.
- Develop your mental strength by deliberately creating uncomfortable circumstances to test yourself. From your task list each day, do the most difficult first, the most stressful, the most challenging. Put yourself forward for a development programme that you will find stretching. Volunteer for those meetings that you find difficult.
- Support the habit of discipline by engaging in sport, craft or activity that requires discipline – whether it's joining a sports team, learning a musical instrument or studying a new language.

Keeping going[11]

Celebrate achievement and success to motivate more of the same. Pat yourself on the back for what has been achieved. Appreciate those you work with and their achievements. As an organization, record and celebrate what has been achieved.

Deal with procrastination immediately. Do what you said you would do, staying the course, regardless of any challenges, temptations or procrastination. Willpower goes up and down with energy levels. Learn what energizes you, don't allow yourself to justify shortcomings. Choosing not to follow a particular discipline once (although easily justifiable) becomes twice and more. A downward spiral away from the chosen goal has begun.

If you want to build relationships across your network – and you let one monthly call to a colleague slip due to work pressures, it doesn't seem so bad really – just one call. Similarly if you let one deadline flex, it's likely to be met with understanding. While individually you might allow your disciplines to flex to circumstances, how much are you really kidding yourself? It's too easy to give up on our disciplines due to "work pressure". If you give up on the principle that leads to achieving your goal, then you will never make the change that you want to make. The more you can stick to your disciplines, the likelihood is that you will enjoy the benefits of that focus more quickly.

Routinize everything that you can, for example, developing a network of colleagues could involve setting reminders to send an email or making a call first thing, just before a lunch break and last thing before going home. Similarly, bad habits can be eliminated by deliberately creating good habits. Precommitment,[12] deliberately avoiding the bad habit in the first place is demonstrated to be more effective than willpower alone for developing good habits. Deliberately set your watch five minutes fast to arrive at meetings on time. The same applies to organizations – create routines around meeting schedules, formats, and behavioural norms.

An organization requires discipline to deliver the right experience to stakeholders. This was personally experienced when working in five-star hotels. As an assistant manager, the first job every day was to visit each of the conference rooms to ensure the rooms were set up correctly. This included making sure that every pencil on every writing pad at every place setting was at the right angle, logo facing upwards.

It is this discipline to ensure the correct standard and attention to detail is delivered every single time that sets Disney and other organizations apart from the majority.

DISCIPLINE AND 31PRACTICES

31Practices provides a framework, enabling practices and disciplines to be formed across the organization that brings the values and purpose of an organization to life. It is the discipline of focusing every day on one aspect of a value through the way you behave. Celebrating success is part of the methodology – supervisors, team leaders and department heads are encouraged to nominate those who live the 31Practices excellently. It is most effective when the 31Practices are built into all aspects of the organization's operating platform, creating the routines that are required to support the ongoing discipline of 31Practices.

The discipline throughout the organization that 31Practices creates where every employee takes an action each day helps embed the Practices more quickly and create a virtuous circle of positive reinforcement.

As noted above, creating an environment that enables people to be disciplined is a challenge – leaders perhaps have to display strong personal disciplines to align themselves with what they are asking others to step up to.

Exercise to support you to develop discipline

How can you as a leadership team develop your own disciplines that will enable a disciplined environment? There is more than one way, but we hope that this simple approach will start the ball rolling.

- What is it that you are striving to achieve as a team? What's the change you want to make?
- Explore the small, perhaps the smallest thing that each of you can do each day that will lead to you moving closer to the change you want to see. Each decide on a task that you are going to do at a certain time of the day that will take the team towards that goal. You don't necessarily have to all do your tasks at the same time. Make it work for you.
- Stick to the schedule for at least two months. Once you've got the hang of this, do more of those things that will support you to achieve the change.
- Keep a record of what you've achieved through the small tasks you've completed – it builds quickly over time.
- Harness the power of routine – build on habits that already occur. When you log on to your PC, reflect on yesterday's achievements or if you drink coffee, make that first cup the time to write out and prioritize your tasks for the day ahead. Share as a team when you come together what has been achieved, where you have moved to.
- Share with other team members what works to help set and create disciplines.
- Review the change you have set yourself. Do you need to refocus? Is there something else emerging that you need to integrate into the change you're achieving?

  In this way, you are going round a cycle of identifying, practising and reflecting on the disciplines you are creating to generate a change, and refocusing/reviewing/refining the changes you are making as you go round the cycle.

Want to know more?

The work of Charles Duhigg on habits probably fits best here as a resource. An engaging writer, he brings the three golden elements of habit formation to life – helping you to understand how to change unwanted habits.

- Charles Duhigg (2012). *The Power of Habit: Why we do what we do in life and business*. Random House
- Chip Heath and Dan Heath (2010). *Switch: How to change things when change is hard*. London: Random House.

PART **4**

THE BROADER CONTEXT

The fourth part of this book highlights why 31Practices makes sense now as a methodology. What makes it particularly relevant at this point and how the 31Practices method fits given the context organizations find themselves in. In Chapters 19–24 we explore *Complexity*, *Change*, *Wisdom*, *Neuroscience*, *Choice* and *Leadership*.

These are common "headlines" in the business world, each one a meaty topic in its own right. Making some sense of these concepts in terms of the practical day-to-day decisions and situations we are faced with is important, in our view.

In Part 3, we have described how our world as individuals is flexible and how we can change how we see, think, feel and act if we choose to do so. In other words, our experience is in a large part made-up, subjective, rather than an objective reality that we can all agree upon. In Part 4, we build on this idea of flexibility and introduce the idea of a systems view, all parts of a system are dependent in some way on each other. Organizations are not fixed entities. The people in organizations act and respond in turn to an ever changing set of circumstances. In a world that is emerging rather than fixed, a style of thinking and working that can navigate this complexity is likely to help people and organizations to thrive.

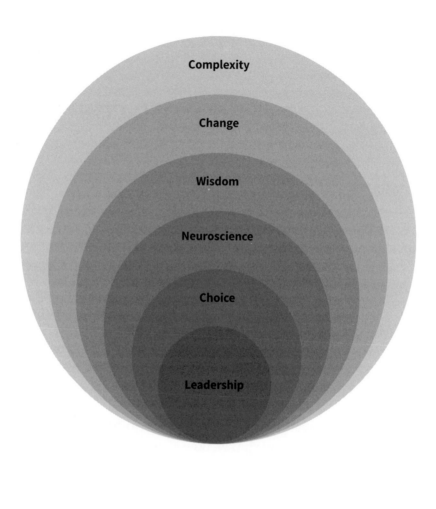

Part 4 moves from the macro to the micro and back out again – from the big picture of complexity down to the inner workings of our physical brain, and outwards again following our moment by moment choices as leaders and leadership. We are complex systems,[1] constantly changing and responding to our internal and external environments. We don't exist in isolation, we exist in relationship to dynamic situations people and ideas. Existing within multiple complex systems as we do requires us to develop personal wisdom to survive and thrive. We have endless choices about what we think, feel and do at any given time. These moment by moment choices create the person we are at any moment in time.

The chapter on Leadership could easily sit apart on its own – certainly, there has been enough written about the subject over the years. Our view of leadership is as part of a system and doesn't exist in isolation. It fits firmly within this part of the book. At the same time, Leadership draws on all of the underpinnings shared in Part 3.

Our intention in sharing these subjects through our 31Practices lens is that we are both provocative and pragmatic, leaving you with greater clarity and confidence about how you are choosing to be.

"In the business world, the rearview mirror is always clearer than the windshield."

Warren Buffett[2]

19

CHAPTER 19   COMPLEXITY

"Snowflakes are one of nature's most fragile things, but just look at what they can do when they stick together."

Source unknown

Organizations are complex adaptive systems. They consist of interconnected, interwoven parts or sets of things that work together as part of a mechanism or interconnecting and dynamic network.[1] Ralph Stacey[2], an eminent figure in the field of complexity, points out that all human systems are "self-organizing" and not open to control. Interactions between humans are co-created and emergent, with multiple possible outcomes at each point of engagement.

A complex environment consists of any number of competing factors, combinations of agents and potential outcomes.[3]

Let's bring this idea of complexity into concrete reality. Just pause and imagine the day in front of you. What are the things competing for your attention? What are the different roles of each of the people you interact with? What different levels of responsibility do you have for the tasks on your plate? What are the multiple contexts within which each of those people, tasks, roles exist? What might the impact be for any one of those people or tasks depending on how you engage with what's needed? Get the picture?

The picture is constantly shifting, depending on what is changing in the relationships between each of the component parts. If I choose to respond to the email requesting a decision about a simple project, other people take action, an output is generated, something now exists that didn't exist before, the system adapts and the patterns recur again and again. It's a bit like looking at life as if it were a kaleidoscope – seeing things shift and move radically as a result of a small movement somewhere in the system.

From this perspective of complexity, very small interventions or chance occurrences in one interaction can have very large, unpredictable or unknown effects. As James Gleick described, the butterfly effect – tiny differences in input can quickly become overwhelming differences in output – a butterfly stirring the air today in Peking can transform storm systems next month in New York.[4]

One small example of the butterfly effect that springs to mind happened very recently. Alex, the head of a function in a very hierarchical organization, was heard musing that it might be a good idea to deploy two people from one departmental team elsewhere to support a project for a short time. No sooner than the words had escaped his mouth, the rumours began, and anxiety started to spread in the department where the two people were currently employed. Eventually, the "decision" (as it had now become) to deploy people out of his team reached Connor, the head of the department in question. A meeting was arranged and through some careful exploration and discussion between Alex and Connor, the decision that had never been made was reversed. What started as an innocent thought spoken out loud had some significantly bigger and unintended consequences for individuals across part of the organization.

Another example is from the restaurant sector. A facelift and new menu had been introduced to a restaurant in London to make it more "current". The changes had been well received by customers and early signs were positive that there would be a significant increase in sales and profitability. One of the senior executives of the owning company visited for lunch and, as he was leaving, mentioned to the local managing director that he thought there could be more grill items on the menu. As a result of this comment, a decision was made to change the menu concept completely to become grill based. What was the impact? For a period, the restaurant was less busy until the menu balance was restored. Just as importantly, the new direction completely demotivated a number of the leadership team who had been responsible for developing the successful new menu concept that the senior executive had commented on.

An example of complexity in action familiar to us all is the viral impact of social media. Those calling for change in the Arab Uprisings in spring and summer of 2011 used social media channels to raise global awareness of events and conditions in countries along the north of Africa and into the Middle East. The viral and uncontrolled use of social media perhaps facilitated a quicker (although not necessarily easier) pathway to change than otherwise might have been the case.

The rise of social media and indeed community platforms in the workplace act as an accelerant for complex processes. In practice, this means that a different, more nimble, skilled and open approach to leadership and management is needed. Achieving effective outcomes is more about people interacting to arrive at an end goal, with a need to adapt to any changes on the way and the ability to add new thinking as it emerges. The approach to making a product where certain people do certain things at certain times as efficiently as possible is no longer fit for purpose and has a limited application.

In the 2010 IBM survey[5] of executives, CEOs noted their primary challenge was operating in an increasingly complex, volatile and uncertain world. And almost exactly half of these high-achievers felt ill-equipped to personally manage the challenge of this complexity and succeed.

A very insightful point was made by Donald Schön[6] decades before: *"managers do not solve problems, they manage messes"*. He points out that problems are extracted from messes by managers through the process of analysis.

Even the problems in front of us are only present from a particular perspective.

SO WHAT?

What does this all mean and what sense can we usefully make of complexity thinking to navigate everyday situations? Here we draw out some core ideas and principles a little further.

Relationships

Complexity thinking offers a radical relational view of the natural world.[7] From this view, things exist in relation to other things and relationships are a core part of the way that we understand the world. Taken a little further, through local interactions (micro interactions) and micro behaviours, big patterns and events unfold and occur.

The reality that we experience is self-organizing, dynamic and emergent.

The parts of a system are forever influencing and being influenced. In sum, the elements of the world exist through their relationships with other elements. We experience the world as sets of related elements and things happen as a result of the relationships between things.

Let's take an example that purposefully changes the view of the relationship we have to each other. Peter Hawkins shares a mantra he uses as he travels on the underground rail network in London.[8] Rather than viewing the people he is thrown together with as strangers, instead he uses the practice of repeatedly reminding himself as he passes people *"you are my brother; you are my sister"*. Have a go yourself when in a crowded space, there is almost a physical shift in your posture as your perspective of the relationship changes.

From a complexity perspective, paying attention to your relationships and how things are connected really is core to enabling things to emerge. The small things you affect in your relationships with others are the root of larger patterns and shifts.

As a different example, take the organization of an event. There is an enormous amount of background preparation that can stretch for 12 months or longer before the event itself, involving teams of people that each have a very small part to play in the creation of the larger whole. How those relationships between the parts emerge can make a significant difference to the experience of organizing the event, the eventual output and the experience of clients on the day.

This relational perspective can be a challenge to understand. In the west, the tendency is to view ourselves as separate to others. But, as individuals, we are actually defined (individually and organizationally) through our interactions with other people and other things.

A view based on our relationship to others emphasizes paying attention to "how" you operate, not necessarily the technical knowledge (the "what") that you bring.

Linearity vs. Chaos

One of the core assumptions that remains pervasively embedded is that things can be reduced down to linear relationships between different things, that these can be measured "objectively", and things can be controlled and predicted with certainty. This assumption of linearity and rationality is a dominant factor in the workings of organizations with little attention paid to the science of self-organization that happens in complex systems, coexisting with the law of linearity. All systems are self-organizing and imposed linearity will be ultimately self-organized and what appears chaotic will fall into or have a self-organizing pattern.

For anyone reading this who's rolled out a process across an organization, there is a familiar chime to the refrain *"well, we know that this was intended to be operated in this particular way, but we've adapted it, as in reality this is how it works best here"*. For a project manager this is frustrating; for a brand, this could be disastrous. So if we accepted the self-organizing nature of systems, how can we build this consideration into process development and project management?

How can you clarify the outcome and vision sufficiently, and create the principles around which a system can self-organize, so that the outcome is aligned and enabled within a particular context?

Feedback loops

It's argued that systems exist in balance and all attempts at change are pulled back towards a general state of equilibrium. The idea of feedback loops is a bit different – Ilya Prigogine[9] talks about positive and negative feedback loops. Positive feedback loops are catalysts which enhance tendencies, and negative feedback loops dampen those down. There are many biological processes which use the output of one positive loop as the input into another positive loop (a self-catalytic loop).

Let's imagine how this might apply to organizations. Take for example, Jo, a local authority director, who has been asked to take responsibility for delivering a particular piece of work by her colleague Mark. In the past, Jo would have said yes, but then would have struggled to deliver due to her very high workload. As a result she would have been depleting her own personal resources though lack of sleep and stress, she would be likely to have missed the deadline, or be too rushed to do the job she would have liked to have done, and possibly failed to do as good a job as expected with her other commitments.

What might have started as a positive is dampened by the reality of the experience of delivering, and the trust and professional relationship between Jo and Mark suffers.

Lets imagine Jo has said *"No"*, shared the reasons why and offered Mark some alternatives. What was a positive decision for Jo and for Mark then builds the relationship between Jo and Mark, increasing the level of trust and certainty between them, leading to a further positive experience. Perhaps an example of a self-catalytic loop.

What positive feedback loops are you creating today? What are you dampening down, reducing, due to a negative feedback loop (real or imagined)? What needs to shift to create more positive energy?

Fractals and patterns

Fractals are irregular, similar (but not always exactly identical) patterns across different scales or sizes. Think about the leaf of a fern or bracken, or a Romanesque broccoli – these are great examples of fractals found in the natural world. In the organizational world, think about the pattern of behaviour of those at the core of the seat of government and how that is reproduced across the different levels of government and out across society. The behaviour of the executive team in a business and how they interact is mirrored throughout the layers of the organization and at the level of one-to-one interactions.

Let's imagine a team heading up a significant part of a global organization. The senior lead is someone who is extremely task-focused, meticulous and detailed. He appreciates the people side, but is not naturally geared to think about the "human side" of business. He doesn't share much about himself personally and doesn't praise people for what they have done well (the assumption is that you are competent and know how good you are, so you don't need to be told). The entire organization is task-focused, it's important to be right and get it done, and at a time of significant change, people are fearful and risk averse. The best way for more junior people to get things done is to delegate upwards as the attention to detail and meticulous quality at the top will "catch" any errors. To shift the culture to one where each person is comfortable taking responsibility, working more creatively and "loosening" some of the fear, less risk-averse behaviour is needed to build the "humanity" – and that means supporting the senior leader to catch himself and to emphasize the people side at every opportunity until it becomes a personal habit and a pattern that is emulated throughout.

You look at a really big system and look down at a really tiny system and see the patterns, not identical, but similar being played out. What you do is important.

From this perspective, what are the patterns that you are creating around you?

WORKING WITHIN COMPLEXITY

Lesley Kuhn[10] offers some ways of working using a complexity perspective which we apply directly here as an aid to consciously working with the complexity around you. We hope that in doing so, we have not taken liberties with Lesley's original intentions.

First, rather than offer recipes or follow the recipes of others, generate your own carefully considered approaches, paying attention to what is happening around you and the quality of relationships at your fingertips.

Second, develop complexity "habits of thought". Rather than forcing yourself to see linearity and cause and effect, notice the interactions, the chain of reactions that follows an event. Look for patterns in things. How are things self-organizing? Where are the self-catalytic loops that are generative, where are the negative dampening effects? What is generative in one space and dampening in another?

Third, be careful not to describe things as they "should be" rather than as they are. Pay attention to what really is happening now rather than what "should be" happening.

Fourth, value humility. No one idea is completely right – as history repeatedly shows. So be curious about how others can support an idea to emerge.

Taken together, these ways of working offer principles (not rigid rules) that can be self-resourcing, and prevent you from falling into the trap of seeing yourself as all-powerful, in control – a heroic leader. As a result, you are more able to see more clearly what might be happening around you. Being able to notice what is emerging is likely to give you some flexibility and nimbleness to navigate the systems you operate within – as well as catch yourself, before you inadvertently set off your own unintended butterfly effect.

COMPLEXITY AND 31PRACTICES

31Practices is not "the answer" to working with complexity, but it is a way to self-author and generate your own recipe for a successful organizational framework, bringing to life the organization values. 31Practices is in synergy with the idea of fractals, the natural interrelated world, that things are emergent and self-organized, and the self-catalytic loops.

The 31Practices methodology supports you to identify your purpose and vision and the principles or values that will enable you to work towards that vision. Each value translates into a set of daily Practices that is performed at a local, individual level and repeated across the organization – creating a visible pattern.

Different parts of the organization are involved in the design of the framework, and ultimately, each individual chooses "how" to live the Practice of the day – choosing what action to take that is linked to the Practice – while being mindful of the overall directional impact they are looking to have.

Once the 31Practices framework is created it is then enabled in organizational routines – allowing things to emerge, with built-in positive feedback loops as stories of behaviours and impact are shared. There are some embedded principles within 31Practices that may resonate with complexity thinking and be of significant, pragmatic use in organizations.

Want to know more?

Writings on complexity can be challenging reads. Among one of the seminal thinkers in this area was Gregory Bateson. If you are interested in reading his work (which is at the "for enthusiasts" end of the spectrum):

- *Mind and Nature: A necessary unity (advances in systems theory, complexity and the human sciences)*. Hampton Press. The 2002 version is a reissue of this classic work.
- For a short introduction to his work there is a video clip on YouTube: http://www.youtube.com/watch?v=AqiHJG2wtPI

CHAPTER 20 CHANGE

"And then one day you find
Ten years have got behind you
No one told you when to run
You missed the starting gun".

Pink Floyd[1]

Change is happening all the time. Change, in its broadest sense, means to cause something to be different (for example, in form, content, future course).[2] This broad definition includes change that requires conscious thought as well as changes that occur by chance.

"Life is like riding a bicycle. To keep your balance you must keep moving"

Albert Einstein[3]

From our perspective, awareness enables change. Once you are aware of where you are (warts and all), change is possible. When you're trying to pretend you're in a different place, you get stuck. This entire book is about change at some level. Through the preceding chapters we have encouraged you to be the shift you are keen to see by raising your awareness. In Part 2 of the book, the focus is on raising your awareness of the purpose you are striving to achieve and from that, the principles that will guide you to that end. Part 3 is designed to raise awareness of your thinking, your emotions and your behaviours. Through this enhanced awareness, you can consider whether they are serving you well – and what would serve you better. Part 4 explores the context that we are in and change at a macro and micro level – from complexity to neuroscience. Much has been written already.

Change is constant and inevitable – it always has been. Did you know that most of the cells in your body are on average only between seven and ten years old? Your cells are in a constant state of flux.[4] This idea of continuous change also underpins our view of the world and our place in it. We don't see an objective reality, we see what we expect to see – and our world view is constantly reinterpreted in the light of new experiences – at any one moment of time, we see things differently to how they were before.[5]

"Nothing endures but change."

Heraclitus[6]

Just recently, a client shared a story about his aged grandfather's passing. For more than 20 years, there had been bitterness between two sides of the family about the inheritance of the family estate, which the grandfather had gifted to his youngest daughter. After his grandfather's death, my client realized on speaking to the youngest daughter what the real cost of that inheritance had been. She had spent the last 25 years of her life as a devoted carer to her father – and in her words, had lost her life from her late twenties through to her early fifties. The bitterness evaporated immediately and the 25 years of pain and hurt were immediately reconfigured in the light of this new awareness.

And yet, we hold on to the idea that things stay the same, we build routines and habits of thinking – creating some sense of certainty against these constant internal and external fluctuations. We are hard-wired to see patterns – to make things connect. This hardwiring enables us to make decisions and navigate what would otherwise be an incomprehensible world.

On top of this changing baseline, there are the actions that we purposefully take to redirect events and make changes to suit our needs.

A colleague was brought up in the South West of England and had a broad, local accent, as did most of his friends. At 16 he believed his accent would cause others to see him as "slow" and "rural", and it would be a disadvantage at university and in business. He made a simple decision "to lose the accent" and started copying people who spoke the way he wanted to speak. Through practice, sometimes with more success than others, eventually the strong accent was lost. This conscious change, brought about by deliberately doing something different, will have led to changes in his perspective, resulting in changes (planned and unplanned) unfolding in his life that would be impossible to track. Did anyone choose to (or not to) employ, befriend or spend time with this person as a result of his accent? No one will ever know.

Change happens within a system and one change in that system (losing the accent, a family member dying) ripples out into the system and those ripples bounce back, providing feedback to the person who made the change in the first place.

Many of the day to day incremental changes that take place go completely unnoticed, undetected. Yet those changes are core to the bigger changes that we aim for. Capturing those small shifts those daily movements towards a different future is key to tracking progress.

Purposeful change in organizations is possible but bby no means straightforward. If you've ever had the role of driving and leading a change project, you will appreciate the challenge of engineering change in a complex system. Change needs leading from the front and supporting from behind. Often, rather than one big change, you get a series of small shifts that become self-reinforcing. This cycle of reinforcement amplifies the small changes taking place, ultimately leading to a felt difference.

What's easier to change at the organizational level includes the structures, the written processes, the actual people occupying particular roles. The tricky bit is to bring about a change in how people behave, to shift ways of working, habits of thinking and doing, and to change attitudes. It's easy to bring in a new process. And it's just as easy for people to ignore the new process, to find a workaround. This difficulty with engineering change is not because people are deliberately obstinate, it's because it's often easier to keep doing what has always been done – and until that balance changes, and the new behaviour is easier than the old one, the old behaviour won't change.

CHANGING PEOPLE IS PERSONAL

*"Change has a considerable psychological impact on
the human mind. To the fearful it is threatening because
it means that things may get worse. To the hopeful it
is encouraging because things may get better. To the
confident it is inspiring because the challenge exists to
make things better."*

King Whitney Jr.[7]

There are many ideas about how change happens and an equal number of
examples indicating how those ideas have failed at some level, somewhere.

This is because how people change is individual and personal. Each of
us approaches change with a set of beliefs about change, about how easy
or difficult a particular change will be, what we personally want to change
or are prepared to change, a set of habits, a context and a set of resources
that enable change to happen or keep us entrenched in current patterns.

Consider Sally, who has "given up smoking" at least 20 times in the
last five years. It would be reasonable to assume that her belief includes *"I
cannot change my smoking habit"*; *"I will always start smoking again, I just
can't persevere long enough"*; *"It's too hard"*.

Let's imagine another person, Les, who moves jobs every two to three
years. When facing a new job, he is excited and optimistic, looking forward
to the new challenges ahead. His beliefs might be along the lines of *"I relish
changing jobs, I look forward to the new learning and understanding I gain".*

And, imagine a third person, Kate, who has to move from a location
she's worked in for 20 years, to a new site, with a new team, to deliver a
reformatted service. She's not slept well since she received the news of the
move three months ago and her performance has dipped at work. Kate's
beliefs might be along the lines of: *"I'm terrified of starting with newco"*; *"I
am not getting a lot of sleep – I wish I was still working for my old company".*

Three personal experiences and belief sets that lead to different
expectations and divergent responses to the changes ahead.

*"It's not that some people have willpower and some
don't. It's that some people are ready to change and
others are not."*

James Gordon[8]

CREATING THE INFRASTRUCTURE AND PLANNING FOR CHANGE: WHAT DO THE EXPERTS SAY?

From systems thinking and complexity theory, we are told what we already know – managing change is not an exact science. The destination imagined at the start is unlikely to be where you end up, and what happens along the way is rarely expected at the outset.

Change frameworks such as those put forward by John Kotter[9] or Jeanenne LaMarsh and Rebecca Potts[10] are incredibly useful. These frameworks don't provide all the answers by any means, but they can offer insight into the necessary infrastructures that support a directional change.

What can you do to make a planned change more likely to happen?[11]

Clarity of vision: *What is the reason for the change? Why bother? What happens if you don't do anything?* Not only is it important to clarify the reason for change, but what does good look like? Not just the organizational vision, but what will the employment process be like in the "new world", what will the communication be like? What will the reward and recognition processes be like?

Awareness and acceptance of the current state of things: *What is the starting point? How are things now? What are the structures in the organization like, what's the culture, what are the capabilities of people, what processes are in place?* It's easy to set off without being clear about where you are starting from, caught up in the excitement of the possibilities promised by the future vision.

Change roles: *Who are the sponsors?* Naturally, sponsorship at the most senior level helps, and for an organization-wide change, is necessary. Potential sponsors, though, exist at every level of leadership and management across the organization – they may not all be on board at the start, or even at the end, so how do you engage across this population? A key role of the sponsors is to remove obstacles.

Who are the change agents? Who will be given specific responsibility to make the change happen? Who are the targets of the change? What is it that they need to change? Everyone is a target in the change process, no one can stay the same when the organization is changing around them. All targets to some extent will feel uneasy, self-conscious, thinking first about what they have to give up, not what they'll gain. When a situation is ambiguous, we look to our leaders, peers, colleagues to provide clues as to how to behave – if the senior leaders are behaving in line with the vision, the vision is more likely to be seen as important and to follow suit. Similarly, those who've been given a formal role as a "change agent" will be under particular scrutiny.

Communication: How and what you communicate is critical. You need to be credible and trusted, bring personal stories and engage people at an emotional level to have impact. Communication is two-way – and not only is it important for people to be heard, but important for them to know that their views and perspective have been heard and actually considered.[12]

Aligning the safety net – empowering action: Doing something different is risky and uncomfortable. If you don't support the changes you want to see – when they start to happen, if, for example, you blame someone for doing something wrong as they try a different approach – old habits will be reinstated. People will go straight back to doing what they've always done – because it's comfortable and more familiar. As a leader of change, share the challenges, difficulties, mistakes you came across (whether real or imagined), praise and support when you see others starting to step up to the new way of doing things – even when they don't get it right.

As well as the personal support you give – align the systems. Align reward and recognition, learning and development and communications directly to support the change that you are introducing. These systems need to positively reinforce the behaviours that you want to see and not give any reinforcement to old habits you're trying to shift. These systems are the cornerstones of the prevailing organizational culture, with each one holding the other in check.

Working with resistance: During change, people go through a series of emotions as they transition the stages from shock and denial that any change is required, to a position where they are able to integrate new ways of being and doing into their repertoire.[13] Resistance is something to engage with, rather than be squashed or limited. What can be learned from resistance, what improvements might the conversations deliver? Approaching resistance with a mindset of enquiry "What's really going on here?" might just be incredibly helpful in ensuring that the change stays on track.

"What you resist, persists."

Carl Gustav Jung[14]

CHANGE AND 31PRACTICES

Clarity of vision: The start point for 31Practices is to clarify the organization's purpose; the purpose being something that is motivating and energizing, that people can engage with at an emotional level and get behind. Within the organization's market niche, what is it that the organization wants to achieve, to deliver, to be known for? Getting this right will create the sense of urgency, the energy around a shared endeavour. Clarification of the values provides the guiding principles.

Change roles: Creating the sponsors and change agents is not only about engaging the senior leadership team; it's also about creating a nominated group across hierarchy and function as guides and allies. These are the people who are closest to the front-line people, working alongside them every day. Together they form a network of "change nodes" throughout the organization.

Aligning the safety net – empowering action: The co-creation workshops for front-line employees provide the input for creating the wording of the 31Practices. When the 31Practices set is reviewed and finalized, a carry card is printed and becomes part of the uniform standard. This communication phase is revisited as stories of impact are shared individually and organizationally, and become part of the fabric of the organization.

31Practices works best when it is connected to a recognition programme. Recognition plays a key role in socializing how the Practices are being adopted, and the impact they have. This positively reinforces the behaviours, encouraging others to follow and the associated stories become part of the organization heritage.

One of the key elements of 31Practices is that people make the choice as to how they are going to "live" the Practice of the day. Each daily Practice is organization-wide, but what each person does to demonstrate that Practice is entirely up to them.

The core values of the organization are embedded into the decision framework for the organization: supporting decision making, prioritization and other day-to-day choices. For 31Practices, various actions take place so that they become part of day-to-day operational process. These activities can range from translating 31Practices into a set of questions to be used at interview, to formulating a meeting protocol, to a screensaver with the Practice for the day.

Finally, because 31Practices is an ongoing programme, it becomes the way people behave, and takes on a life of its own, becoming a way of being for the organization, emerging as the context fluctuates – building a virtuous and reinforcing cycle of behaviour.

"Everyone thinks of changing the world, but no one thinks of changing himself"

Leo Tolstoy[15]

Want to know more?

We've included three books here that offer some insights into the realms of the change literature.

- Ronald A. Heifetz (1994). *Leadership Without Easy Answers: Harvard Business Review Press*. This book explores leading through change and the challenges of leading change.
- It seems appropriate to include a reference from John Kotter, who has done so much in the field of change. His book, John P. Kotter (2012). *Leading Change*. Harvard Business Review Press, is the latest version of his international bestseller. There are also resources available on the John Kotter website: http://www.kotterinternational.com/kotterprinciples/ChangeSteps/
- For a slightly different take on the challenge of change, it's worth looking at Edgar Schein's work. Edgar H. Schein (2010). *Organisational culture and leadership*. San Francisco: Jossey-Bass.

CHAPTER 21   WISDOM

"Knowing others is intelligence;
Knowing yourself is true wisdom.
Mastering others is strength;
Mastering yourself is true power."

Lao Tzu[1]

Lao Tzu, a mystic philosopher of the Zhou Dynasty, is considered a deity in many religious forms of Taoist philosophy, and traditionally viewed as the author of the Tao Te Ching and the founder of Taoism.[2] Lao Tzu perhaps emulates all that it is to be wise.

In this book, we are taking a view of wisdom as meaning a quality of a person or people: specifically, of having experience, knowledge, and good judgement in difficult and uncertain matters of life;[3] of acting with integrity in challenging environments.[4]

A wise person is viewed as sufficiently detached from the problem at hand to make good judgements. A wise person has a well-balanced coordination of emotion, motivation and thought.[5] And, through experience, a wise person has created a habit of making the right decision and taking the right action in a particular context.[6]

The idea of the wise person, the sage, the teacher is part of the mythology of creation, and a core entity of any story – modern and ancient.[7] The search for wisdom reaches back in to the past and forward into millennia yet to come. Philosophy itself means "the love of wisdom".[8]

Wisdom is a pervasive idea and concept that transcends through time, indicating that we are continuously striving to improve. So what are the qualities of wisdom?

Wisdom isn't the same thing as knowing a lot of stuff. Knowledge and knowing things, having expertise and being knowledgeable about something are highly valued qualities. In many education systems, gaining knowledge and assessing the ability to share and apply that knowledge is rewarded through accreditation and qualification. This type of learning and this way of developing is valuable. And yet, this form of knowledge is limited, it does not make us wise. It's a starting point – but it can potentially get in the way of developing the quality of wisdom – as we need to unlearn some of these learned habits in order to allow wisdom to surface.

Wisdom is to do with knowing in different ways – knowing that comes from the experience of life – knowing about the meaning and conduct of life, knowing about uncertainties, knowing what can't be known and how to deal with limited knowledge.[9]

Wisdom is also about self-knowing and self-insight. In this book, we have explored many aspects of self-knowledge and insight in earlier chapters; in Part 3 in particular, many methods of gaining greater self-knowledge are discussed.

WISDOM IN ORGANIZATIONS

In the context of business and organizations, wisdom is a sought-after quality and part of the teaching in business schools the world over. In an environment of significant ambiguity, rapid change, greater mobility and greater information access and exchange, wise leadership is probably required more than "smart" leadership. And leadership in this context does not necessarily equate to authority or seniority – wise leadership can be demonstrated at any level of the organization.

No matter how smart, a leader cannot know the answer or the way forward in every situation that arises. The qualities of a wise leader are about knowing how to manage your own ego, how to navigate uncertainty and ambiguity and remaining open-minded as to what might emerge.

The qualities of a wise leader we suggest include:
• Tolerance and open-mindedness – aware of multiple causes and

multiple solutions in any given situation, aware of paradoxes and contradictions and ability to deal with uncertainty, inconsistency, imperfection and compromise.[10]
- Comfort with ambiguity (knowing that you don't know) – maintaining a view of the bigger picture and the implications of different outcomes.[11]
- Motivation towards the common good.
- Knowing about life, human development, interpersonal relationships; how to live life; different systems and contexts of life; tolerance for difference in values between people; and how to manage uncertainty.

How might such a wise person act in an organizational context? A wise leader might:
- Build with others – understand that the key to long-term success is to intentionally facilitate the success of others.
- Act with integrity – especially when things are not clear or easy. Looking behind what is immediately in front of them at what else might be going on.
- Be calm and self-aware, knowing when to keep quiet and consider their impact before responding – or even choosing not to respond.
- Create a win-win – rather than have the strongest argument make it easier for the other to concede, allow others to exit a debate or discussion with grace.
- Have humility, listen and change as necessary.

It sounds very appealing.

Organizations are in dire need of greater wisdom as the collective wisdom in groups tends to be lower than that of the constituent parts. Social experiments have again and again demonstrated that people behave less ethically when they are part of organizations or groups. While an individual might do the right thing in many personal situations, they behave differently in groups and when under stress. The reasons given? *"I was acting in the company's best interest"*; *"I will never be found out"*; *"I had no other choice"*. This wilful blindness[12] should be a concern.

The size of organizations means they have the capacity to do significant damage as well as good. Cultivating wise leadership avoids you being pulled unintentionally and without thought into group decisions and actions. Developing wise leadership across an organization avoids some of the unintended and damaging consequences of ill-considered decisions. And, without wishing to labour the point, wisdom is not something that sits at the senior levels of hierarchical organizations. Wisdom and wise leadership exists at every level.

CULTIVATING WISE LEADERSHIP

Wisdom, although it can be a quality of a system, emanates from within the individual. A central pillar of the wise leader is the capacity to self-manage, know what we carry into situations, understand the impact of those beliefs, ideas and emotions on ourselves and others, and be clear about what we are there to achieve. This learning process doesn't happen overnight – and you can't get it from a book. Throughout time, leading thinkers, scholars and teachers have pointed to the necessity of experience and learning through life to become wise. Take Confucius as an example:

"By three methods we may learn wisdom: First, by reflection, which is noblest; Second, by imitation, which is easiest; and third by experience, which is the bitterest."[13]

Moving west to Europe, and a few centuries forward, we can look to Albert Einstein:[14]

"Wisdom is not a product of schooling but of the lifelong attempt to acquire it."

Across to Native American wisdom, which points to the challenge and gift of self-mastery. A Native American Prayer includes the words *"my greatest enemy – myself"*.[15] And a quote from Black Elk which is part of a longer teaching:[16]

"The first peace, which is the most important, is that which comes within the souls of people when they realize their relationship, their oneness, with the universe and all its powers."

Wisdom doesn't develop from the outside-in, it comes from the inside out.

John Chambers, Cisco CEO since 1995, sees that just as individual wisdom develops from the inside out, so does organizational wisdom. John has been transforming Cisco from a top-down command/control structure to one of teamwork and collaboration throughout his term as a leader. He achieved this through connecting communities of distributed leaders across Cisco. The result? Cisco has emerged as a distributed ideas engine where leadership emerges organically as ideas grow. "Leading from the middle" is the biggest change in the management of the company.[17]

What a strength! This story is Sir Isaac Newton's quote in action:

"If I have seen further it is by standing on the shoulders of giants."[18]

In order to be wiser, leaders might consider:
- Developing greater self-awareness and self-knowledge
- Developing a clear and compelling purpose
- Developing a beginner mind
- Engaging a mentor

Develop greater self-awareness and self-knowledge

More recent thinkers such as Roger Lehman of INSEAD[19] and Prasad Kaipa[20] echo the point that self-awareness leads to greater wisdom. So what is self-awareness and how do you develop it?

Rich self-knowledge leading to greater wisdom includes awareness of what you can and can't do; awareness of your emotions and goals; and awareness of your sense of purpose or meaning in life. There are clear links between current thinking on wisdom and other areas we have covered in this book, notably Chapter 12, *Happiness* and Chapter 13, *Mindfulness*.

A wise person understands how they personally grow and develop and how they self-manage. They have developed skills of reflection and have insight into what makes them act and feel in a particular way. A wise person accepts and values themselves as a worthy human being – while, holding themselves to critical account. They recognize and manage uncertainties in life, knowing that life is full of uncontrollable and unpredictable events.[21]

To become self-aware means being prepared to look at all the qualities you are happy to admit to and share with others (the "bright side") AND bringing into the light those qualities you would rather not admit to (the "shadow side"). The starting point to greater awareness is acknowledging what you do (warts and all) to yourself. If you don't know yourself, you're more likely to succumb to covering up weaknesses and overplaying strengths instead of practising self-acceptance and being honest.[22]

To develop greater self-awareness:
- Be curious. Research yourself. So today you weren't exactly honest with your customer when you believe that honesty is an important personal value that you hold. Make a note of it, don't hide from it. How important to you is honesty really? What impact will developing more honest interactions have? What stopped you from being honest? What will help you to be more honest?
- Reflect on what you are learning about yourself and what that might mean. Over a week, you notice that you were more honest with those customers you personally liked. How can you be more honest with

those customers that you don't automatically warm to? What do you want to do differently next time?

- Notice the impact of the environment on you. For example, when you make your phone calls in private, you find it easier to relax and try out a more open style of interacting with your customers. Can you secure a private space for all your calls? If not, what is going to help you have excellent calls in the showroom or the open plan office?

When you start to grow your self-awareness, you realize how much "noise" there is that gets in the way of you responding to a situation in the most effective way. Sorting out this noise – what's helpful and realistic from what is clearly unhelpful and unrealistic – takes energy and time, so don't try to do it all at once!

It's through this reflection on you in practice, in a real working context where true experience can lead to learning and greater wisdom. This testing, reflecting and trying again builds learning – not only about who you are – but also about how you develop, bit by bit, as a person.

Develop a clear and compelling purpose

Kaipa sees that wise leaders root themselves in a noble purpose, align it with a compelling vision, and then take action for the rest of their lives. The noble purpose gives direction when the path ahead is hazy.[23] Takeuchi and Nonaka share a similar view.[24] With a clear and compelling purpose, you can act with greater integrity – and be less easily swayed by a situation, context or colleague's agenda.

Who are you and what do you stand for? What is core and important to you? What is the impression you want others to have of you? For more on this, see Chapter 5, *Purpose*.

Develop a beginner mind

"In the beginner's mind there are many possibilities, but in the expert's there are few."

Shunryu Suzuki[25]

Imagine for a moment: you are faced with a situation where one of your team members has expressed dissatisfaction with the way that team meetings are run as there never seems to be any progress. As the leader of that team, you've been following a particular method for running the team meeting. After this feedback – you're going to try out the other two ways of structuring things you know in turn and see what works best. The result – you stumble around testing things out, and the likelihood of one of the solutions you apply improving things is not much better than chance.

This is the "expert mind" in practice. You are the expert and you will find a way to run the meeting that is the right one.

Let's look at the situation again from the perspective of a "beginner mind". As a beginner, you would not be expected to have the answer as to how to run an effective meeting, so you might rightly take a different approach, one with more curiosity. You might ask the member of your team, what would progress look like to them? What suggestions do they have for the way that the meetings need to run? Building on this, you might realize that you each have different expectations of the meeting. Before concluding with a view of how to proceed, you might dedicate the next team meeting to finding out more. What do the other four team members need or want to get out of the meeting, what would the organization see as a successful team meeting? – and what suggestions might the team have as to how the meeting might be run?

The result is that you now know what each of you needs from the meeting and how best to work together to deliver this at this point in time. Your team meetings have a different energetic quality about them, and the "team" feels like a "team" rather than simply a group of people who have a requirement to meet together.

Which scenario suggests greater wisdom?

The beginner mind can lead to the display of greater wisdom. In the second scenario, as the leader of the team you are tolerant of different perspectives, and are demonstrating that you are not concerned about your own brilliance; rather, you have an eye on the bigger picture. What is best for the group here? You accept that you don't know everything and are keen to pool the shared knowledge so that a better solution can be engineered. You know that getting everyone's buy-in will lead to greater motivation for successful team meetings and greater shared responsibility to making sure that that is exactly what happens.

The "don't know" mind advocated by Mary Jaksch[26] may be particularly useful. Rather than prejudging situations by what you do know, keep your mind open and tell yourself that "I don't know" and allow yourself to learn. When you cease to have a fixed idea of people, things, and situations surrounding you, you grow in wisdom because you soak up changes, new ideas, and don't set any person above or beneath you. This is known as the wisdom of the warrior.

From acknowledging that we know very little, to adopting the beginner mind, and starting with "I don't know", we immediately have access to some perspectives and methods that may support the development of wise responses to what is happening.

This idea of the beginner mind chimes with the teachings of the Greek philosopher, Socrates[27]. Rather than demonstrating how much he knew, Socrates was known for his work exposing how little we actually know. To him, questioning what we and others really know was a mark of excellence.

We might know that we don't know – but we are so well programmed to value "being right", being seen as knowing and in control – there's an almost ingrained fear about not knowing. Clearly, placing too much emphasis on what we know and how much we know gets in the way of the curiosity that leads to greater wisdom.

When we accept that every human being in fact knows very little, it is much easier to ask curious questions about the right way forward, rather than to assume that one person (you) is expected to have the answer for every situation that arises.

Engage a mentor

Harnessing the support of a trusted mentor, who in your view displays the qualities of wisdom, may help you on the journey to wise leadership. Many, if not all, of the sages in mythology, philosophy and other stories had students or apprentices with them. Things are no different today.

Engage a mentor who challenges you, but who is not there to show off how great they are. Engage someone who you respect and like!

When you look across your organization, what are you doing to support your leaders to develop greater wisdom?

WISDOM AND 31PRACTICES

The 31Practices methodology, we hope, will build greater individual and organizational wisdom. The approach, aligning employees behind a compelling organizational vision and providing the guiding principles or values that will lead to success, contains components of wisdom. That each employee is required to take responsibility to practise the organizational habits that will lead to success, and notice the impact of those habits, supports individual learning and awareness.

However, 31Practices on its own won't build wisdom – the attention to enabling people to grow, learn and develop through the systems and environment created using 31Practices will be important in the development of greater wisdom.

....

Reviewing your habits of wisdom – from one perspective

Using the rating scale below, to what extent do you do each of the following:

5 = all the time
4 = more often than not
3 = sometimes
2 = rarely
1 = never

1. Align your actions with your ideals (values, principles, morals, beliefs) ☐

2. Create a compelling ideal or purpose with others ☐

3. Take care to facilitate the success of others ☐

4. Make the impossible seem possible ☐

5. Model the kindness you hope to see in others ☐

6. Respond rather than react ☐

7. Prioritize what you "want most" over what you "want now" ☐

8. Choose to defend principles, rather than territory ☐

9. Know when to use logic and reason and when to empathize ☐

10. Deal with issues before they escalate into an impasse ☐

11. Welcome any input that increases your effectiveness ☐

12. Share sincere, verbal appreciation of those around you ☐

13. Take time to contemplate and think more ☐

14. Live your life, rather than live the dreams of those around you ☐

15. Maintain your humility, sharing strengths, but not overblowing your capabilities ☐

16. Embrace your imperfections ☐

How did you do? The good news is that there are no right or wrong answers here. Your journey to wisdom is your own and it would be at odds with the whole idea if there was a "right way" to be wise! Reflecting on your responses, what might you do to develop your personal wisdom?

You can repeat this exercise looking across the patterns in the organization. To what extent does your organization enable the development of wisdom?

Want to know more?

There are a variety of useful authors on wisdom topics.

- The teachings of Shunryu Suzuki are captured in: *Zen mind, Beginner's Mind: Informal Talks on Zen Meditation and Practice*. Shambhala Publications (2011).
- Bob Seelert, CEO of five companies through his career and chairman of Saatchi and Saatchi has collected down-to-earth stories from his career. Bob Seelert (2009). *Start with the answer: And other wisdoms for aspiring leaders*. New Jersey: John Wiley & Sons.

CHAPTER 22   NEUROSCIENCE

"Every man can, if he so desires, become the sculptor of his own brain."

Santiago Ramón y Cajal[1]

Neuroscience is an umbrella term that refers to any of the sciences that deal with the nervous system and includes the study of the anatomy, physiology, biochemistry and pharmacology of the nervous system.

Over the last two decades, our awareness of the nervous system and how it works in conjunction with our thoughts, emotions and behaviours has increased dramatically. Why? Because it is much easier to observe the brain in action due to advances in brain imaging technology. In the past, we would have to wait until the user was dead before careful dissection and thoughtful guesswork.

The explosion in information about the brain has arrived, but understanding is still in its infancy – we are some way off knowing how the brain and nervous system work – and it's unlikely that we will ever be entirely clear. There is a strong appetite for greater understanding. For example, on April 2nd 2013, the US government announced a $100 million dollar research initiative to map the human brain with the end goal being to understand how brain networks function.[2] This fast-growing field of enquiry is moving rapidly, so what we think we know about the brain is in significant flux.

Where the neuroscience moves away from the specific and starts to look at what brain structures mean for people in their everyday lives, the science becomes less exact.

Understanding our brain function, even a little, enables us to see at a physical level:

- How we can learn and change – for example, the process of new habit formation and how we might purposefully unlearn old habits that are no longer serving us.
- The role of emotions – for example, decision making is often emotional rather than rational (especially those bigger, perhaps more important decisions) – even when we think it's rational –rational thoughts are really just a post-hoc rationalization of the decision that we've already made at an emotional level.
- The extent to which we are social beings and connected to those around us consciously and subconsciously. This insight alone may support us to create better, more effective connections and relationships in our daily lives.

Having some insight into how our brains operate empowers us to work "with the brain in mind" (to borrow from the title of David Rock's book[3]). And not surprisingly in such a large field, the opinions of experts within it are not unanimous. Against this context, we've selected aspects and principles from this body of work with some evidence behind them to share here.

We start with some basic physical properties of the brain, from which we go on to explore learning, growth and change; empathy and emotion – and how to live and work with the brain in mind.

THE STARTING POINT

We can actually affect the wiring of our brain by choosing what we expose ourselves to, what we pay attention to and what we actually do.

So, how is our brain wired? As an analogy – the brain is like an incredibly complicated self-generating electrical circuit with neurons instead of wires, gaps (synapses) instead of junctions and chemical messages travelling across the gaps instead of switches. Susan Greenfield, a lifelong researcher of the brain, shares this explanation:[4]

Neurons (nerve cells) are isolated units and between each neuron there is a gap, the synapse. An active neuron generates an electrical blip that enables a nerve cell to communicate with its neighbour. A chemical messenger is needed to transmit the electrical message across the gap to activate the next neuron. The ultimate building-block of operations across your entire nervous system is this chain of electrical – chemical – electrical events.

Those neurons which are coated in a "myelin sheath" work a lot faster than the neurons that aren't – the coating creates a neural "super highway".

Your brain adapts – changing as a result of your experiences (what you pay attention to, what you think about, what actions you take, who you interact with) – throughout your life. The rain is much more changeable in adulthood than was previously thought. Admittedly, there is much more change in the first years of life. The ideas, beliefs and habits we develop and the experiences we have are particularly impactful in these early years.

We only generate new brain cells in very localized brain areas after birth (those associated with memory as far as we currently know).

BUT we develop new connections and new pathways across the existing brain cells constantly.[5]

This changeability, or neuroplasticity,[6] means our brains are being dynamically reconfigured all the time – in response to our internal and external world.

The good news then – you really can learn and adapt at any age.

"Exercising our brains systematically is as important as exercising our bodies. … 'Use it or lose it' should really be 'Use it and get more of it.'"

Dr. Elkhonon Goldberg[7]

Your brain enables the development of your identity – your mind.

Our brains are social organs – hardwired to respond to social stimuli.[8] Through social interaction, our own mind develops[9] and becomes the personalization of our own physical brain.[10] Neither the human brain nor mind exists without social relationships. However, we have multiple selves, multiple identities – multiple ways of being available to us. This is because our sense of our self is highly context-dependent. People's view of themselves is as part of the context they are in – if you move jobs, move reference group, move to another culture – your view of yourself changes. Even our concept of self is socially determined. For example, if you ask an English-speaking Chinese person a question about "self" and a question about "family" in Chinese, there is no difference in brain activity in answering the questions. If you ask the same person the same questions, but in English, there is significantly more activity in response to the question about self – perhaps confirming our observation that "self" is a much more important concept in English-speaking cultures.[11] There is no physical difference in the brain structure; it is purely the socialization of the brain that creates this difference in identity. This insight seems particularly important when considering the process of organizational design and communication, how things are languaged can have significant impact.

Your brain is highly socially sensitive.

Our sense of our self only comes after we are about four to five years old.[12] We develop this sense of self through our interactions with others. A large part of the brain, the medial pre-frontal cortex, is geared to performing relational judgements that affect how we feel and how we perform. Curiously, when we compare ourselves to a group of clever people, our performance goes up on a task where we can assume clever people would do well. However, when we compare our self to an individual clever person, such as Albert Einstein, that comparison reduces our performance on the same task. This effect might occur because we can see ourselves as part of a clever group, but we know we are not Einstein! We are hardwired to compare ourselves – so if you want to improve your performance on a task, imagine a group of people who are generally thought to excel at that task. If you want to reduce your performance, compare yourself to an individual who excels at the task!

What insights does brain research offer?

Understanding how the brain functions can be used in our everyday lives and to support us to drive shifts and changes that we want to see.[13] Whether that change is personal, focused on ourselves as leaders; or interpersonal, focusing on shifting or changing an organization in some way – insight into how brains work may enable us to get past blocks about what "should be happening", to a more accepting understanding of what "is happening". Brain research shows how we:

- Develop new habits
- Are primed for learning
- Channel what we are prepared to experience
- Manage our emotional experience through mindfulness practice

DEVELOPING NEW (AND GETTING RID OF OLD) HABITS

"Neurons that fire together wire together"

Donald Hebb[14]

The more often a pair of neurons "fire" together across a synapse, the stronger that connection becomes. Through different experiences, different connections strengthen.

This is the basis of habit formation – after a repeated conscious intention to perform or think in some new way, the habit becomes "hard-wired" – moving from a place where conscious attention was needed to do something to a habit that is automatic – enabling us to act in a certain way without thinking about it.[15] Our brains are excellent at processing unconsciously – when we have to consciously think about things, our performance slows down.[16] Our emotional and behavioural experience of this process is described in Chapter 16, *Practice*.

Think of the first time you learned a new physical skill, whether it was driving a car, riding a horse, or operating a till or photocopier. When you started, all the things that you had to pay attention to and think about were almost overwhelming. Through repetition – things move from the conscious to the unconscious. Now you get into the car, adjust your seat, mirror, turn on the engine, the lights – and the whole time you've continued to have a conversation with your passenger. You get onto your horse and immediately adopt a balanced position, reins in hand, heels down, shoulders and back straight, connected to your horse through your saddle and leg position. You can navigate your way through the various functions on the till or photocopier without even looking, and at a speed that is more than ten times faster than when you were first shown.

You can't necessarily unlearn old habits, but you can form new ones.[17] Through repeated attention, you can increase the strength of new connections, enabling them to become hard-wired and unconsciously available. The old habits of doing and thinking are still there, but become weaker echoes if not used or attended to. And you have a broader repertoire of skills and choices to draw on.

Through this simple process of habit formation, you can develop your skills as a leader. Through repetition and adjustment, you learn how to connect and build an easy rapport with people, how to take the lead when required, and how to subtly alter words and phrases to enable others to grow and find their own solutions. And you do all this despite the fact that the first time you tried it you were nervous as hell, your inner critique was busy saying *"they'll find you out"*; *"you don't know what you're doing"* – and it felt clunky to be different to normal.

Now you respond skilfully and almost automatically to the situation, without having to remind yourself consciously. What's normal has "shifted".

Even the habit of habit formation can help or get in the way – imagine for example that you're someone who's always going to give up smoking tomorrow; or gives up for two days and always starts again – that's a habit that will get in the way of the change you say you want.

Imagine on the other hand that you choose to start building relationships by talking to people in the office rather than just emailing them – but instead of starting tomorrow, you start right now – today – small goals, easy steps. That is a different pattern of habit development that's more likely to deliver success.

Each time you repeat a new habit, it becomes easier – but habit formation is not instant. It takes time for it to become a hardwired automatic activity. Scott Marcaccio[18] likens habit formation to cutting a path through a dense jungle with a machete, the path quickly become impenetrable again – but with repeated walking and cutting, the path widens and you can more easily walk along it.

PRIMED FOR LEARNING

As we focus and learn, our neural connections don't just strengthen in a linear way – rather, the complexity of each neuron and groups of neurons associated with the task increases.

Each neuron is made up of a central nucleus and a number of branches – a bit like a tree – each branch is called a "dendrite" and the more complex and enriched a neuron, the greater the number of dendrites and the greater number of connections it has with other neurons. This enrichment of the neurons, neural pathways and neural networks further increases the prioritization of those pathways and increases the accessibility of certain understanding, knowledge and memories. Those neural pathways and neurons that are not used will be pruned and deprioritized, becoming simpler in structure.

A relatively recent study demonstrated that the area of the brain associated with working memory (the hippocampus) was larger among London taxi drivers than in those of a similar age and intelligence.[19] Why?

Because London cabbies have to be able to remember the street maps of London without reference to a manual or a satellite navigation system. To become a London taxi driver, each person has to learn and be tested on "The Knowledge". The longer the taxi driver has been working as a London cabbie, the bigger the hippocampus – suggesting it continues to grow over time. This is the only part of the brain that we know of at the moment that develops new cells after birth.

There is evidence that we are primed for learning in other ways. Watching and listening to others and visual rehearsal have been demonstrated by brain research to enhance the development of neural connections.

Social learning – learning through observation of others – has long been evidenced by psychologists.[20] Now we know a little bit more. Humans (and other primates) are blessed with specialized brain cells called mirror neurons[21] which fire their electrical impulses when we observe someone else experiencing an event. Whether it's biting into a crunchy fresh apple, or receiving praise and commendation for a job well done, we experience emotions and memories associated with such an event as if we are experiencing it ourselves. There is no separate section of the brain that processes "self" or "others". The processing is all done together in the same part of the brain. It's not surprising that social learning is powerful and that we strongly assume others are like us.[22]

Storytelling is gaining greater attention as a skill that people are drawing on in order to better communicate experience and share learning with others (see Chapter 15, *Storytelling*). A recent study at Princeton University[23] showed how our brains synchronize when we listen to stories. Using brain-scanning techniques, the researchers could see that the same areas of the listeners' brains were triggered as those that were being accessed in the storyteller's brain, in the same sequence, as the story unfolded. The greater the level of understanding of the story, the more the speaker and listener brain images dovetailed. When there was no understanding of the story – where the same speaker spoke in a different language – no synchronization was seen.

Visualization has long been practised by those in the sporting and personal development arena as a means of focusing towards a desired state or a desired goal. A study explored brain development among adults learning to play the piano. One group just spent part of the day in the same room as a piano, a second group were asked to practise certain finger exercises over five days for two hours a day. After only five days, brain scans showed differences in the brain structure associated with movement of digits. More surprisingly still, a third group who had only "visualized" playing the finger exercises over the same five-day period had almost the same brain level of development as those who had actually played the piano.[24]

So it seems that simply practising a habit by visualizing has a physical impact on the hard-wiring of that habit in your brain. We talk about the importance of visualizing in a number of chapters – it's associated with *Resilience* (Chapter 14), *Practice* (Chapter 16) and *Discipline* (Chapter 18).

CHANNELLING OUR EXPERIENCE – WE SEE WHAT WE EXPECT TO SEE

We create the reality that we see through our choices of what to attend to and what to disregard, what habits to maintain and what habits to lay waste. Neuroscience provides us with an understanding of how this social construction takes place in action through the development of our brains and the configurations and reconfigurations of nerve cells, neural pathways and neural networks as we change, adapt and grow.

Our brains connect past and present experiences into patterns, enabling us to anticipate the future. We create mental maps and schemas, enabling us to make predictions and take action before things happen. This process starts before we are born and continues throughout our lives. We start to recognize and filter against these patterns of experience from about the age of 10.[25]

The result is that we prime our perceptual systems by what we pay conscious attention to – neurons that are expecting a particular input become active before the stimulation arrives. We can even perceive what we expect before it arrives.

Let's fast-forward this idea to one that is familiar to us in an organizational context. When going to present to an audience, if you expect to see colleagues who are happy, pleased to be there, engaged, interested, then that is exactly what you will see and experience. If you're expecting people to be bored, fidgety, disengaged, confused, then that is what you will see and experience.

This is physical evidence for a belief that we have held for many years. If we expect to succeed, we almost experience success before it has arrived, ensuring we are more likely to succeed. If we expect failure, we will experience failure and be more likely to actually fail.

"Whether you think you can or think you can't – you're absolutely right."

Henry Ford[26]

This priming effect also provides a structural basis as to why it's hard to learn in an overly familiar environment – because we don't notice what we're not expecting to notice. In a new environment, we might be less blinkered.

This evidence also gives insight into how two people can have a very different experience of the same event!

There is a wonderful experiment where participants were asked to count the number of times people in a video passed a basketball back and forth – 50% of the people completely failed to notice a gorilla-suited accomplice walking through the action, facing the camera and pounding its chest.[27]

It is so easy to forget that we see our view of the world, not the world itself.

The benefits to the brain of cultivating mindfulness

Mindfulness (of which there are many practices) offers a way of bringing some reflective space between our experience of the world and the decisions we make about how to interact with the world in front of us.

In relation to the brain, mindfulness training can impact on your thinking processes as a whole (your mental "fitness"), supporting you to be able to focus attention with greater success, switch between tasks and more easily pay attention to thoughts and feelings and their impact on decisions and actions.[28]

Mindfulness training can alter your thinking skills – reducing the impact of negative self-talk and building the skills of acceptance and compassion – leading to greater personal happiness. In one particular study of Buddhist monks, Richard Davidson noted that a stronger link between the thinking and emotional areas of the brain occurs with more years of meditation practice. Cultivating feelings of compassion during meditation fires significant activity in areas of the brain associated with happiness. A positive mental state then can be developed through meditation. The topic is explored more fully in Chapter 13, *Mindfullness*.

NEUROSCIENCE AND 31PRACTICES

The 31Practices methodology is aligned to ideas and findings emerging from our increased insight into the workings of our brains as we have seen already from the principles explored in other chapters. Rather than repeat those links here, it's interesting to explore whether there is anything additional that we can glean from neuroscience that would shape the methodology still further. In fact, perhaps current findings simply give more confidence to apply the existing 31Practices methodology.

Exercise – Making the most of your brain

Try this set of activities known as the "healthy mind platter" from Dan Siegel and David Rock designed to optimize your brain effectiveness and create a sense of well-being.[29]

- **Focus Time:** When we closely focus on tasks in a goal-oriented way, we take on challenges that make deep connections in the brain.
- **Play Time:** When we allow ourselves to be spontaneous or creative, playfully enjoying novel experiences, we help make new connections in the brain.
- **Connecting Time:** When we connect with other people, ideally in person, and when we take time to appreciate our connection to the natural world around us, we activate and reinforce the brain's relational circuitry.
- **Physical Time:** When we move our bodies, aerobically if medically possible, we strengthen the brain in many ways.
- **Time In:** When we quietly reflect internally, focusing on sensations, images, feelings and thoughts, we help to better integrate the brain.
- **Down Time:** When we are non-focused, without any specific goal, and let our mind wander or simply relax, we help the brain recharge.
- **Sleep Time:** When we give the brain the rest it needs, we consolidate learning and recover from the experiences of the day.

Want to know more?

- Daniel Siegel's book, *Mindsight*, is worth reading in relation to neuroscience. While he is better known for his work on mindfulness, mind and brain are inseparable, and his work is based in the context of brain research. Daniel J Siegel (2010). *Mindsight: The new science of personal transformation*. New York: Random House.
- From a slightly different angle, we suggest: Frank Amthor (2012). *Neuroscience for Dummies*. Ontario: John Wiley & Sons.
- There are many and varied TED talks that explore the brain. This is a particular favourite from the brain researcher, Jill Bolte Taylor. http://www.ted.com/talks/jill_bolte_taylor_s_powerful_stroke_of_insight.html

CHAPTER 23 CHOICE

"It is our choices, Harry, that show what we truly are, far more than our abilities."

Harry Potter and the Chamber of Secrets, J.K. Rowling[1]

Choice is the right or ability to choose between different things. Choice is a small word that encompasses much that makes us human. Choice equates to freedom – and we always have choice, whatever the circumstances – even if we don't like what we are experiencing, or don't have as much freedom as we would like. This powerful insight was shared so clearly by Viktor Frankl:[2]

"Everything can be taken from a man but one thing: the last of the human freedoms – to choose one's attitude in any given set of circumstances, to choose one's own way."

Choice is important to us as human beings. And life now is all about choices – in fact, we are overwhelmed by choice in all contexts, though we're not always aware of the choices we do have.

In our experience, people respond more positively when they have a choice, when they are involved in defining the course of action rather than being presented with exactly what they have to do.

Curiously, there is a biological basis for the positive impact of choice. Personally making a choice stimulates a part of your brain (the caudate nucleus) that responds in a similar way when we have sex, feel love or eat chocolate.[3] Dr Tali Sharot speculates that our brains evolved this mechanism to reinforce our commitment to our choices. Powerful stuff!

At the other end of the scale, there is startling evidence about the consequences of perceiving no choice. Employees in low-control jobs – jobs where people have to respond to others' demands and timetables with no control or freedom to decide how they respond – have twice the risk of coronary heart disease, and live shorter lives (on average) than workers in high-control positions.[4]

Having choice is linked to greater engagement and well-being, while having very limited choice but lots of "demands" is linked to greater experience of stress and ill health.

WHAT DOES CHOICE DO FOR US?

Choice in the moment has a biological basis – giving us a short-term neural "high". From neuroscience and studies of habit formation, we know when we make the similar choices in similar contexts, we're building strong habits and neural connections that limit our awareness of alternative choices.

"We are our choices."

Jean-Paul Sartre[5]

If, as a project leader, you are always providing the answers to your project team when they come to you for advice, then it's harder to switch to an approach that encourages them to engage their own brains and find the answer themselves. When you are promoted so that you are running five projects in parallel, your choice to be the one who has the answers to all the difficulties and challenges encountered will ensure that you get really bogged down and become a bottleneck, reducing the chance of successful delivery. You can feel really stuck because you have become the person with all the answers – that is part of your personal identity the value that you see you add – and you expect that that is what others want from you. The blinkers are on – and yet, you have to change to survive.

Raising your awareness to look at some of the alternative choices available to you and choosing a different kind of response to the queue of people at your desk will not only free you up and ensure your survival, it will develop the capability and motivation of those working on the projects.

Choice is a motivator – providing greater commitment to a course of action. In cultures where self-expression is more highly valued, having a choice is particularly important – leading to greater ownership of the choice made.[6] Once we've made a decision, we are then ego-bound to defend that decision (for better or worse) – which means we'll invest our energy into the choice we've made.

In this way, we become intrinsically motivated to make our decision the right one. This not only provides a positive feeling about the decision we've made, but brings a level of energy to make it happen.

Take for example the team leader, Linda, who is keen to delegate a particular client presentation. Imagine Linda asks a team member, Joe for help in creating an engaging and impactful presentation to the client – she's going to have to let Joe shoulder much of the responsibility for the content and impact of the presentation – with minimal input on the first and final drafts. She shares one or two examples of successful presentations in the past and what the purpose of the presentation is. Would he be prepared to take it on – does he have the space to take it on?

Consider a different scenario – where Linda tells Joe that he needs to do this presentation for a client – she doesn't care what else he has to deliver, this presentation is a priority. She would like him to give her frequent updates about progress and she needs full sign-off on the final version.

Which approach is going to make Joe feel he has choices? Which one is going to leave Joe feeling motivated? Which one is going to bring out more of Joe's resourcefulness in creating the presentation?

When put like this, it's easy to see the contrast between the "choice" and "no choice" conditions and to feel the impact of the two approaches.

Giving others more choices also requires you to acknowledge that perhaps someone here is able to do this as well as you, better than you, or differently to you. Getting past the small pain of acknowledging that you are not omnipotent and absolutely indispensable pays dividends.

Choice builds learning and capability. Providing a choice about what to do builds people's capability to take the initiative and build their learning. Providing the answer to each query builds dependency (on you). Giving people the chance to use their judgement in applying their knowledge and skills enables them to learn and grow.[7]

Choice defines us. What we choose defines us as people, it defines who we are. Choice gives us power and the opportunity for mastery. Choice also comes with a large helping of responsibility. Making choices and accepting the responsibility that comes with that choice is a part of personal growth and maturity. If we consciously choose a path for ourselves rather than following a path that has been mapped out for us (it may be the very same path), we are taking responsibility for ourselves – we are no longer the victims of a seemingly unfair world.

When you're given choices, it's harder to blame "the organization" (or anyone) when things don't go the way you want them to. You can do something about it by making a different choice. By providing choices, you are enabling others to lead themselves.

"To say you have no choice is to relieve yourself of responsibility."

Patrick Ness[8]

Choice equates to freedom – not the freedom to do exactly what we please regardless of consequences, but the choice to act, mindful of the consequences, and the freedom to find inner peace and well-being whatever happens.

CHOICE AND AWARENESS

It's worth saying something about the combination of choice and awareness. If we are not aware of the range of choice on offer, we inevitably limit ourselves and our possible impact or outcomes we might reach. Choice and awareness, then, go hand in hand. While it's pretty impossible to have full awareness, we can choose to increase our awareness or provide those that are working with us with greater awareness.

In scenario one with Linda and Joe above, Linda gives Joe greater choice, and she shares the parameters: the purpose of the presentation (what it's there to do); how she wants people to feel (impact and engaging); and she provides some examples of what good might look like. In scenario two, Linda provided no resources.

The starting point to increasing your choices is raising awareness – and the decisions to pause, reflect, consider, be curious, rests with you. Throughout this book, we have endeavoured to raise your own personal, interpersonal and contextual awareness – to offer you greater awareness of the choices and consequences of choices at your disposal.

BUILDING THE POSSIBILITY OF CHOICE INTO ORGANIZATIONS

Do you really believe in the power of choice? At a hotel we worked with, vacancies from local competitors were posted on notice boards with the objective of the employees understanding that they were in a good place… and encouraging them to remake that positive choice to stay.

The story of Aruba Networks shares how they used to spend a lot of time and energy tracking and reporting vacations. Today they simply tell every employee to take a vacation when they need it, for as long as they need it, and the only proviso is that they have to make sure that the time off won't interfere with the work getting done.[9]

Bold approaches.

There is a lot you can do to build the possibility of choice into the fabric of your organization. We discuss clarity, culture and work design as three ways that you can increase the possibility of choice through raising awareness and embedding choice into processes and structures.

Clarity

Clarity on your part enables others to make an informed choice. Being clear that what you're offering potential employees is more than just the transactional details (pay, reward, holiday entitlement, working hours etc); your purpose as an organization and how you operate (your organizational values) is likely to make the difference where two organizations are competing for the best recruits. This clarity will make those that make the choice to work with you more committed from the start and less likely to suffer unexpected and uncomfortable "shocks".

Clarity is not just something that happens in the recruitment process, but is something to pay attention to throughout the organization. While clear organizational values and a guiding purpose act as an ongoing anchor, the answers to the questions *"What purpose does this activity serve?"* and *"How do you want this to feel or impact?"* can go a long way to building clarity when delegating. Clarity is part and parcel of your culture.

Culture

To what extent is the culture of your organization geared to maximizing awareness and engaging and empowering employees where possible?

As an example, what culture do you have around providing feedback? Is feedback a once-a-year event associated with the performance appraisal (an extreme example)? Or is feedback a daily occurrence – as and when required, with a strong level of appreciation for what was done well and what would lead to further improvement? A culture which promotes clarity about how well people are doing within a given context provides people with more choices.

If a person knows that they are coming across aggressively during project meetings, they can choose to maintain the current approach, choose a different style of interaction or choose to build a broader repertoire of interpersonal skill. If they are not made aware of their impact on others, they have no basis on which to make a different choice.

A culture which supports leaders to build confidence and self-determination is based on three core principles: choice, decision latitude and personal accountability.[10]

Does your organizational culture reflect a sense of goodwill, or one of fear and mistrust? A more "trusting" culture in general will lead to greater sharing and more appropriate sharing of information and responsibility. As you grow confidence around enabling choice, you can provide more meaningful choice over more substantive issues. A fearful, mistrusting culture will lead people to use knowledge and information as power, as a bargaining chip, reducing the level of openness and, ultimately, the level of engagement.

Whether you ultimately have more control and power over your day or not (you still have to go to work and deliver certain objectives), building greater choice into business as usual will reduce your experience of stress and the negative effects that that has on your body.[11] Belief that you have greater control through greater choice will make you healthier.

Work design

The research evidence around choice and the impact of having more or less choice on our motivation, well-being and mortality that has been gathered over decades and across countries weighs in favour of providing employees with greater latitude. The research suggests that "traditional" command/control approaches will not deliver optimal outcomes – for the organization or the individual.

Command control from the centre does not deliver the required level of agility and speed of response. There has been a move from standardization to individuation and because of this, employees at the point of service delivery are best placed to understand what needs to be done in any given situation. Responsive service and extra employee efforts emerge when people have the necessary leeway to meet customer needs and sufficient authority to serve customer wants.

How can we drive choice down to the front line and control to the person who is well-placed to make a sensible choice? To feel in control of their own work lives, people need to be able to take non-routine action, exercise independent judgement, and make decisions that affect how they do their work, without having to check with someone else.[12]

This does not equate to an absence of leadership; greater leadership is required. But instead of the leader being focused on being personally brilliant, it's about the business leader and leaders of people throughout the organization clarifying the space within which decisions can effectively be made. Clarifying the boundaries and the scope of decision latitude requires a leader to be truly leading, rather than simply reacting from a more informed position. Clarifying the scope of responsibility for others enables the brilliance of others to come to the fore.

Enabling choice and offering greater latitude through the design of work means that you are building the habits of making choices, adaptability, accountability and flexibility into your workforce. Given the emergent, complex and dynamic global context, greater flexibility will pay dividends.

Enabling choice in an organization means being creative and flexible – where you can. It's clearly not always possible to be flexible, but our guess is that there is much more scope than currently exists or you may even imagine.

CHOICE AND 31PRACTICES

The theme of choice runs through the 31Practices approach from beginning to end. To start with, the process begins with co-creation workshops for employees to suggest the specific Practices that they consider would best represent their organizational values and set their organization apart from the competition.

From these workshops, a first draft of the 31Practices is created and reviewed before fine tuning and a formal launch – again, employees across the organization have a chance to contribute to the review.

When the 31Practices are in operation, employees choose the specific way that they are going to fulfil the Practice of the day. For example, if in a hotel the Practice is *"We display meticulous attention to **cleanliness**"*, the receptionist may choose to clear out a cupboard, the engineer when checking the boiler may choose to sweep the plant room, the chef may choose to book the degreasing of the filter, the bar supervisor may choose to check that the glasses are all sparkling.

The 31Practices are owned by the organization and, more importantly, the people that are the organization. The behaviour is therefore authentic and directed towards enabling the organization's greater purpose, in line with organizational values.

"Heroes are made by the paths they choose, not the powers they are graced with."

Brodi Ashton[13]

Exercise: Self and group review

The matrix below, adapted from the work of Derik Mocke,[14] provides a useful way of exploring the level of empowerment , disempowerment (RIP – retired in place), cynicism or simple compliance in your organization. How can you make it easy for employees to choose a positive attitude and high energy?

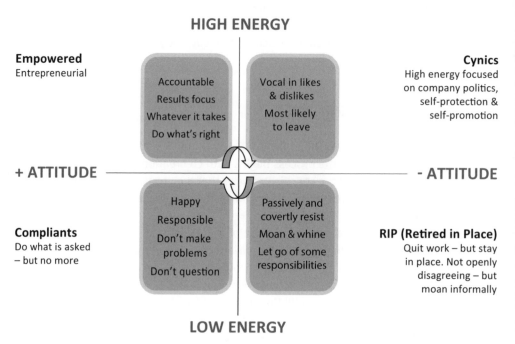

HIGH ENERGY

Empowered
Entrepreneurial

Accountable
Results focus
Whatever it takes
Do what's right

Vocal in likes
& dislikes
Most likely
to leave

Cynics
High energy focused
on company politics,
self-protection &
self-promotion

+ ATTITUDE ———————————————— **- ATTITUDE**

Happy
Responsible
Don't make
problems
Don't question

Passively and
covertly resist
Moan & whine
Let go of some
responsibilities

Compliants
Do what is asked
– but no more

RIP (Retired in Place)
Quit work – but stay
in place. Not openly
disagreeing – but
moan informally

LOW ENERGY

As an individual contributor, where are you on the grid?
- How much time do you spend in the four different quadrants?
- What impact does being in the different quadrants have on your relationships at work, your performance, your enjoyment?
- What happens to move you into the different quadrants?
- What steps can you take to spend more time in the empowered quadrant?

Looking across your team/department/organization – where are others on the grid?
- If you mapped people into the four quadrants, who would be where? What % of employees would be in which quadrant? Noting of course that one person would be unlikely to spend 100% of their time in one "box", where would you put people "in general"?
- What impact does being in the different quadrants have on interpersonal relationships at work, performance, clients, customers?
- What happens in different teams/different departments for those who are in the empowered quadrant? What happens in those areas where people are in the cynics/compliants/RIP quadrants?
- What steps can you take to move more people into the empowered quadrant more of the time?

Want to know more?

The topic of choice seems to have motivated more than one really useful TED talk. So we share two links here:
- Barry Schwartz offers a thought-provoking 20 minutes on the Paradox of Choice. http://www.ted.com/talks/barry_schwartz_on_the_paradox_of_choice.html
- Jeff Bezos, Founder and CEO of Amazon, talks about character being defined by the choices we make over a lifetime. http://www.ted.com/talks/jeff_bezos_gifts_vs_choices.html
- For a highly readable text try Chip and Dan Heath (2013). *Decisive: How to make better choices in life and work.* London : Random House

24

CHAPTER 24 LEADERSHIP

"Leaders honor their core values, but they are flexible in how they execute them."

Colin Powell[1]

A leader is someone who leads, and in organizations, this is more often than not associated with a particular position or function.

We are fascinated with the idea of leadership and what makes a great leader. There are numerous definitions of leadership, diverse models describing the required qualities of leaders, instructions on how to lead across different contexts and much more. Organizations globally spend billions to develop their population of leaders.

Becoming a leader definitely requires attention to models, frameworks and making personal sense of the skills and capabilities required. But this alone will not produce a leader.

As we search for the leadership Holy Grail, we focus on what is external to us; we look to experts and gurus in the field. This approach has its merits, but where are the experts when a decision is required, when action is called for, when a difficult message has to be shared?

In an increasingly unpredictable and uncertain context, where tried and tested methods no longer deliver, command and control is simply not possible (even if it was likely to succeed), content so rapidly changes, and what was true once is rarely repeated, this requires leaders to identify and develop their own model of leadership, and be their own guide.

Rather than looking to experts, you need to work out your own approach, do your own thinking and learn from your own practice. What is your purpose and identity? What is meaningful to you? From this basis, integrate what is helpful and relevant from the swathes of leadership concepts, and through a process of curiosity, explore your own leadership practice and the impact you have on those who you work with.

In this chapter, we don't share formal models of leadership; we want to encourage you to explore your own thinking and approach. What can you do to make sure that you are leading well in the context you find yourself in?

WHAT TO THINK ABOUT

So what might be important to think about? We have covered much already that explores how we think, feel and what we do. From those chapters there is a lot to explore about your inner world and the relationship between your inner landscape and outer experiences.

In this section, looking at complexity, change, wisdom, neuroscience and choice, we suggest that you may like to consider the following:

- things exist in relation to other things, cause and effect is not linear, what we do can enhance the energy in a system or dampen things down, and paying attention to patterns can help us notice how we are doing this. As a leader, it's important to "notice" interactions and patterns. How might you develop your complexity "habits of thought"?
- change is happening all the time, and it is personal. How as a leader do you attend to the personal impact that you have on others in order to facilitate change?
- self-awareness and self-knowledge are core to wise leadership. How might you build your wisdom to enable you to collaborate with others, to act with integrity, to know how (and whether) to respond? How can you cultivate a beginner mind, which offers the possibility of collaboration and exploration, rather than holding onto the view of "leader as expert" which leads to individual heroics?
- choice builds learning and motivation, ownership and responsibility. What might you do to cultivate choice for yourself and others?
- How can you use what we know about the brain and how it's structured? Explore how it "works" in your leadership: develop habits of leadership, optimize your learning and that of those around you; pay attention to the blinkers and expectations that you have that

might get in the way of what is really happening. And, as other leaders are starting to do, perhaps develop your own mindfulness practice so that your brain "fitness" is improved.

From an organizational perspective, leaders are "given" their role, through position. Some do brilliantly, leading in this space; many do a good job; and still others fail miserably – suffering personally. Letting go of the view of the leader as separate to the context in which they are leading is likely to reduce the focus on individual heroics and open up the possibility of a shared endeavour and greater success. Peter Hawkins[2] comments that leadership is relational – leaders are not separate at all from the context in which they lead. Leaders are fundamentally people stepping into a space that requires a leader. Leaders are volunteers responding to a need in the system.

LEARNING TO BE A LEADER

The ability to learn is often quoted as a core trait of successful leadership – our experience working with senior teams underlines this. Learning from adversity is a repeated theme in stories of success that we have witnessed – clarifying priorities and strengths. Whether it's learning through overcoming a difficult childhood or youth, or learning from business failure, learning was a core theme underpinning success in our team assessment work; not only for business leaders, but often for the entire leadership team.

Learning in this way is different to the traditional expert-based learning, and requires you to notice and reflect on what you are doing, making your own meaning of expert input and experience, becoming an active shaper of your development, rather than a passive recipient of the latest fad.

Your own view of leaders and leadership will impact on your approach to learning as a leader. So what do you think about leaders and leadership? We share our position on a number of leadership points below – what is your position?

Is leadership personal or positional? Determined by the individual – a way of being in the world; or determined by the system that the person is in – dependent on position and context? Your position on this dimension will determine where you look for leadership, where you look for input, perhaps who you listen to. It takes no title to be a leader; a leader is someone who people choose to follow. And having the title of leader doesn't mean you automatically become someone people will choose to follow. Leaders emerge from any place in society and are distributed[3] across organizations regardless of position.

"If your actions inspire others to dream more, learn more, do more and become more, you are a leader."

John Quincy Adams[4]

Are leaders born, or do people develop into the leaders you see around you? Your response to this question will dramatically impact on whether you are prepared to invest personally in your own development, and in the development of those you lead. Warren Bennis[5] believes *"leaders are made, not born"*, and that *"there are many possible selves"*.

From our work in the area of Management Due Diligence for private equity investors, we know that leaders are not born. There is such diversity among successful leaders of business teams, it is a challenge to pinpoint a set of characteristics of the "leader" that equates to success.

"The roles we play in the course of our lives have more to do with our successes or failures than our personal histories."

Warren Bennis[6]

How do leaders develop? Through learning a relevant set of skills and behaviours or through development of self-knowledge? Where you sit on this dichotomy will determine what you spend your time investing in and how you assess the leadership qualities of those around you.

Our view is that leadership comes from the person and the situation they find themselves in. A leader has to develop as an individual;[7] this means raising self-awareness and self-knowledge. Self-knowledge requires learning, allowing you to face your vulnerabilities, to grow through success and failure – driving personal integrity and an authentic leadership stance. Yet, different skills are required in different contexts and a core repertoire of interpersonal skills is likely to be useful across a range of situations.

"If you can become the leader you ought to be on the inside, you will be able to become the person you want

on the outside. People will want to follow you. And when that happens, you'll be able to tackle anything in this world."

John Maxwell[8]

To what extent is leadership a quality belonging to individuals, requiring "heroes" or a quality that is enabled through shared endeavour? Your beliefs here will impact on your focus as a leader – how do you try to impact?

We see leadership as fundamentally relational. Leadership happens in the spaces between. Leadership is not something that is possessed by an individual, but is something that is created by the way the leader interacts with those they "lead" (who they are, their history with that leader, assumptions about each other and more). In the words of William Tait[9] *"Leadership is foremost a social activity, an empathic as much as a cognitive pursuit, one conducted through relationships."* A leader is a different leader within a different context, with different followers, colleagues and bosses.

In Management Due Diligence work, it is no mistake that the focus is on the leadership team as well as the leader of that team, and on the context of the business – financial and commercial as well as the team of leaders – neither operates in isolation. Risks inherent in one leader are off-set, minimized or magnified when you look across the whole team, the relationships within the team and the relationship of the leader and leadership team to the context of the organization, market niche and business sector. Investors take a systems view of leadership – because they want the odds stacked in favour of success.

"Leadership requires a leader, followers and a shared endeavour".

Peter Hawkins[10]

SO, WHERE DO YOU START?

Given that the simple answer to most of the questions posed above is "both and", what is the starting point?

You.

LEADERSHIP PURPOSE

Leaders with some form of purpose will have a strong "anchor". The starting point is to build the self-knowledge required to lead with purpose. A leader with purpose can contribute more fully to the organization's purpose, the what and how of the organization's vision.[11]

Some of the big questions to explore: What is your purpose as a leader? What is the difference you want to make? What are you here for? What role does the world need you to fulfil? What inspires you, and in what ways do you want to inspire others? Identifying your core purpose as a leader – what are you here for? – connects with what's really core to you – and raises your self-awareness and self-knowledge.

But leadership of a team, group or an organization is bigger than you. What's the context you are in? What are the qualities of the system? For example, stable or unstable, emerging or established? Who are the stakeholders and what do they need from you as a leader and from your leadership? Who are the stakeholders of the future and what does that future perspective need you to consider here and now?

What is the role that you've been asked to play? Where are you in the leadership pipeline?[12] Are you an individual contributor, functional head, or leader of a global enterprise? What does this level of leadership require you to deliver? What do your followers need from you in this position?

Leadership purpose is not a singular entity – it encompasses you, the organization context, the future context, the system and your role within it.

LEADERSHIP IDENTITY – WHO ARE YOU?

Leading-self comes as part of the leadership of others. But who are you? What's you – what's not you? Knowing more of the answer gives you more power, as you have greater clarity in any context about what you bring, what others are bringing and how to create the path for people to follow.

How do you develop this knowledge? Through a process of working with your own experience and stories[13] – noticing what it is that you are doing, thinking and feeling and how these impact on those around you. Once you've accepted the strengths and the limitations that you bring as a person and a leader, and stopped trying to be omnipotent –

you can show more vulnerability – and in the words of Damien Hughes, vulnerability = power.[14]

It's hard to notice what you do when everything is familiar and comfortable. Instead, you need to step out of your comfort zone. There's no prescription about how far you need to step out, it needs to feel like a safe enough space for you to be stretched a little, feel a little uncomfortable – and not so safe that you can stay firmly wrapped in your personal security blanket of knowledge and expertise. This "learning space" is necessary to notice yourself, and gain insight and awareness. You start to notice what you're holding on to – the ideas and beliefs that you have about yourself and others. It's then a case of sorting through – which beliefs/ideas and notions about yourself are still relevant and helpful given what you have set as your purpose – and which are outdated and get in the way.

One company we have worked with starts the journey of leadership discovery with a group experience that strips away the comfort blanket of technical and professional knowledge and expertise. Instead participants are brought together in a music studio and, with a team of professional musicians, producers and coaches, create a music track that really builds from the individual contributions in the room – no musical capability required.

If you want to understand the things that really get in the way of you being the best that you can be – the internal saboteurs, fears and limiting assumptions that you might be holding onto – this kind of group experience brings that into sharp relief. It also brings out the resourcefulness in you and the strengths that you can build on to formulate the foundations of your leadership.

With careful attention to the wraparound necessary support and contracting, for groups of leaders who are on an ongoing learning journey together, this event fast-forwards people's experience of themselves and provides an increasing self-knowledge that they can build on moving forward. It's not the only method for gaining insight into who you are as a leader – but it is a powerful one.

Understanding who you are, gaining that self-knowledge and insight and embracing all that you are (including the things that you would rather weren't part of you, like that envious streak, the destructive competitor within, the gratifying pleaser, the passionate critic) – enables you to have more control and choice.

LEADERSHIP IMPACT – WHAT HAPPENS AS A RESULT OF YOU?

"If you think you are too small to make a difference, try going to bed with a mosquito in the room."

Anita Roddick[15]

What is your leadership footprint? What impact do you have? This is the point at which it's really useful to carry around a notebook specifically for you to gather data (what really did happen when you set a clear purpose for that team meeting instead of allowing it to drift through the agenda?); and reflect on some of the questions you might be asking yourself about leadership.

Perhaps you've identified your leadership purpose. Once crafted, how do you best voice and communicate that purpose to motivate others? What works even better? What works less well? Noticing yourself – and noting things down (because we really don't remember them) – can provide a new perspective, giving you more ideas on how to build and hone your craft as a leader.

To fast-forward your impact as a leader, be the leader that you want to become. Rather than just having an idea of the leader you are aiming to be – make it real. Step into the "best you" that you are imagining – act the part. Feel what that feels like, sounds like, thinks like – and centre yourself in that experience. This might feel a little odd – it's not a new idea.

Sydney Pollack[16], an actor and director, turned himself into a director by playing the role of a director. *"The first time I directed anything,"* he said, *"I acted like a director. That's the only thing I knew how to do, because I didn't know anything about directing. I had images of directors from working with them and I even tried to dress like a director – clothes that were kind of outdoorsy. If there had been a megaphone around, I would have grabbed it."*

How do you lead a team, lead change? Being a leader is not the end result, leadership is something that changes, needs honing and attention in order to stay fit for purpose.

"Earn your leadership every day."

Michael Jordan[17]

Clarifying your leadership approach and your leadership practice enables you to both understand the type of organizational context in which you thrive and contribute, and also, for any given context, to have greater choice and greater impact on the people you are leading.

LEADERSHIP FEARS AND VULNERABILITY

It's worth noting something about fear and vulnerability as a leader – and worthiness – as these can be critical to success (and failure). Brene Brown has explored the meaning, purpose and power of vulnerability[18] through 12 years of research. She notes that, as social beings, we gain meaning through connecting with others. BUT we fear that we are not perfect and therefore won't be acceptable to others. Fears about not being good enough, and about worth often emerge for those in leadership positions.

This fear is fuelled through TV, film, advertisements and social media – we're bombarded with the message *"You can be perfect if only you focus harder, learn more, be better"*.

So instead of accepting our imperfections (because no one is perfect) – and accepting that some people won't like us (by the law of averages alone), and that life can be tough (and often is), we get more worried about exposing our vulnerabilities – keeping ourselves locked in – hiding what we fear might drive others (and that promotion) away.

Until you can really embrace the idea that you are enough – no matter what gets done and how much remains un-done – you will be bowed down by the possibility of shame and vulnerability.[19] Getting over the fear of shame and vulnerability will unlock your ability to live and lead wholeheartedly. Indeed, we have experienced situations where a leader who is open about their imperfections and exposes their vulnerabilities is respected much more. Authenticity has more power than fabricated perfection. And the choice is yours.

There is a more sinister side to our fears – a legal term described "wilful blindness" discussed by Margaret Heffernan.[20] Wilful blindness is what happens when people are reluctant (fearful) about confronting uncomfortable facts. On the positive side, wilful blindness helps us ignore small blemishes and smoothes social interaction. We are able to maintain optimism in the face of significant difficulties – the optimism can at times help us survive.

At its worst, fear – fear of conflict, fear of change – keeps us living in the dark.

"An unconscious (and much denied) impulse to obey and conform shields us from confrontation and crowds provide friendly alibis for our inertia. And money has the power to blind us, even to our better selves."
Margaret Heffernan[21]

The sheer scale of damage that can e caused by organizations who are wilfully blind makes this issue significant. It is present at every level – and the antidote starts with the individual who is prepared to reveal central truths and ask uncomfortable questions.

LEADERSHIP AND 31PRACTICES

31Practices as a methodology is designed to build the leadership of the organizational system itself – building an enabling (rather than disabling) culture and context within which individual leaders can optimize their leadership impact.

As an example of this, we return to the story of Zappos. The core values identified by Zappos, and the way these values were operationalized and integrated into the culture of the organization, drove a system that enabled Zappos leaders. Core values were important guidelines that managers used in their decision making.[22]

The "hire and fire" criteria applied by Tony Hsieh is one that we use with our clients now in order to refine and prioritize what is truly core to them.

As a leader, 31Practices requires you to embody the values and practices that you expect in others – first you have to lead yourself in order to create an enabling system. To lead others, you need to take the risk – model the daily Practices and share stories of not only what that felt like, but what the impact was – and how you have started to develop your habits. Keep reminding yourself that culture in an organization is the shadow of the leader… your shadow

"Given all the hard work that goes into developing and implementing a solid values system, most companies would probably prefer not to bother. And indeed they shouldn't because poorly implemented values can poison a company' culture."

Pat Lencioni[23]

Want to know more?
- Luis Gallardo (2012) *Brands and Rousers*. London: Lid Publishing.
- Peter Hawkins has written extensively about leadership – and his work offers an insightful read. One of his more recent books is: *Leadership Team Coaching: Developing collective transformational leadership*. Kogan Page, published in 2011.

PART **5**

EVOLUTION

In Part 5, we provide insight into the key stages of the evolution of 31Practices at a number of different levels. We have chosen to present the developments of 31Practices as they occurred, through application in partnership with client organizations. This learning took place with organizations of very different sizes and business contexts. As we support our clients to learn and develop, we continue to refine 31Practices as we learn from each application.

This part also provides insight into the impact of 31Practices in diverse business contexts. We present the application of 31Practices at a single site, private members' club, at multiple sites across the UK for one of the "Big Four" banks, and multiple sites globally for the property division of a blue chip corporate organization.

We finish off with a more in-depth case study at a mixed use property development in the south of England.

The chapters in Part 5 are light and short, designed to give you a flavour rather than detail an exhaustive account.

These multiple insights into the application of 31Practices underline how the approach is tailored for each organization in order for it to be integrated and part of "the way we do things around here".

CHAPTER 25 SITE

A prestigious private members' club has been using 31Practices since 2010. In this particular case, the organization had not articulated its values so this needed to be the starting point. A workshop was facilitated with the leadership team to re affirm the essence of the club and the expectations of all stakeholders, and to create a service promise. Against this backdrop, the leadership team worked through a process to explore, articulate and define the core values of the organization.

The proposed values were presented to the next level (less senior) of management for discussion and were subsequently approved by the chief executive and board of directors.

Following this, a series of high-energy, short workshops were delivered for all members of staff. The limited time available was driven by the operational needs of the business but, as so often when there is a restriction on resources, innovation flourished. As a result, a highly valuable evolution of the 31Practices process was created. As with previous organizations, the workshops were delivered to a mixed audience of function and hierarchy. These were repeated throughout the day to enable as many employees to attend as possible. Because of the short amount of time available, it was critical to engage the audience in a high-tempo style so the approach was based on metaphors of the organization's values with time restrictions to create urgency and speed. This was a great success and has subsequently become an integral part of the 31Practices workshops to generate the best quality output. The whole process was a great example of the *Purpose* and *Identify* stages covered in Chapters 5 and 6.

"The great thing in this world is not so much where we are, but in what direction we are going."

Oliver Wendell Holmes Jr.[1]

Champions were then identified at an operational level to drive the programme forward and a workshop was conducted with this group to equip them with some specific skills for the role focused on leadership qualities and sharing an understanding of how to manage different responses to the initiative.

Another process development in the same client organization was in the areas of performance review: quarterly telephone calls with the senior leadership team were scheduled to review successes, challenges, next steps and support required. A formal annual review visit also takes place, consisting of one-to-one interviews with employees and customers, a group session with the Champions, some desktop review and a session with the Leadership team. An annual review of the 31Practices considers whether they are still relevant or if any changes should be made. The review process supports and reinforces the 31Practices approach as a "journey". The review is wide-ranging, which enables a deeper understanding of successes and challenges and the actions that need to be taken to move forward.

"Progress is not accomplished in one stage."

Victor Hugo, Les Misérables[2]

In February 2013, the club was re-assessed for Investors In People and were congratulated on their achievements over the past three years since the last assessment, which were noted as "very significant".

"When we adopted 31Practices, I wanted a scheme that staff at every level could create and put into practice every day. The effect was instantaneous and provided a real step change in the consistency and pride of our service delivery across all sections of the Club. We received great feedback from Members and most importantly a real morale boost for staff knowing that their efforts were being better recognised by each other as well as Members. Our Investors in People accreditation review hit our highest score to date and it was no coincidence, in my opinion, that our bottom line profit rose by 25% over two years as well!" Marc Newey, Chief Executive, Roehampton Club

CHAPTER 26 NATIONAL

The first version of 31Practices was created for a portfolio of corporate offices for a "Big Four" bank who were pursuing a strategy of developing world-class workplace services solutions in support of the commercial activity on the UK mainland. The aim was to create a new paradigm for the workplace, rather than to incrementally improve what already existed.

A key objective of the service delivery model was to reinforce the organization's brand and values through the service experience in the corporate workplaces and this was achieved through an early version of 31Practices.

In this instance, the senior leadership team translated a values set into 31 behaviours which were then communicated to and adopted by all employees on a daily basis. A pilot of 26 workplaces in Scotland and the north of England was undertaken to validate the concept. This was then rapidly implemented across 120 city-centre locations throughout the UK.

As many of the offices were newly opened, it was recognized that recruitment and retention of front-line people with the right attitude was critical. The 31 behaviours played a key part in the recruitment process so that new employees were clear from the outset about the culture of the organization and the behaviour expected. They were also heavily referred to in a formal induction programme during employees' first 90 days.

Because the people involved in providing the services were from a number of different companies, a single vision and set of common behaviours provided a foundation for a "virtual organization" approach with a focus on shared learning and best practice. This was supported by a schedule of "one team" training, forums, and innovation workshops. Nominations were made for those employees "living" the behaviours and these people were publicly recognized in a monthly newsletter and through an annual awards event in order to positively reinforce the behaviours. A climate of service excellence, empowerment and ownership was supported with robust human resource processes. The leadership style was highly operational and visible to reinforce 31Practices and recognize excellent performance. It was notable that success was faster and more pronounced in newly opened buildings. Starting with a blank sheet, it was easier to implement the approach and progressive leadership, combining the heart, mind and body principles outlined in Part 3. In existing buildings, the "status quo" had to be overcome which took more effort and was a slower process.

"If you tell people where to go, but not how to get there, you'll be amazed at the results."

George S. Patton[1]

Further evidence of the success of the front-of-house initiative was the dramatic improvement in customer satisfaction measurement. On average this moved from 69% to 82%. At the same time, costs were reduced. The achievements were also recognized within the organization in the form of a Customer Service Award, and by an industry sector global innovation award.

We recently met with the client from the time of this project who moved with his organization to the US. He told us that he is still using this version of 31Practices for his supply chain team some ten years after the original introduction.

"Using 31Practices as the foundation and principles that the team live by has enabled me to develop teams, organizations and structures that deliver outstanding results within the UK and Ireland….. and subsequently the US. " Trevor Wigmore, Real Estate Executive, RBS

CHAPTER 27 GLOBAL

The first global application of 31Practices was a key work-stream in a wide-ranging service and culture project for the property division of a blue chip corporate organization. The locations included London, New York, Hong Kong, Singapore, Tokyo, Paris and Frankfurt. The objective was to create a consistent level and style of service to reinforce the organization's brand and values.

This project represented an important development for 31Practices because it was the first time that employee workshops were used to help create the set of Practices. As always, there were some sceptics who referred to cultural differences being a barrier to such an approach but, in hindsight, this proved to be no more than an imaginary obstacle. The key is in the style of delivery which must be respectful and sincere.

The first workshops were held in London, followed by New York, then back to Europe before the Asia-Pacific locations. All the workshops were delivered over a two-month period. The participants were cross-functional and across hierarchies, including supply chain partner companies. The objective was to identify behaviours that were directly connected to the values, that could be adopted globally, and, together, would set the behaviour of the organization's people apart from other organizations.

The output from the workshops was distilled down into a draft version of 31Practices and circulated through the business for review and comment. This part of the process allowed a preview of the 31Practices and also the ability to suggest final changes. Because of this, when the final version of 31Practices was launched, everybody was familiar with them and adoption was straightforward.

"Without involvement, there is no commitment. Mark it down, asterisk it, circle it, underline it."

Stephen Covey[1]

A global recognition programme was set up, but importantly, managed on a regional basis by supervisory-level staff. The programme encouraged nominations for those living the Practices well; each quarter, the best examples were recognized in an internal newsletter. The newsletter had a core global content with the balance produced regionally. Supervisors, rather than a communications department or senior management, took responsibility as they were best placed to see what was happening on a daily basis. It also made 31Practices more real, owned within the business rather than centrally – resulting in a high level of engagement and interest.

Some of the rich stories of 31Practices from this case include the story about a member of the cleaning team who rescued an office employee's engagement ring that had slipped down the waste pipe from a hand basin; and another about a security guard who drove an employee home after they had lost their wallet. These were great examples of how stories (Chapter 15, *Storytelling*) can be so powerful in reinforcing the positive behaviours you're looking to foster.

Two examples from New York about three months after the launch typify the success of the programme: first, we have previously mentioned the post-room employee saying: *"Look, Number 16, I suggested that in our workshop"* and secondly an engineer (ex-Marine) saying *"when this whole thing started I thought it was a crock of shit, but you know, I think it is the best thing I have seen in my working career"*. You will see connections with the themes referred to in Chapter 11, *Inspiration*.

After the programme was launched in Asia, the head of business from Bangkok called the London office and asked *"What happened? This place is buzzing"*. And this is typical of the impact that 31Practices has. Many jobs are repetitive and the workplace can become "routine", with people operating on auto-pilot. 31Practices provides an opportunity to focus on a behaviour each day and "wake people up" to be mindful, conscious of their behaviour and live this one behaviour excellently. 31Practices continues to be used in parts of the organization all over the world, from London to Paris to Singapore to Mumbai five years after the formal programme.

"31Practices is a great tool that provides simple, yet powerful, methods for service staff to enhance the brand experience. The tool is cost effective and easy to implement, yet its impact is significant and cumulative over

time. It is a tangible, pragmatic approach to enhancing client satisfaction and loyalty – hugely important but often overlooked as critical to a firm's economic success." Steve Flaim, Global Head of CRES, Barclays Capital.

CHAPTER 28 CASE STUDY

This case study is based on a mixed use property development in the south of England. The development consisted of designer outlets, bars and restaurants, leisure and entertainment facilities, a marina, a hotel and car parking.

It is a very good example of a virtual organization because there is a team of people employed by the landlord operating together with the teams of a variety of service partners (security, cleaning and technical services). From a customer perspective, however, the complexity of the organizational structure is irrelevant. Customers regard all of the employees as being there to provide the appropriate customer service and will form their perception of the organization accordingly.

In early 2011, as part of the customer service strategy, 31Practices was adopted.

A number of workshops were held with a cross-section of employees, including management and service providers. The workshops focused on what the values and vision meant to this group, developing the 31Practices eventually adopted so that all staff (management and service providers) could identify with them.

A team of Customer Service Champions was created specifically to assist with the day-to-day deployment of the approach. Their first task was to work with the resulting 31Practices to ensure the "language" was easy for every employee to understand and apply.

Workshops for all staff from the various service partners were led by the Customer Service Champions to encourage two-way communication and allow feedback right from the beginning of the initiative. The workshops were organized for small groups at different times of the day to make it easy for people to attend, irrespective of their hours of work. A celebratory lunch and dinner were provided to launch the programme and carry cards (see Chapter 1, *Introduction*) were given to every member of staff, becoming part of the uniform standard.

The on-the-job training was embraced by all members of the "virtual organization" and reinforced in a number of different ways; for example, a daily email of the Practice for the day, and a flip-over calendar of Practices in the restroom.

Once 31Practices was in place, nominations were requested about what team members had done and how they had demonstrated and personalized the various Practices. The aim was to highlight the "day-to-day" rather than just the heroics, allowing everyone to take part and make a personal contribution. The nominations were posted in a central location so that everybody could see how others had contributed. At the end of the month, the best nominations were shortlisted, and the Customer Service Champions met and reviewed the month and voted in a confidential ballot to select the month's winner. This assisted in bringing all service partners together, working as one team, and highlighted all the good examples of how people were making a contribution. The winner of the previous month was then invited to join the voting for the following month. Each winner was awarded a certificate and gift card in recognition of what they had done. A newsletter provided details of why the winner had been chosen; however, all the other shortlisted nominations were also described. In effect, this created the "heritage" of the organization through stories and positively reinforced desirable behaviour.

The regular (daily) feedback meant that the programme was kept at the forefront of people's minds and while the budget was not available for a team-building exercise off-site, this "on-the-job" approach gave a greater understanding and appreciation of what other employees were doing at the Centre. The Customer Service Champions (training team) worked together to further develop the programme during the period, learning from their experiences and fine tuning it to ensure momentum was maintained so that it kept the wider teams' motivation high.

Nominations highlighting the successes from across the virtual organization promoted positive team relations and helped to create an engaged team keen to offer the best customer service.

This project highlighted the importance of many of the topics referred to in Chapter 18, *Discipline*. There was a significant amount of planning,

administrative process management and monitoring on an ongoing basis
that helped 31Practices to be so successful.

*"It was character that got us out of bed, commitment
that moved us into action, and discipline that enabled
us to follow through."*

Zig Ziglar[1]

THE IMPACT?

Customer service is an intrinsic part of the development's product and
experience. This commitment to excellent customer service is the key to
ensuring customer retention, which in turn drives sales. The 2011 exit poll
showed customers had 89% satisfaction with their experience with service
polling at 87%. Visit time increased and despite a difficult economic
climate, 2011/12 sales increased +10% on the previous year, compared to
+8% in 2011.

845 31Practices nominations were made during 11 months, from all
departments and service providers. There was 100% participation and
at least one winner from each of the service partner companies. 92 of
these nominations were shortlisted during the period, giving an average
of eight each month, which meant that each month, a broad variety of
nominations were received from around the business.

100% of staff attended workshops carried out at different times of the
day and week to enable all shift workers to gain an understanding of the
programme and what was required of them. 95% of staff attended either
the launch lunch or dinner; they were put on at different times to ensure
maximum attendance of the team working different shifts.

An Employee Engagement Survey took place in November 2011. The
results highlighted that the level of engagement was 11 points above the
Towers Watson UK High Performance Norm. When asked if they felt able
to impact customer satisfaction within their role, this was +33 compared
to the Group. In addition, the team's results of "feeling energized to go the
extra mile" were +27 compared to the High Performance Norm.

The programme was seen to encourage greater appreciation and
understanding of other team members' roles working at different times of
the day and give greater motivation to provide fantastic customer service.

Over 80 new ideas were suggested through the programme, two of which were winners for their respective months. This included the introduction of a temporary disabled user badge in the car park, which allowed visitors with a temporary disability, such as a broken leg, to park in a disabled space, allowing them easier access to the lifts and facilities normally only granted to visitors who are registered disabled. In addition, for site evacuations or exercises, one of the cleaning team suggested that temporary stickers should be placed on occupiers' doors to confirm they were empty and had been checked, which would assist in speed and greater efficiency when confirming building clearance. Both ideas were implemented at low cost and regarded as great successes.

Finally, in addition to the hard measures mentioned above, positive feedback was received through mystery shopper visits, testimonials from a variety of staff from different service providers and customer feedback (increased from five entries from 11/8/09 to 31/12/10 to 59 from 1/1/11 to 28/02/12).

In summary, this example highlights how effective the 31Practices tool is in translating an organization's core values into practical day-to-day behaviour and the measurable impact that can be achieved by giving ownership to operational teams supported by a robust recognition programme.

29

CHAPTER 29 MY31PRACTICES

"An ounce of practice is worth more than tons of preaching."

Mahatma Gandhi[1]

In Chapter 1, *Introduction*, the current frontier for 31Practices is described as the development of a personal application of 31Practices: my31Practices. In the "perfect storm" that is globalization, economic uncertainty, family fragmentation, enhanced pace of business, instant communications, unlimited connectedness – we find that we are endlessly busy, both at work and in our social lives. Against this context, it is very easy to "do" without mindful awareness of what we are doing all of this for. The result? We end up "doing" without much thought about how we are behaving – caught in habits of thinking and action that are at best unsustainable, and, at worst, destructive. Under this pressure, we can very easily feel out of control and lose touch with our personal core values, our core purpose and what creates meaning for us.

But there is another way… People can often see the benefit in joining a gym or creating a fitness regime to be the best they can be from a physical perspective. Might it then be possible that people would benefit from developing mental and behavioural fitness in a more holistic way? To do this starts with discovering and reconnecting with our personal core values… what's really important to us. The next step is to align the way we think, feel and behave, and this is where my31Practices can help by releasing the power of your personal values through a set of very practical behaviours every day. In this way, people can be the best they can be or the best version of themselves.

"Knowledge is of no value unless you put it into practice."
Anton Chekhov[2]

But why should we bother? As the humanist Carl Rogers[3] noted, we are our own best experts, resourceful and whole. Looking within ourselves to find our "inner compass" of guiding values is useful and significantly helpful.

"Just trust yourself, then you will know how to live."
Johann Wolfgang von Goethe[4]

Our own values are not immediately obvious to us. They show up in our behaviour, what we move towards, what we move away from. They show up in our language, stories and traditions. Some people work with a coach to help them identify their core values.

You don't necessarily need to employ a professional thinking partner to help you work out what your core values are. But, for some people, it can help. And a quick conversation with an insightful friend can help to get you started, or a moment to reflect with some provoking questions can be just as fruitful.

Looking back over your own life events can provide a realization of what is actually important for you. A significant life event can be a rich source of insight. If you have had the pleasure of listening to Tony Robbins[5], you'll hear in his story that a significant event that occurred when he was 11 was key in defining his values model. As his family was given food, a fact that his father could not accept, Tony talks about the human need to contribute, to give to others. This experience informs a core part of Tony Robbins' life purpose.

Our core values provide us with a clearer path when faced with choice and ambiguity – if you are someone who values "creativity and freedom", you might be more likely to value others' opinions and so spend a little more time listening to others as a matter of course. Why is this important? In simple terms, when our behaviour is aligned with our values, we are happy and, when they are not, we feel stressed. In our modern society, people are increasingly uncomfortable with how they behave compared to the way they would want to.

To demonstrate this point, few people reading this will be unaware of the Tiger Woods story over the last few years (mentioned in Chapter 6, *Identify*). He went from the most successful golfer in history, and the highest paid athlete in the world for over a decade, to somebody shunned by businesses, friends and the general public, struggling to regain form. When he was interviewed on ESPN about the issues that have been well documented, Tiger said, *"I had gotten away from my core values"*. Up until his "transgression", Tiger Woods was known all over the world as consistent, powerful, dedicated and a loyal family man. But the moment his behaviour and actions betrayed this picture, the whole thing crumbled. As he said himself, he became removed from his "core values" as a person, husband, and father. Because Tiger had abandoned his core values, his world came crashing down.

In this case, the destructive impact of what happened was easier to see and quantify because Tiger Woods is a "personal brand" which focuses on the individual, in this case a "performance brand" in the public spotlight. The importance of his behaviour being aligned with his core values is therefore more magnified, but nevertheless serves as a good reminder to the rest of us of how important it is to align our behaviour with our core values and why 31Practices can be so helpful. Just think of somebody you know that you thought stood for certain values and then did something that seemed to betray this. How did you feel about them after this? How strong were your feelings? How long would it take for them to regain your trust?

So how does my31Practices work? Well, the principles are exactly the same as for the organization version of 31Practices, following the framework outlined in Chapter 4, *Framework*. First it is necessary to understand and articulate your personal core values. Once we understand our core values, it really helps to bring these values to life in our day-to-day behaviour. In this way we can powerfully combine the resources of our mind, heart and body. This is what my31Practices does. It helps translate the higher-level values into practical actions and behaviours – creating a virtuous circle around what we believe, how we behave and how we feel. Just as for the organization version of 31Practices, the idea is for you to focus on just one Practice each day so it is easy to do. Over time we learn through practising and repetition, and our behaviour becomes consistent and habitual. Of course, this is easier said than done! We all know how we can start new things full of enthusiasm with good intentions, whether this is a New Year's resolution or a fitness programme or a diet. But then, for some reason, our intentions seem less important and other things take over. This is because we are too "busy", both at work and in our social lives.

Our lives become full of "doing" with little time or thought for "being". We are swept along on a current of "busyness" rather than making choices based on what is meaningful to us.

"You can't hire someone to practice for you."

H. Jackson Brown, Jr.[6]

Mindful of the above and the central role that technology plays in our lives, we thought that a technology platform that could be used on mobiles, tablets, laptops and PCs would be invaluable and this is how it works:

The first thing to do is identify your five core values. You might want to refer to Chapter 2, *Values* and apply this technique to your personal values. There are a number of ways to do this depending on your preference; you can simply select five from a list of values, complete an online questionnaire or even have a conversation with a personal coach. You then simply enter the values into the values field.

Second, for each value, you work out six practical behaviours that would show you were living the value. The fun, creative bit is using your own experience and ideas to do this. For example if you value "honesty", what to you represents the very best example of "honesty"? A judge? Mother Theresa? Your best friend? Your mother? When you have chosen the example(s), think of all the behaviours they display that makes you think of them as "honest" in your mind's eye: these might be that they look you in the eye when talking, give you bad news as well as good, always listen to all points of view before making a decision. When you have a good long list, think which six of those you want to adopt to "live" the value of honesty and enter them into your 31Practices list. There is a particular style to follow when writing the Practices: Use "I" to start, then write the behaviour you are going to adopt in the present tense. Finally, highlight one or two key words in bold; for example, "I look out for **strangers** who may be in need and offer to **help**". You can update your list at any time so you can refine the wording as you go.

You don't have to have all 31 Practices before you start. You can have just one practical behaviour for each of your five values and then you're off – adding more as you go along. To keep it easy, every day, you will be reminded of your Practice for that day. You can even set the time to receive your reminder – so it really works for you. And if you are less into technology, you can design and print your own my31Practices carry card or crib sheet to refer to.

You can also reinforce each Practice by adding other things to inspire you – a photograph, a video clip or a quote/piece of prose. For example, if your value is "Caring" and your Practice is "I look out for **strangers** who may be in need and offer to **help**" you could attach a photograph of a stranger you met on holiday, a video of the song "Strangers in the night", or the quote *"Strangers are just friends you haven't met yet"*.

Have you heard the phrase: what gets measured gets done? This is another built-in feature of my31Practices. At the end of each day (again, you can set the time if you want to), you will be asked to rate how you did on a scale of 1 to 6. Nobody is going to check so it is completely down to you. If you want to, you can set some performance levels with rewards and at the end of each month you can see what reward you've earned.

You can also capture your experiences by recording "what" you did and how this made you feel, and the impact your behaviour had. For example, *"I was walking through the station when I noticed an old lady struggling to open her purse and then spill coins all over the floor. I helped her pick them up, she thanked me for my help and we had a chat about her being on a pension. Her name was Enid. As I walked away, I noticed that I felt uplifted."* Over time, you will collect all the things you have done under each of your Practices, so you can just scroll through what you have done to bring your values to life – you may be pleasantly surprised at just how much you have done. You can sort by Practice number or value. You can also share your Practice and what you have done to "live" your Practice with friends through Twitter, Facebook and email.

It's fun, you develop much greater awareness of what's important to you and how to "live it", it's quick and easy to do each day and everything is there at your fingertips through your mobile phone.

And that is it, my31Practices: release the secret of your personal values every day.

The web application is being beta tested and launched in 2013 at www. My31Practices.com

One exercise to help you identify your values

This exercise has been adapted from one shared by Laura Whitworth and her colleagues.[7]

Get a large blank sheet of paper, write in pencil – keep an eraser to hand.

Group similar ideas/words together and don't worry if no one else would put those words together – this is entirely yours.

Peak Moment: think about peak moments: times when you have been really energized and motivated, you felt you had endless resources to apply to whatever it was you were engaged in – who was present, what was going on, what values were being "honoured" at that time.

Low Moments: think about those moments when you were angry, upset, frustrated. Perhaps frustrated about how someone else was treated. We might not recognize our values until something or someone gets in the way.

Must Haves: what is that you "must have" in your life in order to be fulfilled? e.g. creative self-expression? Excitement?

Critical Decision Moments: at times when you've had to make a decision that you found particularly difficult to make, what was it finally that persuaded you in one direction?

As you become aware of each instance, what was it that led to the "peak moment", to the "frustration", to the "must have" to the final decision? What does this say to you about what you value?

Aim for a list of between five and ten values. Don't worry that they are not perhaps perfect, or that you are not 100% sure that they are the values that are important to you (yet); this is not a "one time only opportunity to state who you are". We believe that while our core values are pretty stable, it can take some time to become really aware of what's critical to us.

Can you prioritize this list of values? What are the top five?

"I made my own assessment of my life and began to live it. That was freedom."

Fernando Flores[8]

CHAPTER 30 SUMMARY

As we come to the end of this book, we trust that you have found it enjoyable, thought provoking and a helpful read... and will continue to revisit various chapters from time to time.

"The only thing that is constant is change."

Heraclitus[1]

The key context for organizations is that the pace of change has never been faster and continues to accelerate. This situation is fuelled by our ability to communicate information at lightning speed to millions of people. We have a voracious appetite for new knowledge and live in a world of unprecedented complexity. Collaboration and outsourcing has created more and more virtual organizations.

But against this dynamic landscape blurred by speed and change, we remain, at our core, human beings with some basic and simple characteristics. We are emotional beings in need of a sense of purpose and a sense of belonging. These base needs are very powerful.

The traditional role of the organization was to bring order, direction and control. But as the world becomes more dynamic, this approach is less and less relevant. It is more appropriate to have flexibility of objectives, action and reaction; to be able to adapt, to be agile. It takes too long for the traditional command and control approach to respond. Decentralized decision making is needed but within a constancy of "way" or core personality. As organizations are judged on the behaviour of the people representing them, authenticity is the new Holy Grail for organizations. We have been aware of the potential repercussions of failing to be authentic since as long ago as the Enron scandal and before, but in our more dynamic environment, this can now happen more often, more quickly and on a larger scale.

Of course, values alignment is no mean feat to achieve: connecting organizations from the boardroom to the front line, aligning the hearts, minds and bodies of perhaps thousands of individuals to come together to represent a common "way"; overcoming the barriers of individual interests, functions, different companies, geographies, and cultural differences; and doing this consistently, where any failure or shortfall may be communicated to millions in a flash. No mean feat indeed – but if it was easy to do, everybody would be doing it already.

While it may not be easy to achieve in practice, we believe that it is nonetheless very straightforward and consists of a number of key steps:

1. Establish a clear sense of purpose that engages hearts and minds.
2. Identify a set of values and be clear about what the words mean.
3. Establish the "way things work around here", constantly nourish and cultivate this and do not allow anything to contaminate it.
4. Use the 31Practices tool (or similar approaches) to make the values part of the daily conversation and embed them into the fabric of the organization. Use them as a reference for decision making.
5. Make it an organization-wide agenda, not owned by a function like Human Resources or Communications.
6. Have the mindset of taking a journey rather than delivering a project.
7. Lead by example: the more senior the individual, the more magnified their behaviour is (both positively and negatively).
8. Recognize the behaviours that represent the values to positively reinforce them throughout the organization and create the organization "heritage".
9. Assess the impact of the way people are behaving at a quantitative level but recognize the limitations of measurement. Also, pay attention at a more granular "cause and effect", qualitative level.
10. Refine the approach, strengthening what is working well.
11. Involve employees across hierarchies and functions throughout the process.
12. Be aware of the underpinning psychological, sociological and philosophical principles that are at play: the Heart Principles, focused on being; the Mind Principles, focused on knowing; and the Body

Principles, focused on doing. We can't actually separate with hard lines what is heart, mind and body; all are part of each other – just like a holograph.
13. Recognize that we do not operate in a vacuum and that there is a broader system and context that leaders and organizations find themselves in.
14. Learn from the experience of others but always apply these learnings to your own particular circumstances which are unique to you. Make it your own – don't just put someone else's version into your organization.

As we say, very straightforward. You may wonder which of these steps is the most important but we believe that chance of success is optimized only by doing ALL of the above. The challenge is in the relentless pursuit and obsession with authentic delivery: every action, every person, every day… and practice makes more perfect!

As the song we quoted at the beginning of Chapter 2, *Values* says: *"It ain't what you do, it's the way that you do it, that's what gets results."*[2]

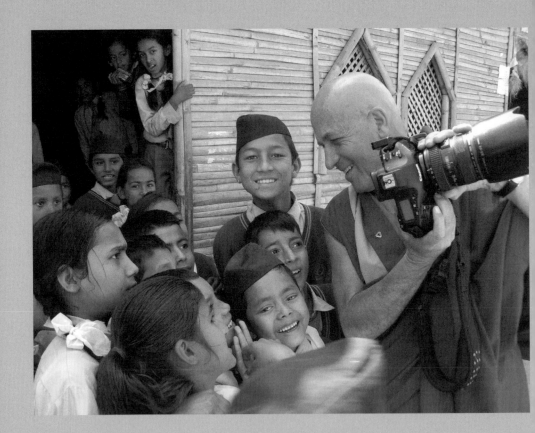

CHAPTER 31   PHOTOGRAPHY

"Matthieu's spiritual life and camera are one, and from this spring these images, fleeting yet eternal."

Henri Cartier-Bresson[1]

When we were thinking about this book project, of course we wanted to create something that people wanted to read. We wanted the book to be of interest at a very practical level and also at a level that was thought provoking. But we also wanted the book to be more than that, to be special. Early on in the project, we had the idea of the structure of 31 chapters and decided to seek out a photographer whose work we could feature at the beginning of each chapter. We explored a number of possibilities and then (thanks to Google!) we discovered Matthieu Ricard. You will see from the below that, apart from his beautiful photographs, Matthieu is a perfect "fit". We are honoured that he has chosen to support our book and, in turn, we are keen to support his Karuna-Shechen Foundation so please consider making a contribution.

Matthieu Ricard is a best-selling author, translator, photographer, and Buddhist monk highly regarded for his scholarship and knowledge of Buddhism and Tibetan culture. He has lived, studied, and worked in the Himalayan region for over 40 years.

The son of French philosopher Jean-François Revel and artist Yahne Le Toumelin, Matthieu was born in France in 1946 and grew up among the personalities and ideas of Paris' intellectual and artistic circles. He earned a Ph.D. degree in cell genetics at the renowned Institute Pasteur under the

Nobel Laureate Francois Jacob. In 1967, he travelled to India to meet great spiritual masters from Tibet.

After completing his doctoral thesis in 1972, he left his scientific career to concentrate on Buddhist contemplative practice. Since then, he has lived in India, Bhutan, and Nepal and studied with some of the greatest teachers of that tradition, Kangyur Rinpoche and Dilgo Khyentse Rinpoche.

He is the author of several best-selling books including *The Monk and the Philosopher*, a dialogue with his father; *The Quantum and the Lotus*, a dialogue with the astrophysicist Trinh Xuan Thuan; *Happiness: A Guide to Developing Life's Most Important Skill*; and *The Art of Meditation*. His books have been translated into over 20 languages.

Matthieu's intimate knowledge and unprecedented access to Tibetan teachers and culture has enabled him to capture on camera the spiritual masters, landscapes, and people of the Himalayas. He is the author and photographer of *Journey to Enlightenment, Buddhist Himalayas, Monk Dancers of Tibet, Tibet: An Inner Journey, Motionless Journey*, and *Bhutan, Land of Serenity*. His work has been exhibited throughout the world.

Henri Cartier-Bresson said of his photographs: *"Matthieu's camera and his spiritual life are one, and from this spring these images, fleeting yet eternal."*

Matthieu Ricard has dedicated his life to the study and practice of Buddhism following the teachings of the greatest Tibetan spiritual masters of our time. He has been the French interpreter for the Dalai Lama since 1989. He is the author of several volumes of Buddhist texts translated from the Tibetan, such as *The Life of Shabkar: The Autobiography of a Tibetan Yogin, The Heart Treasure of the Enlightened Ones*, and *The Heart of Compassion: The Thirty-seven Verses on the Practice of a Bodhisattva* (teachings by Dilgo Khyentse Rinpoche).

He is an active member of the Mind and Life Institute, an organization dedicated to collaborative research between scientists and Buddhist scholars and meditators. He is engaged in research on the effect of mind training and meditation on the brain at various universities in the USA and Europe.

In addition to receiving the French National Order of Merit for his humanitarian work, he has been the guest speaker at TED and many other conferences throughout North America and Europe, as well as guided seminars and talks on happiness, compassion and meditation. When he is not travelling, Matthieu resides at Shechen Monastery in Nepal.

Karuna-Shechen

In 2000, Matthieu Ricard founded Karuna-Shechen, a global non-profit humanitarian organization. Based on the ideal of "compassion in action",

Karuna-Shechen develops education, medical, and social projects for the most destitute populations of the Himalayan region. Under his guidance, the organization has initiated and managed over 120 humanitarian projects in India, Nepal, and Tibet. The photographs in this book are taken in areas where the projects are located.

Karuna-Shechen's beneficiaries live in remote and isolated areas and have little or no other access to essential services. Over 90,000 beneficiaries have been helped. They range in age from young children to the elderly. Special attention is given to the education and empowerment of women. Services are offered on a sliding scale according to means and free of charge to the poorest patients. Karuna-Shechen's activities have a significant direct impact on individuals, families, and communities. Its programmes are developed in direct response to their needs and aspirations by working directly in the field with local partners. Projects range from a large clinic in Nepal to small dispensaries in Tibet, from schools for 3,000 children to helping village grandmothers become solar engineers, and caring for the abandoned elderly to helping individual children in need.

Widespread poverty in India and Nepal makes access to even basic healthcare extremely difficult; in Tibet, remote regions do not have adequate medical facilities. Karuna-Shechen helps 16 medical clinics in eastern Tibet, operates a large medical clinic and dispensary in Nepal, and a mobile clinic and medical centre in India. Its outreach programmes include health education in schools and slum areas of Nepal, basic medical help to villages and the destitute in Bihar, India, and programmes in Tibet to help disaster victims. The majority of the patients are women and children.

Almost 50% of Karuna-Shechen's resources are used for education with an emphasis on the education of girls who are often not given the opportunity to go to school. In Nepal, Karuna-Shechen builds bamboo schools to educate thousands of poor children. In India, it facilitates non-formal education to women in rural villages. In Tibet, it offers scholarships to students for higher education and builds and supports schools for Tibetan children.

Its social service programmes include support of the elderly, a hospice, vocational training, and help for disadvantaged individuals. Karuna-Shechen also supports a number of cultural preservation projects in Tibet.

All Matthieu Ricard's proceeds from his books, photographs, and events are donated to Karuna-Shechen. Support also comes from individual donors and foundations and online contributions. For further information on these wonderful projects and to learn how you can participate, please go to www.karuna-shechen.org.

GLOSSARY OF PHOTOGRAPHS

Chapter 1: Introduction
Two Tibetan monks at the banks of the icy Lake Yilung Lhatso in eastern Tibet, not far from Derge. The engraving on the rock reads "Om Mani Padme Hum", which is the mantra of the Buddha of Compassion, Avalokiteshvara (Chenrezig in Tibetan). 2005.

Part 1: Laying the groundwork

Chapter 2: Values
High in the mountains of eastern Tibet, five elaborately dressed young nomad women, their dresses lined in fur (chubas), attend the festival of Mani Gengok.

Chapter 3: Journey
Even in August, the path around the sacred mountains of the Amnye Machen range in the Golok province in eastern Tibet remains covered in snow. With its peak rising 18,000 feet above sea level, the mountain is regarded as one of the holiest in Tibet. Thousands of pilgrims trek around it each year, taking as long as nine days to do so. The mountain's melted snows become the Yellow River, the great mother waterway of China. 2001.

Part 2: 31Practices: the underpinning framework

Chapter 4: Framework
Dilgo Khyentse Rinpoche (1910–1991), one of the main teachers of the Ancient Tradition (Nyingmapa) of Tibetan Buddhism, visits Thangboche Monastery, near Everest base camp in Nepal. From his window he watches sacred dances being held in his honour in the courtyard below. Next to him, his host, Thangboche Rinpoche. From the monastery, one has spectacular views of the mountains. 1989.

Chapter 5: Purpose
Hundreds of monks of Shechen Monastery in eastern Tibet work in orchestrated teams to pitch the vast tent in which the sacred dance festival will take place. Some 15 monks worked for more than a week to stitch together the thick white cotton. 1988.

Chapter 6: Identify
A nomad family from the region of Dzachuka in Kham, eastern Tibet. 2005.

Chapter 7: Action
On the first day of the main festival of sacred dance at Shechen Monastery in eastern Tibet, the monks rehearse in plain monastic

dress, adding some simple yellow scarves. Only on the second day will they wear their full costumes of brocade and wooden masks. A large crowd of enthusiastic lay spectators has already gathered. 1985.

Chapter 8: Impact
A nomad rider firing blanks at a target as he gallops past, during the Mani Genkok festival in Kham, eastern Tibet. Following the grand opening, the riders ride past the crowd in turn and perform all sorts of acrobatics with their old muskets. Then, spurring their horses into a gallop, they fire blanks at a paper target extended between two posts stuck in the ground. When they hit the bull's eye, a jet of powder shoots out of a cannon and the target collapses in clouds of white smoke. When they miss, the onlookers laugh good-naturedly.

Chapter 9: Refine
Red-beaked Himalayan Magpie flies over Shechen retreat centre in Namo Buddha, Nepal. 2006.

Part 3: Section 1: The heart principles

Chapter 10: Emotion
A Tibetan traditional doctor takes the pulse of a nomad girl from Tsatsa, eastern Tibet, in a clinic supported by Karuna-Shechen's humanitarian program. 2005.

Chapter 11: Inspiration
Tibetan and Bhutanese monks from Shechen Monastery in Nepal enjoy the snow on a summit overlooking Lake Geneva in Switzerland during a European tour of sacred dances. 1997.

Chapter 12: Happiness
Young novice monks in Darjeeling, India. 1975.

Part 3: Section 2: The mind principles

Chapter 13: Mindfulness
Lamas and monks at the Shechen Retreat Center in Nepal. 2005.

Chapter 14: Resilience
This man from Kham, eastern Tibet, has come with the rest of this crowd to greet Dilgo Khyentse Rinpoche. His face expresses all the fierce courage and unwavering, visceral devotion of a people who have succeeded in preserving their dignity and their strength of purpose in the face of overwhelming tragedy. 1985.

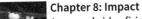

Chapter 15: Storytelling
Dilgo Khyentse Rinpoche and a group of lamas at the end of a ceremony that has lasted nine days and nine nights without interruption, in the

mountainous valley of Bumtang, in Bhutan. Having created the ritual mandala using coloured powders, they are now preparing to scatter the powders in the river. Dissolving the mandala in this way symbolizes the ephemeral nature of all things. 1981.

Part 3: Section 3: The body principles

Chapter 16: Practice
Dressed in a "black hat" costume, a Buddhist monk performs a sacred dance at the Tibetan monastery of Shechen in Nepal. 2006.

Chapter 17: Strengths
A woman doctor in Kham, eastern Tibet working at a clinic supported by Karuna-Shechen. 2004.

Chapter 18: Discipline
The fourteenth Dalai Lama meets the young reincarnation of one of his main spiritual teachers, Dilgo Khyentse Rinpoche (1910–1991), at Bodhgaya in India. For the photographer, this image symbolizes the ever-flowing loving kindness and compassion that characterizes the fourteenth Dalai Lama. 2000.

Part 4: The broader context

Chapter 19: Complexity
Aerial view of terraced fields in the Amdo province of Tibet (now the Chinese province of Qinhai). 2004.

Chapter 20: Leadership
A great Tibetan master, Kyabje Trulshik Rinpoche, arrives in Bir, India, as night falls. He is received by a procession of monks, who escort him to his residence. 2004.

Chapter 21: Neuroscience
One of the ten incarnate Tibetan lamas (tulkus) who are studying at Shechen Monastery in Nepal participates in the butter-lamp offering ceremony at the end of the year. He is wearing the "pandita hat" emblematic of his rank. 1987.

Chapter 22: Wisdom
At Mindroling Monastery, one of the six main Nyingma monasteries in Tibet, on his return to Tibet after over 30 years in exile, Dilgo Khyentse Rinpoche meets one of his close friends. The old man is the former retreat master of the famous Kangri Thokar hermitages, wh ere the great fourteenth-century scholar and saint Longchen Rabjam practised. 1985.

Chapter 23: Change
A jeep serves as spectators' seats at the great festival of Mani Genkok, in eastern Tibet – the first in ten years. Thousands of Tibetan nomads dressed in their best clothes and ornaments camp out in the plains during the summer festival. During the festival, which is dedicated to the legendary Gesar of Ling, masked monks perform dances that re-enact the great episodes in the king's life. 2004.

Chapter 24: Choice
Two young Bhutanese children. 1985.

Part 5: Evolution

Chapter 25: Site
In the centre of every Bhutanese province, here in the Paro Valley, there is an impressive edifice built of stone, beaten earth, and wood, called a "dzong", one half of which generally houses a monastery, the other half reserved for the seat of the local government. These buildings also served as fortresses that protected against chance invaders. 2007.

Chapter 26: National
The high valley of the Yangtze, at the level of Denkhok. The Yangtze rises on the high plateaus of eastern Tibet, where it is known as the Drichu. Two celebrated masters of Tibetan Buddhism were born here: to the left (south) of the valley, Dilgo Khyentse Rinpoche (1910–1991), and to the right (north), the sixteenth Karmapa (1924–1982). 1985.

Chapter 27: Global
The Himalayan Langtang Range above a sea of clouds in the morning. Seen from Namo Buddha, Nepal. 2006.

Chapter 28: Study
Morning mist in a Himalayan valley in Nepal. Karuna-Shechen has implemented rainwater harvesting and medical projects in the area. 2006.

Chapter 29: my31Practices
Contemplating the beauty of eastern Bhutan. 2007.

Chapter 30: Summary
A performance of sacred dance in a courtyard in Bhutan. 2007.

Chapter 31: Photography
Matthieu Ricard photographs the beneficiaries of the humanitarian projects of Karuna-Shechen. In this photo he shows his camera to the children of the Bamboo School in Milanchi, Nepal. Karuna-Shechen has built eight bamboo schools that educate over 11,000 poor children in Nepal. 2011.

NOTES

Chapter 1: Introduction

1 Leonardo da Vinci (1452–1519), an Italian artist, scientist and engineer. He was an all-round genius whose paintings and inventions changed the world. http://www.bbc.co.uk/science/leonardo/ (accessed 4th February 2013).

2 This statistic is quoted at Engaged Marketing: Our thinking. http://www.engagedmarketing.com.au/our-thinking.html (accessed 1st August 2013).

3 Ipsos Mori article. Consumers voting with their feet: Nearly one in six say poor dealings with staff put them off from purchasing. http://www.ipsos-mori.com/researchpublications/researcharchive/1848/Consumers-Voting-With-Their-Feet-Nearly-One-In-Six-Say-Poor-Dealings-With-Staff-Put-Them-Off-From-Purchasing.aspx (accessed 1st August 2013).

4 Dr Kathryn Waddington, Head of Department, of Psychology, University of Westminster, London UK. Feedback received June 2013, personal communication.

5 31Practices® is a registered trademark owned by SERVICEBRAND GLOBAL Ltd.

6 Ross Peat, CEO, KlickEx, feedback received on the draft Manuscript, personal communication.

Part 1

1 Ursula K. Le Guin (born 1929): author, poet, novelist.

Chapter 2: Values

1 In fact, the original version is a calypso song written by jazz musicians Melvin "Sy" Oliver and James "Trummy" Young. It was first recorded in 1939 by Jimmie Lunceford, Harry James, and Ella Fitzgerald.

2 Rosanna M. Fiske: www.blogs.hbr.org/cs/2011/07/the_business_of_communicating.html by Rosanna M. Fiske (accessed 28th July 2013).

3 Barrett Values Centre: Values Overview. http://www.valuescentre.com/values/?sec=values_overview (accessed 8th February 2013).

4 Values shift: a guide to personal and organizational transformation, Twin Lights Publishers, 1994.

5 Netflix, the world's leading internet television network. http://netflix.com.

6 Netflix website: http://jobs.netflix.com/jobs.html.

7 Antony Jenkins, CEO, Barclays, interviewed on the 17th January 2013. http://www.telegraph.co.uk/finance/newsbysector/banksandfinance/9808042/Antony-Jenkins-to-staff-adopt-new-values-or-leave-Barclays.html (accessed 28th July 2013).

8 Ivan Misner (2012) In Business, Culture Eats Strategy for Breakfast; 27th September 2012. FOXBusiness http://smallbusiness.foxbusiness.com/legal-hr/2012/09/27/in-business-culture-eats-strategy-for-breakfast/#ixzz2CkyBVqMi (accessed 28th July 2013).

9 IBM (2012). Leading through connections: Insights from the IBM Global CEO Study http://www-935.ibm.com/services/us/en/c-suite/ceostudy2012/ (accessed 28th July 2013).

10 David Rock (2011). The Business of Values. www.blog.hbr.org/cs/2011/06/the_business_of_values.

11 Heidegger, M. (1962). Being and Time. Trans. J Macquarie and E Robinson. San Francisco: Harper.

12 Thomas Peters and Waterman (1982) As long ago as 1982, McKinsey consultants Tom Peters and Robert Waterman popularized culture as a management tool with their analysis of the best US companies, In Search of Excellence.

13 Ken Blanchard and Phil Hodges (2003). The Servant Leader. Tennessee: Thomas Nelson Inc.

14 Deloitte. Core Beliefs and Culture: Chairmans Survey Findings http://www.deloitte.com/view/en_US/us/About/Leadership/1fe8be4ad25e7310VgnVCM1000001956f00aRCRD.htm (accessed 28th July 2013).

15 CIPD (2012). Employee Outlook. CIPD http://www.cipd.co.uk/binaries/6030%20EmpOutlook%20Autumn%202012%20WEB.pdf (accessed 28th July 2013).

16 Enron scandal at-a-glance, reported by the BBC, 22nd August, 2002. http://news.bbc.co.uk/1/hi/business/1780075.stm (accessed 1st August 2013).

17 Ken Blanchard, Michael O'Connor, Michael J O'Connor Ph.D., Jim Ballard (1997) Managing by Values. San Francisco: Berrett-Koehler Publishers.

18 CIPD (2012). Employee Outlook. CIPD http://www.cipd.co.uk/binaries/6030%20EmpOutlook%20Autumn%202012%20WEB.pdf (accessed 28th July 2013).

19 CIPD (2012). Employee Outlook. CIPD http://www.cipd.co.uk/binaries/6030%20EmpOutlook%20Autumn%202012%20WEB.pdf (accessed 28th July 2013).

20 Peter Cheese, CEO of the Chartered Institute for Personnel and Development (CIPD) in the UK.

21 Tony Hsieh (2010). Delivering Happiness: A Path to Profits, Passion, and Purpose. US:Hachette Publishing.

22 Tony Hsieh (2010). Delivering Happiness: A Path to Profits, Passion, and Purpose. US:Hachette Publishing.

23 Pulitzer Prize winner Carl Bernstein reports on Murdoch's Watergate at The Daily Beast (9th July 2011). He demystifies Murdoch Culture and the excessively aggressive tactics it promotes. Bernstein's experienced journalistic point of view allows for considerable insight into exactly why and how this approach to journalism and company culture is so appalling. http://mag.newsweek.com/2011/07/10/murdoch-s-watergate.html (accessed 1st October 2013).

24 Margaret Heffernan (2011). Wilful Blindness: Why we ignore the obvious at our peril. London: Simon & Schuster.

25 Sir John Whitmore (2009) Coaching for Performance: GROWing human potential and purpose, 4th Edition. London: Nicholas Brealey Press.

26 Jim Collins and Jim Poras (2005). Built to last: Successful habits of visionary companies. London: Random House (ppxiii–xiv).

27 Flamholtz, Eric. "Corporate Culture and the Bottom Line." European Management Journal Vol. 19, No. 3 (2001): 268-275.

28 Laura Chamberlain (2012). Four key enablers to employee engagement, Personnel Today, 27th January 2012. http://www.personneltoday.com/articles/27/01/2012/58291/four-key-enablers-to-employee-engagement.htm (accessed 4th February 2013).

29 Anne Marie Lohuis (2008). The communicative ins-and-outs of core values: A qualitative analysis of the communication process of "innovation" as a core value in organizations. Masters Thesis, University of Twente.

Chapter 3: Journey

1 Edgar Schein is Professor Emeritus at the MIT Sloan School of Management. He is a leading thinker, researcher and author in the field of organisational culture.

2 Will Durant (1885–1981): a prolific American writer perhaps best known for The Story of Civilization which consists of 11 volumes; and highly regarded for his work The Story of Philosophy.

3 Confucius (551–479 BC) was a Chinese teacher, editor, politician, and philosopher of the Spring and Autumn Period of Chinese history. The philosophy of Confucius emphasized personal and governmental morality, correctness of social relationships, justice and sincerity.

Chapter 4: Framework

1 E.E. Cummings (1894–1962). American poet, painter, essayist, author and playwright. Writing poems from the age of 8, he explored ideas such as purpose and inner strength among many others.

2 Jon Kabbat-Zinn a scientist, writer and meditation teacher and Professor of Medicine at the University of Massachusetts.

3 Jon Kabbat-Zinn (2005). Coming to our senses: Healing ourselves and the world through mindfulness. London: New York: Piatkus.

4 W. Edwards Deming (1986). Out of the Crisis: MIT Centre for Advanced Engineering.

5 Walter A. Shewart. (1939). Statistical Method from the Viewpoint of Quality Control. New York: Dover.

6 Jim Collins and Jim Poras (2005). Built to last: Successful habits of visionary companies. London: Random House (ppxiii–xiv).

Chapter 5: Purpose

1 Antoine De Saint Exupery (1900–1944) author and airman. His most famous work includes "The Little Prince".

2 Richard Ellsworth Professor of Management at the Peter F. Drucker and Masatoshi Ito Graduate School of Management. Professor Ellsworth is the author of Leading with Purpose (2002) Stanford University Press.

3 Mike Munro Turner. Coaching on Purpose http://www.mentoringforchange.co.uk/articles_mentpurpose.php#mentp (accessed 28th July 2013).

4 The list of characteristics of purposefulness come from the work of Assagioli R, (1973), The Act of Will, Turnstone Press, the contextualization of those characteristics are the authors' alone.

5 Replace current ref 5 with: 5 Bruce MacEwen writing for Adam Smith Esq covered some of this territory in Thoughts on IBM's 100th: Idea or Product. Quoted in "The Purpose Driven Organisation" a blog by Deb Lavoy. http://aboveandbeyondkm.com/2011/07/the-purpose-driven-organization.html (accessed 1st October 2013).

6 Charlotte Rainer, Professor of HR Management at Portsmouth Business School: (CIPD, Shared Purpose: The Golden Thread, 2010). CIPD podcast series.

7 Ian Mintram, HR Vice President Europe Consumer at GlaxoSmithKline. CIPD podcast series.

8 Jim Collins and Jerry L Porras (2005). Built to last: Successful habits of visionary companies. London: Random House.

9 Charlotte Rainer, Professor of HR Management at Portsmouth Business School: (CIPD, Shared Purpose: The Golden Thread, 2010). CIPD podcast series.

10 Sculley J, 1988, "Odyssey", Collins.

11 Why would anyone want to be an Olympic volunteer? Sean Gregory, Time World, 19th February 2010.

12 Senior Vice President and Global Head of Quality, Talent Transformation and Leadership Development, Anand Pillai, CIPD podcast series: http://www.cipd.co.uk/podcasts.

13 Bruce Temkin Examining Apple Stores and Employee Engagement. 13th July 2012 http://bx.businessweek.com/voice-of-the-customer/view?url=http%3A%2F%2Fexperiencematters.wordpress.com%2F2012%2F07%2F13%2Fexamining-apple-stores-and-employee-engagement%2F (accessed 28th July 2013).

14 Frances Hesselbein and Paul M. Cohen (1999). Leader to Leader: Enduring Insights on Leadership from the Drucker Foundation's Award Winning Journal. San Francisco: Jossey-Bass.

15 Simon Sinek (2010). How Great Leaders Inspire Action. http://www.ted.com/talks/simon_sinek_how_great_leaders_inspire_action.html (accessed 28th July 2013).

16 Jim Collins and Jerry L. Porras (2005) Built to last: Successful Habits of Visionary Companies. London: Random House.

17 Steve Pavlina (2005). How to discover your life purpose in about 20 minutes. http://www.stevepavlina.com/blog/2005/01/how-to-discover-your-life-purpose-in-about-20-minutes/ (accessed 6th February 2013).

18 Peter Hawkins. (2011). Leadership team coaching: Developing collective transformational leadership. London: Kogan Page.

Chapter 6: Identity

1 Tiger Woods, professional golf player, winning the US Masters aged 21 with a record score. He was the youngest man to earn the title.

2 Brian Tracy is a motivational speaker and author. He has written more than 50 books, having studied economics, business, philosophy, psychology and history.

3 Martin Selligman (2003). Authentic Happiness: Using the new positive psychology to realise your potential for deep fulfillment. Nicholas Brealey Publishing: London.

4 Badaracco, J. (1998). The Discipline of Building Character. Harvard Business review, March – April.

5 Tiger Woods interviewed by Tom Rinaldi, ESPN, November 2009. Interview transcript available at: http://www.weiunderpar.com/post/464360113 (accessed 28th July 2013).

6 IBM (2012). Leading through connections: Insights from the IBM Global CEO Study http://www-935.ibm.com/services/us/en/c-suite/ceostudy2012/ (accessed 28th July 2013).

7 Chris Kelly, Paul Kocourek, Nancy McGaw and Judith Samuelson (2005). Deriving Value from Corporate Values. The Aspen Institute and Booz Allen Hamilton Inc.

8 Groupthink is a term first used in 1972 by Irving L. Janis that refers to a psychological phenomenon in which people strive for consensus within a group. In many cases, people will set aside their own personal beliefs or

adopt the opinion of the rest of the group. People who are opposed to the decisions or overriding opinion of the group as a whole frequently remain quiet, preferring to keeping the peace rather than disrupt the uniformity of the crowd (http://psychology.about.com/od/gindex/g/groupthink.htm accessed 1st October 2013).

9 Richard Barrett (2010). The Seven Levels of Organisational Consciousness. Barrett Values Centre. http://www.valuescentre.com/uploads/2010-07-06/The%207%20Levels%20of%20Organisational%20Consciousness.pdf (accessed 8th February 2013).

Chapter 7: Action

1 William B Sprague (1830–1915). Elected governor of Rhode Island in 1859 and became a US Senator in 1763.

2 Action definition from the free online dictionary. http://www.thefreedictionary.com/action (accessed 8th February 2013).

3 Rudolph Virchow 19th Century German pathologist, anthropologist and statesman: 1821–1902.

4 Mel Robbins (2012). Follow the five-second rule. http://www.success.com/articles/1865-----get-a-move-on--follow-the-five-second-rule (accessed 8th February 2013).

5 Badaracco, J. (1998). The Discipline of Building Character. Harvard Busines review, March–April.

6 Peter Nivio Zarlenga (1941-2007) American businessman.

7 Mel Robbins (2012). Follow the five-second rule. http://www.success.com/articles/1865-----get-a-move-on--follow-the-five-second-rule (accessed 8th February 2013).

8 Napoleon Hill (1883–1970), an American author and an early producer of personal success literature.

9 John Locke (1632 – 1704). British philosopher, Oxford academic and medical researcher.

10 Sir Thomas More, author, statesman and martyr, 1478-1535.

11 Albert Einstein (1879–1955) was a German-born theoretical physicist, often regarded as the father of modern physics, and the most influential physicist of the 20th century.

12 LaMarsh and Associates (2005) Master of Managed Change Handbook. Chicago, Illinois: LaMarsh and Associates.

13 Michael Jordon (b. 1963). Born in Brooklyn, New York – Drafted into the Chicago Bulls, he eventually became the most decorated player in the NBA, leading the Bulls to six national championships.

14 Pat Mesiti, American speaker and coach.

15 Peter Marshall (b. 1946), a British historian, philosopher, biographer, travel writer and poet. http://www.petermarshall.net/biography.cfm (accessed 8th April 2013).

Chapter 8: Impact

1 Napoleon Hill (26th October 1883– 8th November 1970) was an American author, one of the earliest producers of the modern genre of personal-success literature (http://en.wikipedia.org/wiki/Personal-success_literature). He is widely considered to be one of the great writers on success.

2 Carlos Fernando Flores Labra (born 9th January 1943, Chile), an engineer, entrepreneur and politician. He is a former cabinet minister of president Salvador Allende, before being imprisoned under the Pinochet regime. He has continued in politics and education.

3 Oxford Dictionary Online: http://oxforddictionaries.com/definition/english/impact.

4 Simon Caulkin (2008). The Rule is simple: Be careful what you measure. Observer Newspaper, 10th February 2008.

5 Barack H. Obama is the 44th President of the United States, born 1961, sworn into office in January, 2009.

6 Henry Mintzberg quoted by Simon Caulkin (2008). The Rule is simple: Be careful what you measure. The Observer, Sunday 10th February 2008 http://www.guardian.co.uk/business/2008/feb/10/businesscomment1 (accessed 29th July 2013).

7 Stemming from ideas about experiential learning, for more background and research into learning, see Kolb, D. A., Boyatzis, R. E., & Mainemelis, C. (2000). Experiential Learning Theory: Previous Research and New Directions. In Perspectives on cognitive, learning, and thinking styles. Sternberg & Zhang (Eds.). NJ: Lawrence Erlbaum. And Kolb, D. A. (1984). Experiential learning: Experience as the source of learning and development. New Jersey: Prentice-Hall.

8 John E. Jones, US Lawyer and Federal Judge in Pennsylvania.

9 Charles Duhigg (2012) The power of habit: Why we do what we do in life and business. William Heinemann. London.

10 Ivan Pavlov (1849–1936), a famous Russian physiologist. He won the Nobel Peace Prize for Physiology in 1904.

11 Burrhus Frederic "B. F." Skinner (20th March 1904 – 18th August 1990) was an American psychologist, behaviorist, author, inventor, and social philosopher. He was the Edgar Pierce Professor of Psychology at Harvard University from 1958 until his retirement in 1974.

12 Charles Duhigg (2012) The power of habit: Why we do what we do in life and business. William Heinemann. London.

13 Charles Duhigg (2012) The power of habit: Why we do what we do in life and business. William Heinemann. London.

Chapter 9: Refine

1 Albert Einstein (1879–1955) was a German-born theoretical physicist, often regarded as the father of modern physics, and the most influential physicist of the 20th century.

2 Oxford Dictionaries Definition on line: http://oxforddictionaries.com/definition/english/.

3 Kolb, D. A. (1984). Experiential learning: Experience as the source of learning and development. New Jersey: Prentice-Hall.

4 Royce Holloway (2012). Adaptive Action, same and different. Human Systems Dynamics Institute. www.HSDInstitute.org.

5 Joseph Conrad (1857–1924), a Polish author regarded as one of the greatest novelists in English.

6 Ronald Moen and Clifford Norman (2001). Evolution of the PDCA Cycle. http://kaizensite.com/learninglean/wp-content/uploads/2012/09/Evolution-of-PDCA.pdf (accessed 8th April 2013).

7 Ron Ashkenas (2012). It's time to rethink Continuous Improvement. Harvard Business Review Blog Network, 8th May 2012. http://blogs.hbr.org/ashkenas/2012/05/its-time-to-rethink-continuous.html.

8 Vijay Govindajaran, Earl C. Daum Professor of International Business at the Tuck School of Business, Dartmouth

College, New Hampshire. Regarded as a leading business thinker, Vijay specialises in globalization, innovation & execution. Quoted in Ron Ashkenas.

9 Ron Ashkenas (2012). It's time to rethink Continuous Improvement. Harvard Business Review Blog Network, 8th May 2012. http://blogs.hbr.org/ashkenas/2012/05/its-time-to-rethink-continuous.html.

10 Included in a presentation by Professor Rob Briner (2012). Evidence-based coaching psychology: What would it look like and how close are we? Presented at the Special Group in Coaching Psychology Annual Conference, Aston, December 2012. Rob Briner is Professor of Organisational Psychology at the University of Bath School of Management in the UK.

11 W. Edwards Deming (1900–1993) an American statistician, professor, author and consultant. His thinking is incorporated into a number of industrial methods. He is perhaps best known for the Plan-Do-Check- Act cycle.

Part 3 – Exploring the principles

1 Thomas Merton (31st January 1915 – 10th December 1968) was an Anglo-American Catholic writer and Trappist monk.

2 Johann Wolfgang von Goethe (1749–1832), a German writer, artist and politician. A literary celebrity, he was one of the key figures of German literature.

3 For example, the work of Martin Heidegger (1927/1962). Being and Time. Translated by J Macquarrie and E. Robinson. New York: Harper and Row.

Chapter 10: Emotion

1 Dale Carnegie (1888–1955) an American writer and lecturer, famous for books and courses in self-improvement, public speaking and interpersonal skills.

2 Emotion Definition from Oxford Dictionaries Online: http://oxforddictionaries.com/definition/english/emotion (accessed 11th February 2013).

3 Kahlil Gibran (1883–1941) a Lebanese-American artist, poet and writer. Probably best known in the English-speaking world for his book The Prophet. Gibran is the third best-selling poet of all time (behind Shakespeare and Lao-Tzu). http://en.wikipedia.org/wiki/Kahlil_Gibran (accessed 15th May 2013).

4 Daniel Goleman (1995). Emotional Intelligence: Why it can matter more than IQ. London: Bloomsbury.

5 Gabriele Lakomski (2008). Cognitive versus Emotion? Revising the rationalist model of decision-making. Organization Learning, Knowledge and Capabilities Conference, 2008, 28th–30th April, 2008 Copenhagen, Denmark.

6 Friedman, Howard S. & Riggio, Ronald E. (1981). Effects of individual differences in nonverbal expressiveness on transmission of emotions. Journal of Nonverbal Behavior, 6, 96-102.

7 Albert Mehrabian, Professor Emeritus of Psychology, UCLA. From his well known work: Mehrabian, Albert (1971). Silent Messages (1st ed.). Belmont, CA: Wadsworth.

8 Lea Winerman (2005). The Minds Mirror. Monitor on Psychology, October 2005, American Psychological Association. http://www.apa.org/monitor/oct05/mirror.aspx (accessed 4th March 2013).

9 Rizzolatti G., Fadiga L., Gallese V., Fogassi L. (1996). Premotor cortex and the recognition of motor actions. Cognitive Brain Research, 3, 131-141.

10 Paul Ekman (2004). Emotions Revealed: Understanding Faces and Feelings. London: Phoenix.

11 Daniel Siegel (2007). The Mindful Brain: Reflection and attunement in the cultivation of well-being. New York: W.W. Norton & Co.

12 Whitworth, L., Kimsey-House, K., Kimsey-House, H. and Sandahl, P. (2009). Co-Active Coaching: new skills for coaching people toward success in work and life. Davis Black: London.

13 Joseph LeDoux, A neuroscientist, the Henry and Lucy Moses Professor of Science, and Professor of Neuroscience and Psychology at New York University.

14 Bennett Voyles (2007). Beyond Loyalty: Meeting the challenge of customer engagement. A report for the Economist Research Unit, Part 1.

15 Circle Company Associates (2010). Turning Emotion into Engagement: Utilizing the power of emotion to connect customers to your brand. White paper.

16 Nikki Blacksmith & Jim Harter (2011). Majority of American works not engaged in their jobs. http://www.gallup.com/poll/150383/majority-american-workers-not-engaged-jobs.aspx (accessed 28th February 2013).

17 Jeremy Scrivens of the emotional economy at work http://www.theemotionaleconomyatwork.com/#!service (accessed 28th February 2013).

18 For example: Richard Barrett (2010). The Seven Levels of Organisational Consciousness. Barrett Values Centre. http://www.valuescentre.com/uploads/2010-07-06/The%207%20Levels%20of%20Organisational%20Consciousness.pdf (accessed 8th February 2013).

19 Rollin McCraty, Annette Deyhle and Doc Childre (2012) The Global Coherence Initiative: Creating a coherent planetary standing wave. Global Advances in Health and Medicine 1(1) 64-77.

20 Saveloy. P. and Mayer. J.D (1990). Emotional Intelligence. Imagination, Cognition and Personality, 9 p. 185–211.

21 Daniel Goleman (1995). Emotional Intelligence: Why it can matter more than IQ. London: Bloomsbury.

22 Daniel Siegel (2007) The Mindful Brain: Reflection and attunement in the cultivation of well-being. New York: W.W. Norton & Co.

23 Daniel Siegel (2007) The Mindful Brain: Reflection and attunement in the cultivation of well-being. New York: W.W. Norton & Co.

24 Brian Tracy is a motivational speaker and author. He has written more than 50 books, having studied economics, business, philosophy, psychology and history.

25 Diagram adapted from two sources: Richard Layard (2005) Happiness: Lessons from a new science. London: Allan-Lane and Lucy Ryan of Positive insights presented as part of Advanced Positive Psychology masterclass, November 2011.

Chapter 11: Inspiration

1 Leo Babauta (born 1973) describes himself as a writer, runner and vegan. Author of one of the top 25 blogs and top 50 websites: www.zenhabits.net.

2 Richard Barrett (2010). The six modes of decision making. Barrett Values Centre http://www.valuescentre.com/uploads/2010-07-06/Six%20Modes%20of%20Decision%20Making.pdf (accessed 28th February 2013).

3 Scott Barry Kaufman (2011). Why Inspiration Matters. Harvard Business Review Blog network. http://blogs.hbr.org/cs/2011/11/why_inspiration_matters.html (accessed 28th February 2013).

4 Martine Wright is a high profile survivor the London 7/7 bombings where she lost both her legs and 80% of her blood. She has gone on to marry, have a family, and become a Paralympian.

5 Todd M. Thrash and Andrew J. Elliot (2003). Inspiration as a Psychological Construct. Journal of Personality and Social Psychology 84(4) p871-889.

6 Carl R. Rogers (2004/1961). On becoming a person: A therapist's view of psychotherapy. London: Constable and Robinson.

7 Louis Leo Lou Holtz (born 1937) is a retired American football coach, and active sportscaster, author and speaker. http://en.wikipedia.org/wiki/Lou_Holtz (accessed 15th May 2013).

8 Deci, E.L., & Ryan, R.M. Self-Determination theory: An approach to human motivation and personality http://selfdeterminationtheory.org/theory (accessed 4th March 2013).

9 Whybrow, A. and Wildflower, L. (2011). Humanistic and Transpersonal Psychology in L. Wildflower and D. Brennan (Eds) The Handbook of Knowledge Based Coaching. London: John Wiley & Sons.

10 Csikszentmihalyi, M. (1990). Flow: The Psychology of Optimal Experience, New York: Harper & Row.

11 Todd M. Thrash and Andrew J. Elliot (2003). Inspiration as a Psychological Construct. Journal of Personality and Social Psychology 84(4) p.871-889.

12 Marina Milyavskaya, Iana Ianakieva, Emily Foxton-Craft, Agnes Colantuomi, and Richard Koestner (2012). Inspired to get there: The effects of trait and goal inspiration on goal progress. Personality and Individual Differences, vol.52 (1), p.56-60.

13 Scott Barry Kaufman (2011). Why Inspiration Matters. Harvard Business Review Blog network. http://blogs.hbr.org/cs/2011/11/why_inspiration_matters.html (accessed 28th February 2013).

14 Scott Barry Kaufman (2011). Why Inspiration Matters. Harvard Business Review Blog network. http://blogs.hbr.org/cs/2011/11/why_inspiration_matters.html (accessed 28th February 2013).

15 Deci, E. L., & Ryan, R. M. (1985). Intrinsic motivation and self-determination in human behavior. New York: Plenum.

16 Terry Barber is Chief Inspiration Officer at Performance Inspired, a consultancy focused on creating inspiring work environments, based in Atlanta, USA.

17 Gregory Dess and Joseph Picken (2000). Changing Roles: Leadership In The 21st Century, Organisational Dynamics, Vol.28(3)pp 18-34 http://psycnet.apa.org/psycinfo/2000-03079-002 (accessed 1st March 2013).

18 Terry Barber is Chief Inspiration Officer at Performance Inspired, a consultancy focused on creating inspiring work environments, based in Atlanta, USA.

Chapter 12: Happiness

1 Freya Stark (1893–1993) was a British Explorer and travel writer. Writing more than two dozen books on her travels, she was one of the first non-Arabians to travel through the southern Arabian deserts.

2 Oxford Dictionary – definition of happiness. http://oxforddictionaries.com/definition/english/happiness (accessed 5th March 2013).

3 See the work of Paul Eckman For example: Paul Eckman (2004). Emotions Revealed: Understanding faces and feelings. London: Phoenix.

4 Richard Layard (2005) Happiness: Lessons from a new science. London: Allan-Lane.

5 Danner, D., Snowden, D. and Friesen, W. (2001) Positive emotions in early life and longevity: findings from the nun study, Journal of Personality and Social Psychology, 80, 804-13.

6 Alejandro Braun (2009) Gross National Happiness in Bhutan: A Living Example of an Alternative Approach to Progress, University of Pennsylvania (http://www.schoolforwellbeing.org/download/GNH%20Paper%20Final.pdf).

7 Dr Ross McDonald (2004). Television, materialism and culture: An exploration of imported media and its implications for GNH, Journal of Bhutan Studies, vol 11(4) pp 68–88.

8 John Helliwell, Richard Layard and Jeffrey Sachs (Eds). (2012). World happiness report http://www.earth.columbia.edu/sitefiles/file/Sachs%20Writing/2012/World%20Happiness%20Report.pdf (accessed 30th July 2013).

9 Edington D.W., Yen L.T., Witting P. The financial impact of changes in personal health practices. Journal of Occupational and Environmental Medicine. (1997); vol 39 pp 1037-1046.

10 Wendy Lynch (2003). Optimal health and productivity: Mutually exclusive or redundant. Paper in the European Newsletter of the Institute for Health and Productivity management. February 2003, Volume 1, No.1 p. 7-8.

11 Gallup Study: Engaged Employees inspire company innovation http://businessjournal.gallup.com/content/24880/gallup-study-engaged-employees-inspire-company.aspx (accessed 5th March 2013).

12 Julie Gebauer (2010). Key Findings: An interview with Julie Gebauer on Towers Perrin's just released global workforce survey. http://www.towersperrin.com/tp/showhtml.jsp?url=global/publications/gws/key-findings.htm&country=global (accessed 5th March 2013).

13 John Helliwell, Richard Layard, and Jeffrey Sachs (Eds.) (2012) World Happiness Report.

14 Ronald J Siegel is assistant clinical professor of psychology at Harvard Medical School and editor of Harvard Health Publications special health report, Positive Psychology: Harnessing the power of happiness, personal strength and mindfulness (2013). See also http://www.health.harvard.edu/video/positive-psychology/what-it-takes-to-be-happy.htm (accessed 15th May 2013).

15 Richard Layard (2005) Happiness: Lessons from a new science. London: Allan-Lane.

16 Richard Layard (2005) Happiness: Lessons from a new science. London: Allan-Lane.

17 Ross McDonald (2004). Television, materialism and culture: An exploration of imported media and its implications for GNH, Journal of Bhutan Studies, vol 11(4) pp 68 – 88; Tim Kasser (2004) in Ross Mcdonald.

18 Kennon M, Sheldon and Sonja Lyubomirsky (2004). Achieving Sustainable Happiness: Prospects, Practices and Prescriptions. In A. Linley & S. Joseph (Eds.), Positive psychology in practice (pp.127-145). Hoboken, NJ: John Wiley & Sons. http://sonjalyubomirsky.com/wp-content/themes/sonjalyubomirsky/papers/SL2004.pdf.

19 Richard Layard (2005) Happiness: Lessons from a new science. London: Allan-Lane.

20 www.poverty.ac.uk.

21 Richard Layard (2005) Happiness: Lessons from a new science. London: Allan-Lane.

22 As an example, see Richard Layard, Guy Mayraz and Stephen Nickell (2009) Does Relative Income Matter? Are the Critics Right? (Paper No' CEPDP0918. cep/lse.ac.uk/_new/publications/).

23 Bhutan's foreign minister, Lyonpo Jigmi Thinley, at a United Nations Development Programme (UNDP) meeting in Seoul, Korea, in 1998. Quoted in an article by Orville Schell (2002) Gross National Happiness – http://www.pbs.org/frontlineworld/stories/bhutan/gnh.html.

24 Tim Kasser (2004) cited in in Ross Mcdonald (2004). Television, materialism and culture: An exploration of imported media and its implications for GNH, Journal of Bhutan Studies, vol 11(4) pp 68 – 88; Tim Kasser (2004) in Ross Mcdonald.

25 Jose Mujica: The world's poorest president, BBC news 15th November 2012. http://www.bbc.co.uk/news/magazine-20243493 (accessed 5th March 2013).

26 Abraham Lincoln (born 1809 – assassinated 1865): he came from a poor family and had a reputation for being ambitious, energetic, generous and charitable. He was the 16th President of the United States of America (1861–1865). http://www.whitehouse.gov/about/presidents/abrahamlincoln (accessed 15th May 2013).

27 Mahatma Gandhi (1869–1948), born in Gujarat. The leader of the Indian Nationalist movement against British rule and widely considered the father of his country. His doctrine of non-violent protest has been hugely influential.

28 Oliver Burkeman (2012) The Antidote: Happiness for people who can't stand positive thinking. Cannongate: Edinburgh.

29 Tensin Gyatso is the 14th Dalai Lama. He is the Head of State and the Spiritual Leader of Tibet. Born on the 6th July 1935 to a farming family, he was recognised as the reincarnation of the 13th Dalai Lama at the age of two. He has lived in exile since 1959, authored more than 72 books and received over 84 awards, honorary doctorates and prizes in recognition of his work for peace. http://www.dalailama.com/biography/a-brief-biography (accessed 15th May 2013).

30 Kennon M, Sheldon and Sonja Lyubomirsky (2004). Achieving Sustainable Happiness: Prospects, Practices and Prescriptions. In A. Linley & S. Joseph (Eds.), Positive psychology in practice (pp.127-145). Hoboken, NJ: John Wiley & Sons. http://sonjalyubomirsky.com/wp-content/themes/sonjalyubomirsky/papers/SL2004.pdf.

31 For example: Ryff, C.D., & Singer, B. (2003). The role of emotion on pathways to positive health. In R.J. Davidson, K.R. Scherer, & H.H. Goldsmith (Eds.), Handbook of affective sciences. New York: Oxford University Press.

32 Ryff, C.D., & Singer, B. (2003). The role of emotion on pathways to positive health. In R.J. Davidson, K.R. Scherer, & H.H. Goldsmith (Eds.), Handbook of affective sciences. New York: Oxford University Press.

33 Viktor E. Frankl (1945/2004). Man's Search for Meaning. London: Random House.

34 Ryff, C.D., & Singer, B. (2003). The role of emotion on pathways to positive health. In R.J. Davidson, K.R. Scherer, & H.H. Goldsmith (Eds.), Handbook of affective sciences. New York: Oxford University Press.

35 Jeremy Scrivens (2009). The emotional economy at work. http://theemotionaleconomy.com/ (accessed 30th July 2013).

36 Stephen M.R. Covey (2006). The Speed of Trust: The one thing that changes everything. London: Simon & Schuster.

37 Adam Grant (2013). Give and Take: A Revolutionary Approach to Success. London: Weidenfeld & Nicolson.

38 Randolph Nesse (2000), 'The Evolution of Hope and Despair', Journal of Social Issues 66: 429-69.

39 Penedo, F.J. & Dahn, J.R. (2005). Exercise and well-being: a review of mental and physical health benefits associated with physical activity. Current Opinion in Psychiatry. Mar;18(2):189-93.

40 General Satisfaction Survey (http://www3.norc.org/gss+website/).

41 James Oppenheim (1882–1932), an American poet, novelist and editor. See quotes on: http://www.goodreads.com/author/show/483496.James_Oppenheim (accessed 15th May 2013).

42 Jose Mujica: The world's poorest president, BBC news 15th November 2012. http://www.bbc.co.uk/news/magazine-20243493 (accessed 5th March 2013).

43 Thich Nhat Hanh (1997). Stepping into Freedom: Rules of Monastic Practice for Novices. Berkeley, CA : Parrallax Press.

44 Andy Gibson (2012), What's the 5-a-day for your mind? speaking at Action for Happiness, 18th October 2012.

45 Gratitude and appreciation is part of Jewish Practice, see page 170 in Rabbi Kerry M. Olitzky and Rabbi Daniel Judson (2002). The Rituals and Practices of a Jewish Life: A Handbook for Spiritual Renewal. Woodstock: Jewish Lights Publishing.

Section 2: The Mind Principles

1 Antoine De Saint Exupery (1900–1944) author and airman. His most famous work includes "The Little Prince".

2 Susan Greenfield (2009). ID: The Quest for Meaning in the 21st Century. London: Hodder and Stoughton.

Chapter 13: Mindfulness

1 Eckhert Tolle (2005). The Power of Now: A guide to spiritual enlightenment. Namaste Publishing : Canada.

2 Jon Kabat-Zinn (2003). Mindfulness-based interventions in context: Past, present and future. Clinical Psychology: Science and Practice 10(2). 144-156.

3 David Rock & Linda Page (2009). Coaching with the Brain in Mind: Foundations for Practice. John Wiley & Sons. New Jersey.

4 Tang, Y.-Y., Ma, Y., Wang, J., Fan, Y., Feng, S., Lu, Q., et al. (2007) Short-term meditation training improves attention and self-regulation. Proceedings of the National Academy of Sciences of the United States of America, 104. 17152-17156.

5 David Rock and Linda Page (2009). Coaching with the Brain in Mind: Foundations for Practice. John Wiley & Sons. New Jersey.

6 George Bernard Shaw (1856–1950), was a playwright originally from Ireland. He wrote over 50 plays over his lifetime, with the final play completed a few months before his death. Nobelprize.org. 18 March 2013 http://www.nobelprize.org/nobel_prizes/literature/laureates/1925/shaw-bio.html.

7 Daniel J Siegel (2007). The Mindful Brain: Reflection and attunement in the cultivation of well-being. New York. Norton.

8 Daniel J Siegel (2007). The Mindful Brain: Reflection and attunement in the cultivation of well-being. New York. Norton.

9 Caitlin Kelly (2012) OK Google, Take a Deep Breath, writing for New York Times, 28th April 2012.

10 Bill Duane, Google Engineer quoted in Kelly (2012).

11 Mr Allan, Mr Tan's line manager at the time he developed the mindfulness programme. Quoted in Kelly (2012).

12 Janice Maturano, quoted in David Gelles (2012) The Mind Business. Financial Times, 24th August 2012 (accessed on 21st January 2013).

13 David Gella (2012). The Mind Business. The Financial Times, 24th August 2012. http://www.ft.com/cms/s/2/d9cb7940-ebea-11e1-985a-00144feab49a.html#axzz2IeYHYxYE (accessed 30th July 2013).

14 Stephen R. Covey (2004). The 7 habits of highly effective people: Powerful lessons in personal change. London: Simon & Schuster UK Ltd.

15 Thich Nhat Hanh (1997). Stepping into Freedom: Rules of Monastic Practice for Novices. Berkeley, CA: Parrallax Press.

16 Dave Crenshaw (2008). The Myth of Multitasking: How doing it all gets nothing done. San Francisco: Jossey Bass.

17 BBC report (2005) Infomania worse than marijuana, 22 April 2005. http://news.bbc.co.uk/1/hi/uk/4471607.stm (accessed 30th July 2013).

18 Lord Chesterfield: Philip Stanhope, 4th Earl of Chesterfield (1694–1773) in Letters to his Son on the Art of becoming a Man of the World and a Gentleman. See Lord Chesterfield & David Roberts (2008). Lord Chesterfield's Letters. Oxford University Press: Oxford.

19 Jon Kabat-Zinn (2003). Mindfulness-based interventions in context: Past, present and future. Clinical Psychology: Science and Practice 10(2). 144-156.

20 Senge, P., Jaworski, J., Scharmer, C.O., and Flowers, B.S. (2005). Presence: Exploring profound change in people, organisations and society. London: Nicholas Brealey.

21 Staudinger, U. M. (2008). A psychology of wisdom: History and recent developments. Research in Human Development, 5, 107-120.

22 Tog-me Zong-po (1245–1369) 37 Practices of a Bodhisattva: A summary of how an awakening being behaves. Tog-me the monk, a teacher of scripture and logic, composed this text in a cave near the town of Ngülchu Rinchen for his own and others' benefit. http://www.unfetteredmind.org/37-practices-of-a-bodhisattva (accessed 1st October 2013).

23 Cited in Encyclopaedia Britannica online http://www.britannica.com/EBchecked/topic/70982/bodhisattva (accessed on 21st January 2013).

24 Sharon Salzberg (2011), Real Happiness: The Power of Meditation. New York: Workman Publishing Co.

25 Lao-Tzu or Laozi was a philosopher of ancient China best known perhaps as the author of the Tao Ti Ching which has led him to be traditionally considered as the founder of philosophical Taoism http://en.wikipedia.org/wiki/Laozi (accessed 15th May 2013).

Chapter 14: Resilience

1 Confucius (551–479 BCE), a Chinese teacher, editor, politician and philosopher of the Spring and Autumn Period of Chinese history. He authored many classic Chinese texts. His thoughts and teachings were further developed into Confucianism. http://en.wikipedia.org/wiki/Confucius (accessed 19th March 2013).

2 Oxford English Dictionary definition of Resilience http://oxforddictionaries.com/definition/english/resilience (accessed 19th March 2013).

3 Grotberg, E.H. (2003). What is resilience? How do you promote it? How do you use it?, in E.H. Grotberg (ed.) Resilience for Today: Gaining Strength From Adversity. Westport, CT: Praeger.4 Michael Neenan (2009). Developing Resilience: A cognitive-behavioural approach. London: Routledge.

5 Alessandro "Alex" Zanardi (born 23rd October 1966) is an Italian racing driver and paracyclist.

6 Michael Watson, MBE (born 15th March 1965 in Hackney, London) is a retired British boxer whose career ended prematurely as a result of near-fatal injury sustained in a title fight in September 1991.

7 Walter Elias "Walt" Disney (5th December 1901 – 15th December 1966) was an American business magnate, animator, film producer, director, screenwriter, and actor.

8 Colonel Harland David Sanders (1890–1980). http://www.articlesbase.com/entrepreneurship-articles/colonel-sanders-story-of-perseverance-entrepreneurship-100394.html?utm_source=google&utm_medium=cpc&utm_campaign=ab_paid_12&gclid=CNfx6pfliLYCFf9LLtAod6zsAtg (accessed 19th March 2013).

9 Jean-Dominique Bauby (1952–1997), a well-known French journalist, author and editor of the French fashion magazine, ELLE. In December 1995, aged 43, he suffered a massive stroke leaving him paralyzed apart from his left eyelid (called locked-in syndrome). It was through blinking his left eye that he dictated "The Diving Bell and the Butterfly". http://en.wikipedia.org/wiki/Jean-Dominique_Bauby (accessed 15th May 2013).

10 Real Business (2010). From the streets to startup success. 1st December. http://realbusiness.co.uk/article/5061-from_the_streets_to_startup_success (accessed 1st August 2013).

11 Michael Neenan (2009). Building Resilience: A cognitive behavioural approach. London: Routledge.

12 Tom Morris (2004). The Stoic Art of Living: Inner resilience and outer results. Illinois: Carus.

13 Persaud, R. (2001). Staying Sane: How to make your mind work for you. London: Bantam Press.

14 The World Health Report (2001). Mental Health: New Understanding, New Hope Geneva: World Health Organisation.

15 Halliwell, Ed., Main, Liz, and Richardson, Celia (2007). The Fundamental Facts: The latest facts and figures on mental health. Mental Health Foundation.

16 Confederation of British Industry (2005). Who cares wins: absence and labour turnover 2005 London: CBI.

17 Health and Safety Executive (2008) www.hse.gov.uk.

18 Rosch, P. J. (Ed.). (2001, March). The quandary of job stress compensation. Health and Stress, 3, 1-4.

19 Ralph Waldo Emerson (1803–1882), a founder of the Transcendental movement and the founder of a distinctly American philosophy emphasizing optimism, individuality, and mysticism, Emerson was one of the most influential literary figures of the nineteenth century. http://www.rwe.org/biography.html (accessed 19th March 2013).

20 Dr Srikumar Rao, speaker, author and former business school professor; talks to Google: http://www.youtube.com/watch?v=u20VVbhpM50 (accessed 8th march 2013).

21 Michael Neenan (2009). Building Resilience: A cognitive behavioural approach. London: Routledge.

22 Southwick SM, Vythilingam M, Charney DS (2005). The psychobiology of depression and resilience to stress: implications for prevention and treatment. Annual Review of Clinical Psychology.1:255-91.

23 Sir Edmund Hilary (1919–2008), a New Zealand bee keeper, developed a passion for climbing. One of the first people to conquer Mount Everest in 1953 with Tenzing Norgay, a Nepalese climber. Their success followed the failure of five major expeditions to conquer the peak between 1920 and 1952. From the 1960's he became concerned with Nepalese welfare, building clinics, hospitals and 17 schools. He was a key figure in attracting the funding to create the National Park around Everest to protect the environment. http://www.achievement.org/autodoc/page/hil0bio-1 (accessed 15th May 2013).

24 A.A. Milne (1882–1956) an English author best known for his children's books featuring Christopher Robin and Winnie the Pooh. ThinkExist.com Quotations. "A. A. Milne quotes". ThinkExist.com Quotations Online 1st April 2013 – 15th May 2013. http://en.thinkexist.com/quotes/a._a._milne/.

25 Albert Einstein (1879–1955) was a German-born theoretical physicist, often regarded as the father of modern physics, and the most influential physicist of the 20th century.

Chapter 15: Storytelling

1 John Kotter, a former Professor at Harvard Business School, and in 1996 authored the best-selling text, Leading Change, Harvard Business School Press.

2 Oxford Dictionaries Online http://oxforddictionaries.com/definition/english/story (accessed 21st January 2012).

3 Blake Mycoskie is an American entrepreneur and author. He is best known as the Founder and Chief Shoe Giver of TOMS Shoes.

4 Philip Pullman is an English writer. In 2008 he was named by The Times among the 50 greatest British writers since 1945.

5 How long have we been here? The Natural History Museum. http://www.nhm.ac.uk/nature-online/life/human-origins/modern-human-evolution/when/index.html (accessed 22nd January 2013).

6 Lisa Kron (2012). Wired for Story: The writer's guide to using brain science to hook readers from the very first sentence. New York: Ten Speed Press.

7 Peter Guber is a film producer. His repertoire includes: Rain Man, Batman, The Color Purple, Gorillas in the Mist, Midnight Express, The Witches of Eastwick and more. He is quoted from a short article in Psychology Today, The Inside Story, March 2011. http://www.psychologytoday.com/articles/201103/the-inside-story (accessed 22nd January 2013).

8 Jason Hensel (2010). Once upon a time: Story telling and your quest for business success, Feb. 2010. http://www.mpiweb.org/Magazine/Archive/US/February2010/OnceUponATime (accessed 22nd January 2013).

9 Pamela Rutledge (2011). The Psychological power of story telling: Stories leapfrog technology, taking us to authentic experience. In Psychology Today, January 2011. http://www.psychologytoday.com/blog/positively-media/201101/the-psychological-power-storytelling (accessed 22nd January 2013).

10 Chris Hurn (2012). Stuffed Giraffe shows what customer service is all about. Huffington Post. http://www.huffingtonpost.com/chris-hurn/stuffed-giraffe-shows-wha_b_1524038.html (accessed 20th March 2013).

11 Stephens, G.J, Silbert, L.J. & Hasson, U. (2010). Speaker-listener neural coupling underlies successful communication. PNAS, 27th July. http://psych.princeton.edu/psychology/research/hasson/publications.php (accessed 23rd January 2013).

12 Peter Guber is a film producer. His repertoire includes: Rain Man, Batman, The Color Purple, Gorillas in the Mist, Midnight Express, The Witches of Eastwick and more. He is quoted from a short article in Psychology today, The Inside Story, March 2011. http://www.psychologytoday.com/articles/201103/the-inside-story (accessed 22nd January 2013).

13 Michael Gazzaniga, Professor of Psychology and the Director for the SAGE Center for the Study of Mind at the University of California Santa Barbara. He oversees an extensive and broad research program investigating how the brain enables the mind. Quoted in Peter Guber, The Inside Story, March 2011.

14 For more on the use of story in coaching, see David Drake.

15 Peter Guber is a film producer. His repertoire includes: Rain Man, Batman, The Color Purple, Gorillas in the Mist, Midnight Express, The Witches of Eastwick and more. He is quoted from a short article in Psychology today, The Inside Story, March 2011. http://www.psychologytoday.com/articles/201103/the-inside-story (accessed 22nd January 2013).

16 Dave Carroll (2010) United Breaks Guitars. http://www.youtube.com/user/sonsofmaxwell?feature=watch (accessed 20th March 2013).

17 Erin Morgenstern (2011). The Night Circus. London: Vintage Books.

18 Pamela Rutledge (2011). The Psychological power of story telling: Stories leapfrog technology, taking us to authentic experience. In Psychology Today, January 2011. http://www.psychologytoday.com/blog/positively-media/201101/the-psychological-power-storytelling (accessed 22nd January 2013).

19 Peter Guber (2011). Tell to Win: Connect, Persuade, and Triumph with the Hidden Power of Story. London: Profile Books.

20 Joseph Campbell (1988) The Hero with a Thousand Faces. London: Paladin.

21 Mooli Lahad (2000). Creative Supervision. London: Jessica Kingsley.

22 Julie Allan, Gerard Fairtlough and Barbara Heinzen (2001). The Power of the tale: Using Narratives for Organisational Success. Chichester: John Wiley & Sons Ltd.

23 Harold Goddard (1878–1950) was a professor of English and Head of the English department at Swathmore College, Pennsylvania.

24 Harold Clarke Goddard (1960). The Meaning of Shakespeare, Volume 2. University of Chicago Press.

Section 3: The Body Principles

1 Lilias Folan, the 'first lady of yoga' is regarded as one of America's most knowledgeable and beloved master yoga teachers. She hosted a ground breaking TV series, Lilias, Yoga and You in 1972.

2 Johann von Goethe (1749–1832) German poet, playwrite, novelist and natural philosopher. At the age of 25, his novel, The Sorrows of Young Werther, achieved cult status and gave him world wide fame.

Chapter 16: Practice

1 Gary Player, nicknamed the "black knight", is regarded as one of the great players in the history of golf.

2 Mahatma Gandhi (1869–1948), born in Gujarat. The leader of the Indian Nationalist movement against British rule and widely considered the father of his country. His doctrine of non-violent protest has been hugely influential.

3 Practice, as defined by the Oxford Dictionary Online. http://oxforddictionaries.com/definition/english/practice (accessed on 27th January 2013).

4 Martha Graham, American dancer, teacher and choreographer of modern dance, 1894–1991.

5 Kirk Mango (2012). Becoming a true champion: Achieving athletic excellence from the inside out. Maryland: Rowman & Littlefield.

6 Charles McGrath (1997). Elders on Ice . The New York Times Magazine. http://www.nytimes.com/1997/03/23/magazine/elders-on-ice.html?pagewanted=all&src=pm (accessed 1st August 2013).

7 Malcolm Gladwell (2005). Blink: The Power of Thinking Without Thinking. London: Penguin.

8 Matthew Syed (2011). Bounce: The Myth of Talent and the Power of Practice. New York: Harper Perennial.

9 Malcolm Gladwell (2011). Outliers: The Story of Success. London: Penguin.

10 Donald Schon (1991). The Reflective Practitioner. Aldershot: Ashgate Publishing Ltd.

11 Eric Lindros (b.1973) Canadian professional ice hockey player.

12 This curve is a combination of Elizabeth Kubler-Ross's cycle of grief which is commonly referred to as the change cycle and the competence cycle described by W. Lewis Robinson, which builds on others work and ancient traditions. See W. Lewis Robinson (1974). Conscious Competency – The Mark of a Competent Instructor – The Personnel Journal – Baltimore, Volume 53, PP538-539; and Kubler-Ross, E. (1973) On Death and Dying. London: Routledge.

13 Jim Gillette Stages of competence – http://www.personal-growth-and-freedom.com/competence.html (accessed 18th April 2013).

14 Publilius Syrus, 1st century B.C. A Syrian, brought as a slave to Italy, but through his wit and talent won the favour of his master who freed and educated him.

15 Ed Macauley (b.1928), American basketball player.

16 Lawrence Peter "Yogi" Berra (b.1925) baseball player and coach http://www.yogi-berra.com/ (accessed 21st March 2013).

17 Matthew Syed (2011). Bounce: The Myth of Talent and the Power of Practice. New York: Harper Perennial.

Chapter 17: Strengths

1 Abdul Kalam, born in 1931, a successful scientist and engineer, was elected as the 11th President of India 2002–2007.

2 Oxford Dictionary Online http://oxforddictionaries.com/definition/english/strength (accessed 28th January 2013).

3 P. Alex Linley & Susan Harrington (2006). Playing to your strengths. Psychologist, 19(2) pp. 86-89.

4 Martin Seligman (2002). Authentic Happiness: Using the new positive psychology to realise your potential for deep fulfilment. London: Nicholas Brealey Publishing.

5 Susan Tardanico is a cofounder of Authentic Leadership Alliance, and works with leaders and women in business http://www.authenticleadershipalliance.com/about/.

6 Susan Tardanico (2011). Stop worrying about your weaknesses. Focus on your strengths. http://www.forbes.com/2011/04/27/employer-employee-focus-on-strengths-not-weaknesses.html (accessed 30th January 2013).

7 Carol Kauffman, Ilona Bonniwell and Jordan Silberman (2010). The Positive Psychology Approach to Coaching. In Elaine Cox, Tatiana Bachkirova and David Clutterbuck (Eds.). The Complete Handbook of Coaching. London: Sage.

8 Professor Barbara Fredrickson is the Kenan Distinguished Professor of Psychology at the University of North Carolina.

9 Martin Seligman (2002). Authentic Happiness: Using the new positive psychology to realise your potential for deep fulfilment. London: Nicholas Brealey Publishing.

10 Albert Einstein (1879–1955) was a German-born theoretical physicist, often regarded as the father of modern physics, and the most influential physicist of the 20th century.

11 David Rock & Linda Page (2009). Coaching with the brain in mind: Foundations for Practice. New Jersey: John Wiley & Sons.

12 Hill, J. (2001). How well do we know our strengths? Paper presented at the British Psychological Society Centenary Conference, Glasgow.

13 Seligman, M.E.P. & Csikszentmihalyi, M. (2000). Positive psychology: An introduction. American Psychologist, 55, 5–14.

14 Hodges, T.D. & Clifton, D.O. (2004). Strengths-based development in practice. In P.A. Linley & S. Joseph (Eds.) Positive psychology in practice (pp.256–268). Hoboken, NJ: Wiley.

15 Buckingham, M. & Clifton, D.O. (2001). Now, discover your strengths: How to develop your talents and those of the people you manage. London: Simon & Schuster.

16 Steve de Shazer and Insoo Kim Berg, founders of solution-focused therapy, have brought their influential thinking from its origins in family therapy to the world of individual and organisational change and development with significant success – many practitioners and consultants in this field draw on these underpinning principles to support change.

17 David L. Cooperrider and Diana Whitney, A positive Revolution in Change: Appreciative Inquiry http://appreciativeinquiry.case.edu/uploads/whatisai.pdf (accessed 28th January 2013).

18 Gregory Bateson (1904–1980) – Anthropologist, Social Scientist, Cyberneticist – one of the most important social scientists of 20th century.

19 Barbara Fredrickson (2001). The role of positive emotions in positive psychology: The broaden-and-build theory of positive emotions. American Psychologist, 56(3) p218-26.

20 Lyubomirsky, S., King, L., and Diener, E. (2005). The benefits of frequent positive affect: Does happiness lead to success? Psychological Bulletin, 131(6), p803-55.

21 Ursula Staudinger (2008). A Psychology Wisdom: History and recent developments. Research in Human Development vol 5(2). p.107-208.

22 Martin Seligman (2002). Authentic Happiness: Using the new positive psychology to realise your potential for deep fulfilment. London: Nicholas Brealey Publishing.

23 The Polyanna principle is the tendency for people to be overly optimistic. http://en.wikipedia.org/wiki/Pollyanna_principle (accessed 4th February 2013).

24 Thomas Edison (1847–1931) considered one of the most prolific inventors in history http://www.biography.com/people/thomas-edison-9284349.

25 Corporate Leadership Council. (2002) Building the high-performance workforce. Washington, D.C.: Corporate Executive Board.

26 Daniel M. Cable, Francesca Gino and Bradley R. Staats (2013). Reinventing Employee Onboarding. MIT Sloan Management Review, Spring. http://sloanreview.mit.edu/article/reinventing-employee-onboarding/ (accessed 2nd August 2013).

27 James K. Harter, Frank, L. Schmidt and Corey L.M. Keyes (2003). Well-being in the work place and its relationship to business outcomes: A review of the Gallup Studies. In Corey L.M. Keyes & Jonathan Haidt (Eds.). Flourishing: The positive person and the good life (Chapter 9, pp.205-224). American Psychological Association.

28 Asplund, J., Lopez, S.J., Hodges, T., & Harter, J. (2009). The Clifton StrengthsFinder® 2.0 Technical Report: Development and Validation [technical report]. Lincoln, NE: Gallup.

29 Rath, T., & Conchie, B. (2008). Strengths based leadership. New York, NY: Gallup Press.

30 Fredrickson, B. L. & Losada, M. (2005). Positive affect and the complex dynamics of human flourishing. American Psychologist, 60(7), 678-686.

31 Losada, M. & Heaphy, E. (2004). The role of positivity and connectivity in the performance of business teams: A nonlinear dynamics model. American Behavioral Scientist, 47(6), 740-765.

32 Leonardo da Vinci (1452–1519), an Italian artist, scientist and engineer. He was an all-round genius whose paintings and inventions changed the world. http://www.bbc.co.uk/science/leonardo/ (accessed 4th February 2013).

33 Losada, M. & Heaphy, E. (2004). The role of positivity and connectivity in the performance of business teams: A nonlinear dynamics model. American Behavioral Scientist, 47(6), 740-765.

34 Martin Seligman (2002). Authentic Happiness. London: Nicholas Brealey.

35 P. Alex Linley & Susan Harrington (2006). Playing to your strengths. Psychologist, 19(2) pp. 86-89.

36 Richard Barrett is the Founder and Chairman of the Barrett Values Centre. He is an internationally known thought leader on values, culture, leadership and consciousness. One of the tools developed measures the different between individual and organisational values, the impact of this and what might be done to create alignment. http://www.valuescentre.com/products__services/?sec=cultural_transformation_tools_(ctt) (accessed 4th February 2013).

37 Mahatma Gandhi (1869–1948), born in Gujarat. The leader of the Indian Nationalist movement against British rule and widely considered the father of his country. His doctrine of non-violent protest has been hugely influential.

Chapter 18: Discipline

1 Dr. Louis Leo "Lou" Holtz (born 6th January 1937) is a retired American football coach, and active sportscaster, author, and motivational speaker.

2 Discipline definition Oxford Dictionaries online http://oxforddictionaries.com/definition/english/discipline and Latin root:http://www.latin-dictionary.net/search/latin/disciplinare (accessed 21st March 2013).

3 Lou Holtz in his paper: Winning ways Discipline: Showing you care. http://chialphapeoria.com/welcome/resources/louholtz.pdf (accessed 22nd March 2013).

4 Lou Holtz in his paper: Winning ways Discipline: Showing you care. http://chialphapeoria.com/welcome/resources/louholtz.pdf (accessed 22nd March 2013).

5 Harry S. Truman (1884–1972) was the 33rd President of the USA in office from 1945–1953.

6 Al Hirschfield (1903–2003) an American caricaturist, famous for his simple black and white caricatures. He also worked at Disney. http://www.alhirschfeldfoundation.org (accessed 21st March 2013).

7 Tammy Parlour, owner of Changs Hapkido Academy London, along with her students, discuss mental training for martial arts. http://www.changshapkido.net/category/mental-training-for-martial-arts/ (accessed 31st July 2013).

8 Lucius Anneas Seneca (Seneca the younger) (4 BC–AD 65) Roman leader and philosopher.

9 Mohamed Ali, Born Cassius Clay in 1942, Kentucky USA, professional boxer, philanthropist and political activist. He was awarded the Presidential Medal of Freedom in 2005 – the highest US civilian honour.

10 Napoleon Hill (1883–1970). He spent his life writing teaching and lecturing about the principles of success.

11 Chip Heath and Dan Heath (2010). Switch: How to change things when change is hard. London: Random House.

12 Molly J. Crockett, Barbara R. Braams, Luke Clark, Philippe N. Tobler, Trevor W. Robbins, and Tobias Kalensher (2013). Restricting Temptations: Neural Mechanism of Precommitment. Neuron, Vol. 79 (2) p. 391-401.

Part 4 – The broader context

1 We simply define system as a set of things working together as parts of a mechanism or an interconnecting network; a complex whole. This is taken from the oxford dictionary http://oxforddictionaries.com/definition/english/system (accessed 31st July 2013).

2 Warren Buffett (born 1930) is an American business magnate, investor and philanthropist. At the time of writing is widely considered the most successful investor of the 20th Century. http://www.biography.com/people/warren-buffett-9230729 (accessed 15th May 2013). This quote came from http://www.brainyquote.com/quotes/quotes/w/warrenbuff385064.html (accessed 15th May 2013).

Chapter 19: Complexity

1 System: a set of things working together as parts of a mechanism or an interconnecting network; a complex whole. This is taken from the oxford dictionary http://oxforddictionaries.com/definition/english/system (accessed 31st July 2013).

2 Ralph Stacy (2012). Comment on debate article: Coaching Psychology Coming of Age: The challenges we face in the messy world of complexity. International Coaching Psychology Review, vol 7(1), p.91-95.

3 Bob Hodge (2012). Coaching for a complex world. International Coaching Psychology Review, vol 7(1), p.109-113.

4 Gleick, J. (1988). Chaos: Making a New Science. London: Heinemann.

5 IBM Corporation (2010). Capitalising on complexity: Insights from the Global Chief Executive Officer Study. Somers, NY: IBM Global Business Services.

6 Donald A. Schön (1983). The reflective practitioner (p.15-16). New York: Basic Books.

7 Lesley Kuhn (2012). Epistemological reflections on the complexity sciences and how they may inform coaching psychology. International Coaching Psychology Review, vol 7(1), p114-118.

8 Peter Hawkins (2013). Foreword In Liz Hall (2013) Mindful Coaching: How mindfulness can transform coaching practice. London Kogan Page.

9 Ilya Prigogine & I. Stenners (1984) Order out of Chaos. London: Flamingo.

10 Lesley Kuhn (2012). Epistemological reflections on the complexity sciences and how they may inform coaching psychology. International Coaching Psychology Review, vol 7(1), p114-118.

Chapter 20: Change

1 Pink Floyd, Gilmour, Mason, Waters, Wright (1976). Time, Dark Side of the Moon.

2 The free online Dictionary (2012) http://www.thefreedictionary.com/change.

3 Albert Einstein (1879–1955) was a German-born theoretical physicist, often regarded as the father of modern physics, and the most influential physicist of the 20th century.

4 Kirsty L. Spalding, Ratan D. Bhardwaj, Bruce A. Buchholz, Henrik Druid, Jonas Frisén (2005). Retrospective Birth Dating of Cells in Humans. Cell. Vol 122(1) p.133-143.

5 Julie Allen & Alison Whybrow. (2007). Gestalt Coaching. In S. Palmer & A. Whybrow (Eds). Handbook in Coaching Psychology: A guide for practitioners. London: Routledge.

6 Heraclitus (540 BC–480 BC), from Diogenes Laertius, Lives of Eminent Philosophers.

7 The only reference to King Whitney Jr is this quote. If you do know him (if you are him), please do contact us – we would be delighted to reference him properly.

8 James S. Gordon, MD, is a Harvard-educated psychiatrist and a renowned expert in using mind-body medicine to heal depression, anxiety, and psychological trauma.

9 Kotter, J.P. (1996). Leading Change. Harvard Business Review Press; Kotter, J.P. (2006). Our Iceberg is Melting. Macmillan Press: Oxford.

10 Potts, R. & LaMarsh, J. (2004). Managing Change for Success: Effecting change for optimum growth and maximum efficiency. Duncan Baird Publishers: London.

11 Alison Whybrow and Victoria Henderson (2007). Concepts to support the integration and sustainability of coaching initiatives within organizations. In S.Palmer and A Whybrow (Eds). (2007). Handbook of Coaching Psychology: A Practitioners Guide.

12 McFarlin, D. B. and Sweeney, P. D. (1992) Distributive and procedural justice as predictors of satisfaction with personal and organisational outcomes. Academy of Management Journal 35(3): 626–637.

13 Kubler-Ross, E. (1973) On Death and Dying. London: Routledge.

14 Carl Gustav Jung (1875 -1961), a Swiss Psychologist and Psychiatrist who founded analytic psychology. Encyclopaedia Britannica http://www.britannica.com/EBchecked/topic/308188/Carl-Jung (accessed 27th March 2013).

15 Leo Tolstoy (1828–1910), a Russian author, was the youngest of four boys. His first great novel was the epic War and Peace. His second best-known novel was Anna Karenina.

Chapter 21: Wisdom

1 Lao-Tzu or Laozi was a philosopher of ancient China best known perhaps as the author of the Tao Ti Ching which has led him to be traditionally considered as the founder of philosophical Taoism http://en.wikipedia.org/wiki/Laozi (accessed 15th May 2013).

2 Lao-Tzu in Wikipedia. https://en.wikipedia.org/wiki/Laozi. (accessed 31st July 2013).

3 Definition of wisdom (1933). Oxford Dictionary.

4 Baddeley, S. and James, K. (1987), "Owl, Fox, Donkey, Sheep: Political Skills for Managers", Management Education and Development, 18, pp. 3-19.

5 Ursula Staudinger (2008). A Psychology Wisdom: History and recent developments. Research in Human Development vol 5(2). p.107-208.

6 Hirotaka Takeuchi and Ikujiro Nonaka (2011). The Wise Leader. Harvard Business Review.

7 Joseph Campbell (1988) The Hero with a Thousand Faces. Paladin: London.

8 Douglas J. Soccio (2009) Archetypes of Wisdom: Introduction to Philosophy. Wadsworth: CA.

9 Sternberg, R.J. (1990). Wisdom: Its nature, origin and development. New York: Cambridge University Press.

10 Ursula Staudinger (2008). A Psychology Wisdom: History and recent developments. Research in Human Development vol 5(2). p.107-208.

11 Sternberg, R.J. (1998). A balance theory of wisdom. Review of General Psychology, 2 347-365.

12 Margaret Heffernan (2011). Wilful Blindness: Why we ignore the obvious at our peril. London: Simon & Schuster.

13 Confucius (551–479 BC) was a Chinese teacher, editor, politician, and philosopher of the Spring and Autumn Period of Chinese history. The philosophy of Confucius emphasized personal and governmental morality, correctness of social relationships, justice and sincerity.

14 Albert Einstein (1879–1955) was a German-born theoretical physicist, often regarded as the father of modern physics, and the most influential physicist of the 20th century.

15 Translated by Lakota Sioux Chief Yellow Lark (1887) Published in Native American Prayers – by the Episcopal Church. http://www.sapphyr.net/natam/quotes-nativeamerican.htm (accessed 13th November 2012).

16 Black Elk, Oglala Sioux & Spiritual Leader (1863–1950).

17 Bronwyn Fryer interviews Cisco CEO John Chambers on Team work and Collaboration. HBR Blog Network. October 24 2008. http://blogs.hbr.org/hbr/hbreditors/2008/10/cisco_ceo_john_chambers_on_tea.html (accessed 15th May 2013).

18 Sir Isaac Newton (1676) quoted in a letter to Robert Hooke. Original wording: If I have seen further it is by standing on ye sholders of giants http://www.phrases.org.uk/meanings/268025.html (accessed 4th February 2013).

19 Roger Lehman is Affiliate Professor of Entrepreneurship and Family Enterprise at INSEAD.

20 Prasad Kaipa, Senior Research Fellow and Executive Director Emeritus at The Center for Leadership, Innovation and Change, Indian School of Business in Hyderabad. Quote in The Wise Leader, By Alvin Lee, Web Editor | 8th November 2012 http://knowledge.insead.edu/leadership-management/the-wise-leader-2320.

21 Ursula Staudinger (2008). A Psychology Wisdom: History and recent developments. Research in Human Development vol 5(2). p.107-208.

22 How to by wise. Edited by Sarah Eliza and 30 others. http://www.wikihow.com/Be-Wise. (accessed 31st July 2013).

23 Prasad Kaipa, Senior Research Fellow and Executive Director Emeritus at The Center for Leadership, Innovation and Change, Indian School of Business in Hyderabad. Quote in The Wise Leader, By Alvin Lee, Web Editor | 8th November 2012 http://knowledge.insead.edu/leadership-management/the-wise-leader-2320.

24 Hirotaka Takeuchi and Ikujiro Nonaka (2011). The Wise Leader. Harvard Business Review.

25 Shunryu Suzuki (1904-1971) was a soto Zen monk and teacher who helped popularize Zen Buddhism in the United States and is renowned for founding the first Buddhist monastery outside Asia. His teachings are captured in: Zen mind, Beginner's Mind: Informal Talks on Zen Meditation and Practice. Shambhala Publications (2011).

26 Mary Jaksch, author, Zen Master and Psychotherapist and contributor to http://www.wikihow.com/Be-Wise. (accessed 31st July 2013).

27 Socrates (c. 469 BC – 399 BC) was a classical Greek Athenian philosopher, credited as one of the founders of Western philosophy.

Chapter 22: Neuroscience

1 Santiago Ramón y Cajal (May 1852–October 1934) was a Spanish pathologist, histologist and neuroscientist. His pioneering work exploring the microscopic structure of the brain led many to consider him the father of modern neuroscience.

2 Stephanie Pappas (2013). Obama Announces Huge Brain-Mapping Project. LiveScience. http://www.livescience.com/28354-obama-announces-brain-mapping-project.html (accessed 15th May 2013).

3 David Rock and Linda J Page (2009). Coaching with the Brain in Mind. London: Wiley.

4 Susan Greenfield (2009). ID: The quest for meaning in the 21st Century. London: Hodder and Stoughton.

5 Spalding, K.L., Bhardwaj, R.D., Buchholz, B.A., Druid, H. and Frisen, J. (2005). Retrospective Birth Dating of Cells in Humans. Cell, Vol. 122, 133–143, 15th July 2005.

6 Definition and description of Neuroplasticity taken from: http://www.medterms.com/script/main/art.asp?articlekey=40362 (accessed 11th March 2013).

7 Dr. Elkhonon Goldberg, neuropsychologist, clinical professor of neurology at New York University School of Medicine, and disciple of the great neuropsychologist Alexander Luria.

8 David Rock and Linda J Page (2009). Coaching with the Brain in Mind. London: Wiley.

9 Leslie Brothers (2002). Mistaken Identity: The Mind-Brain Problem reconsidered New York: SUNY Press.

10 Susan Greenfield (2009). ID: The quest for meaning in the 21st Century. London: Hodder and Stoughton.

11 Dr Geoff Bird (2013). Neuroscience and Leadership: The self and others. Presentation at Friends Meeting House, Euston Road London. 26th April 2013.

12 Dr Geoff Bird (2013). Neuroscience and Leadership: The self and others. Presentation at Friends Meeting House, Euston Road London. 26th April 2013.

13 Dr Srikumar Rao, speaker, author and former business school professor; talks to Google: http://www.youtube.com/watch?v=u20vVbhpM50 (accessed 8th March 2013).

14 Donald Hebb (1904–1985). A Canadian psychologist influential in neuropsychology where he sought to understand the function of neurons contributed to psychological processes such as learning. http://en.wikipedia.org/wiki/Donald_O._Hebb (accessed 11th March 2013).

15 David Rock & Linda Page (2009). Coaching with the brain in mind: Foundations for Practice. New Jersey: John Wiley & Sons.

16 Dr Geoff Bird (2013). Neuroscience and Leadership: The self and others. Presentation at Friends Meeting House, Euston Road London. 26th April 2013.

17 Schwartz, J.M. & Begley, S. (2002). The mind and the brain: Neuroplasticity and the power of mental force. New York: Regan Books, Harper Collins.

18 Scott Marcaccio, formally a health and fitness advisor, writing on http://scottmarcaccio.com/how-to-change-a-habit-using-neuroscience/ (this link is no longer available).

19 Katherine Woollett & Eleanor Maguire (2012). Exploring anterograde associative memory in London taxi drivers. Neuroreport, 23(15). p.885–888.

20 Bandura, A. (1977). Social Learning Theory. New York: General Learning Press.

21 Giacomo Rizzolatti and Luciano Fadiga (2005). The mirror-neuron system and action recognition. In Freund, H.J., Jeannerod, M. and Hallett, M. (Eds). Higher order motor disorders: from Neuroanatomy and Neurobiology to Clinical Neurobiology. New York: oxford University Press.

22 Dr Geoff Bird (2013). Neuroscience and Leadership: The self and others. Presentation at Friends Meeting House, Euston Road, London. 26th April 2013.

23 Stephens, G.J, Silbert, L.J. & Hasson, U. (2010). Speaker-listener neural coupling underlies successful communication. PNAS, 27th July. http://psych.princeton.edu/psychology/research/hasson/publications.php (accessed 23rd January 2013).

24 Pascual-Leone A. 1996. Reorganization of cortical motor outputs in the acquisition of new motor skills. In Recent Advances in Clinical Neurophysiology, ed. J Kinura, H Shibasaki, pp. 304–8. Amsterdam: Elsevier Sci.

25 Susan Greenfield (2009). ID: The quest for meaning in the 21st Century. London: Hodder and Stoughton.

26 Henry Ford (1863–1947) was an American industrialist, founder of the Ford Motor Company and sponsor of the assembly line technique of mass production. His cars revolutionized transportation.

27 Simons, D.J. and Chabris, C. (1999). Gorillas in our midst: Sustained inattentional blindness for dynamic events. Perception, vol 28 pp 1059-1074.

28 Slagter, H.A., Davidson, R.J., and Lutz, A. (2011). Mental training as a tool in the neuroscientific study of brain and cognitive plasticity. Frontiers in Human Neuroscience. Vol 5. pp 1-12.

29 David Rock and Daniel Siegel (2011). Healthy mind platter, for optimal brain matter. http://drdansiegel.com/resources/healthy_mind_platter/ (accessed 13th March 2013).

Chapter 23 Choice

1 J.K.Rowling (1998). Harry Potter and the Chamber of Secrets. London: Bloomsbury. Albus Dumbledore speaking to Harry Potter about destiny and choice.

2 Viktor E. Frankl (1945/2004). Man's Search for Meaning. London: Random House.

3 Tali Sharot (2011).The Optimism Bias: A Tour of the Irrationally Positive Brain. New York: Random House.

4 Dr Ruth Bell, Dr Annie Britton, Dr Eric Brunner, Dr Tarani Chandola, Dr Jane Ferrie, Ms Miriam Harris, Ms Jenny Head, Professor Sir Michael Marmot, Ms Gill Mein and Dr Mai Stafford. (2004). Work, Stress and Health: The Whitehall II Study. London: CCSU / Cabinet Office.

5 Jean-Paul Sartre (1905–1980), was a French existential philosopher, playwright, novelist, screenwriter, political activist, biographer and literary critic. He was awarded the Nobel Prize for literature in 1964.

"Jean-Paul Sartre – Biography". Nobelprize.org. 15th May 2013 http://www.nobelprize.org/nobel_prizes/literature/laureates/1964/sartre-bio.html (accessed 31st July 2013).

6 Kim, H.S. and Sherman, D.K. (in press). Express Yourself: Culture and the Effect of Self-Expression on Choice. Journal of Personality and Social Psychology.

7 James Kouzes and Barry Posner (2012). The Leadership Challenge: How To Make Extraordinary Things Happen In Organizations. John Wiley & Sons.

8 Patrick Ness (2010). Monsters of Men: Chaos Walking. Walker Books: London.

9 James Kouzes and Barry Posner (2012). The Leadership Challenge: How To Make Extraordinary Things Happen In Organizations. John Wiley & Sons.

10 James Kouzes and Barry Posner (2012). The Leadership Challenge: How To Make Extraordinary Things Happen In Organizations. John Wiley & Sons.

11 Susanne E. Weinstein, Karen S. Quigley and J Toby Mordkoff (2002). Influence of control and physical effort on cardiovascular reactivity to a video game task. Psychophysiology Vol 39(5) pp 591-598.

12 James Kouzes and Barry Posner (2012). The Leadership Challenge: How To Make Extraordinary Things Happen In Organizations. John Wiley & Sons.

13 Brodi Ashton is an author of young adult novels. The quote comes from: http://www.goodreads.com/author/quotes/4384465.Brodi_Ashton (accessed 15th May 2013).

14 Derik Mocke: Employee Empowerment. http://www.sustainable-employee-motivation.com/employee-empowerment.html (accessed 1st April 2013).

Chapter 24: Leadership

1 Colin Powell, born in 1937, is an American statesman and retired as a four-star General in the US Army.

2 Peter Hawkins (2011). Leadership Team Coaching: Developing collective transformational leadership. London: Kogan Page.

3 Richard Bolden (2008). Distributed Leadership. In A Maturano & J. Gosling (eds.). Leadership: The Key Concepts. London: Routledge. pp. 42-45.

4 John Quincy Adams (1767–1848). 6th President of the United States. Quote shared by Art Jonak@ArtJonak.

5 Warren Bennis (1925), a professor at the University of California, he is an influential authority on leadership, and has been consulted by at least four American presidents, among others.

6 Warren Bennis (2010). Still Surprised: A memoir of a life in leadership. Jossey-Bass.

7 Tim Hindle (2012). Guide to Management Ideas and Gurus. The Economist.

8 John C Maxwell (2007). Talent is never enough: Discover the choices that will take you beyond your talent. Workbook. Tennessee: Thomas Nelson.

9 William Tate (2012). Managing Leadership from a systemic perspective. London Metropolitan University: Centre for Progressive Leadership white paper.

10 Peter Hawkins (2011) Leadership Team Coaching: Developing collective transformational leadership. Kogan Page, p.17.

11 John Baldoni (2011). Leading with Purpose gets the best results. CBS news http://www.cbsnews.com/8301-505125_162-57329556/leading-with-purpose-gets-the-best-results/ (accessed 30th January 2012).

12 Ram Charan, Stephen Drotter & James Noel (2001). The Leadership Pipeline: How to build the leadership powered company. San Francisco: Jossey-Bass.

13 Robert Warwick & Douglas Board (2012). The social development of leadership and knowledge: re-thinking research and practice. Centre for Progressive Leadership white paper.

14 Damian Hughes (2009). Liquid Leadership: Inspirational lessons from the world's great leaders. Chicester: Capstone Publishing.

15 Anita Roddick (1942–2007) was a British business-woman, human rights campaigner and environmental activist. This quote is from: http://thinkexist.com/quotation/if-you-think-you-re-too-small-to-have-an-impact/532763.html (accessed 15th May 2013).

16 Sydney Pollack, (1934–2008), an American director, producer and actor. Perhaps best known for Tootsie and Three days of the Condor.

17 Michael Jordan (born 1963) is an American former professional basketball player and active entrepreneur.

18 Brene Brown (2010). The power of vulnerability. TED talk available on: http://www.ted.com/talks/brene_brown_on_vulnerability.html (accessed 1st February 2013).

19 Brene Brown is an inspirational speaker and writer. She has written three books. The latest is 2012: Daring Greatly: How the courage to be vulnerable transforms the way we live, love, parent and lead. New York: Penguin books.

20 Margaret Heffernan (2011). Wilful Blindness: Why we ignore the obvious at our peril. London: Simon & Schuster.

21 Margaret Heffernan (2011). Wilful Blindness: Why we ignore the obvious at our peril. London: Simon & Schuster.

22 Tony Hsieh (2010). Delivering Happiness: A path to Profits, Passion and Purpose. Mundelein Illinois: Roundtable Companies.

23 Pat Lencioni (2002). Make Your Values Mean Something. Harvard Business Review.

Chapter 25: Site

1 Oliver Wendell Holmes, Jr. (8th March 1841 – 6th March 1935) was an American jurist who served as an Associate Justice of the Supreme Court of the United States from 1902 to 1932.

2 Victor Marie Hugo (26th February 1802 – 22nd May 1885) was a French poet, novelist, and dramatist of the Romantic movement.

Chapter 26: National

1 George Smith Patton, Jr. (11th November 1885 – 21th December 1945) was a general in the United States Army best known for his command of the Seventh United States Army, and later the Third United States Army, in the European Theatre of World War II.

Chapter 27: Global

1 Stephen Richards Covey (24th October 1932 – 16th July 2012) was an American educator, author, businessman, and keynote speaker. His most popular book was The Seven Habits of Highly Effective People.

Chapter 28: Case study

1 Hilary Hinton "Zig" Ziglar (6th November 1926 – 28th November 2012) was an American author, salesman, and motivational speaker.

Chapter 29: my31Practices

1 Mohandas Karamchand Gandhi 2nd October 1869 – 30th January 1948), commonly known as Mahatma Gandhi, was the preeminent leader of Indian nationalism in British-ruled India. Employing non-violent civil disobedience, Gandhi led India to independence and inspired movements for non-violence, civil rights and freedom across the world.

2 Anton Pavlovich Chekhov (29th January 1860 – 15th July 1904) was a Russian physician, dramatist and author who is considered to be among the greatest writers of short stories in history.

3 Carl Rogers (1967–2004). On becoming a person: A therapist's view of psychotherapy. London: Constable & Robinson.

4 Johann Wolfgang von Goethe (1749–1832), a German writer, artist and politician. A literary celebrity, he was one of the key figures of German literature.

5 Tony Robbins (2006). Why we do what we do. TED talks. http://www.ted.com/talks/tony_robbins_asks_why_we_do_what_we_do.html. (accessed 31st July 2013).

6 H. Jackson Brown, Jr. is an American author best known for his inspirational book, Life's Little Instruction Book, which was a New York Times bestseller (1991–1994).

7 Laura Whitworth, Henry Kimsey-House, Karen Kimsey-House & Phil Sandahl (2007) New skills for coaching people towards success in work and life. Nicholas Brealy Publishing: London.

8 Fernando Flores (born 1943), a Chilean engineer, entrepreneur and politician. Finance Minister alongside President Salvador Allende, he was imprisoned after the military coup of Augusto Pinochet in 1973, and forced into exile in 1976. http://en.wikipedia.org/wiki/Fernando_Flores. This quote comes from: http://www.brainyquote.com/quotes/authors/f/fernando_flores.html (accessed 15th May 2013).

Chapter 30: Summary

1 Heraclitus of Ephesus (c. 535–c. 475 BCE) was a pre-Socratic Greek philosopher.

2 In fact, the original version is a calypso song written by jazz musicians Melvin "Sy" Oliver and James "Trummy" Young. It was first recorded in 1939 by Jimmie Lunceford, Harry James, and Ella Fitzgerald.

Chapter 31: Photography

1 Henri Cartier-Bresson (22nd August 1908 – 3rd August 2004) was a French photographer considered to be the father of modern photojournalism.

ABOUT THE AUTHORS

Dr Alison Whybrow

Alison is an award winning Chartered and Registered Psychologist and Supervisor who coaches senior and high potential leaders across industry sectors. Alison works with individual and system strengths, combining theoretical depth and pragmatism. She brings academic and practical depth with 20 years of experience working with clients in heavy industry, banking, health and media.

Alison has a depth of technical knowledge, underpinned by her Doctorate exploring the Employment Relationship and Organisational Design. She is well known as a contributor in coaching circles and passionate about good practice.

In her work, Alison acts as a catalyst to enable her clients to see more clearly their impact, discover and pursue their core purpose, and deliver. Her work with individuals and groups enables them to develop resources and abilities to coach themselves when faced with future challenges. She brings rigor, a systemic lens and challenge.

Alison works across sectors with global brands. Her clients include individuals from financial organisations, Private Equity investment executives, Partners in Law firms, Military Commanders, Senior Civil Servants, individual Entrepreneurs, Learning and Development specialists, and emerging talent. Client organisations include the MoD, NATO, NHS based organisations (including NHS trusts), BSkyB, CitiBank.

Alison holds a degree and doctorate in Psychology, is professionally qualified as a Chartered and Registered Psychologist, an accredited Master of Change with La Marsh & Associates, holds a foundation in counselling from Regents College (London) and is accredited to use diverse profiling tools. Alison received an Achievement Award for her Distinguished Contribution to Coaching Psychology from peers in the British Psychological Society in 2009.

Alan Williams

Alan coaches service sector organizations, internationally and in the UK to deliver inspiring service for competitive advantage. He created the 31Practices concept and approach.

With more than 20 years senior leadership experience in customer service based businesses, Alan has a track record of success in devising holistic SERVICEBRAND strategies and then using deep operational experience to turn the creative thinking into sustainable, practical reality. Alan has applied this approach as a consultant and a Board director, in operational and functional support roles and for global blue chip organizations as well as smaller entrepreneurial companies. He has enjoyed roles with InterContinental Hotels, Whitbread, Compass/RBS and Marriott International before founding SERVICEBRAND GLOBAL in 2005. His projects have delivered remarkable business impact across a balanced scorecard of measures.

Alan is at his best when given the opportunity to push the boundaries to inspire groups of people across functions, organizations and hierarchy to be proud of their role in delivering memorable customer experience. He thrives on leading the transformation of service, culture and behaviour and is an expert facilitator of experiential learning workshops.

Alan graduated in Hotel & Catering Administration at Surrey University where he has been a visiting lecturer, was a global train the trainer for the Marriott International Spirit to Serve programme and attended the Whitbread Leadership Course at London Business School. He served as President of the Meetings Industry Association, is a Fellow of the Institute of Hospitality, a Board member of the British Quality Foundation and a Steering Group member of the recently formed UK Values Alliance.